THE SMART GUIDE TO

Bridge

BY BRENT MANLEY

The Best Game Ever

It is estimated that 20 million people in North America play some form of bridge. Most play social, or party, bridge at home with friends, where the atmosphere is relaxed and informal. A much smaller number venture to clubs for rubber bridge, played for money, sometimes with very high stakes.

Still others play duplicate bridge—a more competitive form of the game—in clubs and at tournaments. The American Contract Bridge League (ACBL), with national headquarters in the Memphis, Tennessee, area, has more than 166,000 members. It is the largest bridge organization in the world.

Tournament Tested

The ACBL sanctions more than 1,200 tournaments every year and puts on three major tournaments that attract the best players from around the world. If you go to one of the 3,200 bridge clubs affiliated with the ACBL, you can play in a a mini bridge tournament. Some clubs are open seven days a week.

Most bridge contests in the United States do not have cash prizes for the winners, as is common in other parts of the world, but there is one big cash tournament each year in Las Vegas—the Cavendish Invitational Pairs—where the total purse usually exceeds $1 million.

Log On to Play

A growing number of players get their "bridge fix" on the Internet, where popular bridge-playing sites provide a competitive venue for aficionados from around the world. Many top stars practice with each other online every day. There are dozens of bridge games every day, around the clock, on the three major online bridge sites: www.bridgebaseonline.com, www.okbridge.com, and www.swangames.com.

Bridge Lingo

Have you ever played bridge against—or even with—a robot? If not, you could try it in one of the Internet bridge sites. A robot is a computer program that knows how to play at a basic level. You can actually sit at a virtual table on the Internet and play with a robot as your partner and two robots as opponents.

Dr. Zhivago's Game

The list of celebrity bridge players is long and impressive and includes actor Omar Sharif, a genuine expert at the game. Sharif often lists bridge as his true passion. Acting, he says, is just a job. His name is still on a syndicated bridge column that appears in many U.S. newspapers.

Other famous players include Don Adams (TV's *Get Smart*) and comedian George Burns, who played bridge every day right up to the day he died at age one hundred. Before his death in 1999, former NBA star Wilt Chamberlain had become hooked on duplicate bridge and was a regular at a bridge club in Los Angeles. Tennis star Martina Navratilova is another inveterate player, as is Hall of Fame baseball player Paul Molitor.

When the ACBL held its big summer tournament in Washington, D.C., in 2009, one of the competitors was U.S. Supreme Court Justice John Paul Stevens, still a year away from retirement.

Bridge Facts

Microsoft founder Bill Gates and investment guru Warren Buffett—two of the world's richest men—are major fans of bridge. Gates regularly attends bridge tournaments organized by the ACBL, and Buffett admits to playing rubber bridge just about every day. Dwight Eisenhower played bridge from his command post in Europe as a U.S. Army general during World War II and in the White House as president.

A Game for a Lifetime

There are roughly 5,000 experienced bridge teachers in North America, and most are busy year-round. Some take occasional breaks to teach and run games on cruise ships, but their primary work in the early twenty-first century is introducing the game to the thousands of baby boomers now entering retirement and looking for a stimulating and interesting hobby.

The beauty of bridge is that it can be played for a lifetime, well after the knees or elbows have given out, ending golf and tennis careers. Oswald Jacoby, one of the all-time greats of the game, won a major championship at the age of eighty-one.

Bridge is the ultimate game of logic with some of the bluffing elements of poker, but you must always remember that it is, in the end, a partnership game.

Where to Play

Decades ago—before the advent of television, computers, and video games—virtually everyone played cards at home, and bridge was king of the family games. You didn't have to go farther than your living room to find a game, and many young people learned after being drafted by their parents. Even as late as the Sixties, bridge games were commonplace at most colleges. Those days are long gone, and the powers that be are scrambling to recruit a new generation of young players to fill the gaps in the future.

That said, if you want to find a bridge game, there are many ways to do so. Most cities of medium size or larger have at least one bridge club, and games are almost always available at country clubs.

Need to Know

If you want formal instruction in the game of bridge, your best resource is the ACBL home page (www.acbl.org), where you can click on "Find a Teacher" to get started.

If you find a teacher and take lessons, your fellow students will be candidates for taking part in games you organize at home. In fact, home-based clubs—with rotating hosts—are common.

Most medium to large duplicate clubs have regular lessons and games for beginners as a way of recruiting new members, but taking lessons at a duplicate club does not obligate you to continue with that style of play. The information you take in during lessons at a duplicate club will serve you just as well for your games at home.

Vacation Play

A great way to combine leisure time with learning bridge is to sign up for a bridge cruise. Many are hosted by famous bridge players such as Eddie Kantar and Larry Cohen, who are also two of the most respected bridge writers in the world. The lectures they give are entertaining and useful, and the celebrity lecturer is usually available to answer all your questions. Every bridge cruise includes daily games.

If the idea of bridge at sea does not appeal to you, consider a "land cruise," which has a format similar to a bridge cruise but on dry land, often at a college or resort hotel.

Another interesting way to combine bridge with a vacation is to take a bridge trip—usually comprised of of a couple dozen or more players—that covers multiple cities and has bridge games scheduled at all the stops. It's a great way to satisfy your urge to play while meeting local players and learning their customs.

Bridge Lingo

At one time, the term *little old lady* (*LOL*) was used in duplicate settings to describe a less-than-expert older woman player. Lately it has taken on a different meaning: a seemingly innocent competitor who can and will eat your proverbial lunch if you are not careful or respectful. Watch out for the LOLs!

Games Galore

The ACBL measures the volume of play in bridge games that it sanctions in terms of tables, one table being four people playing one session of bridge at a club, tournament, or on the Internet. In 2010, for the third year in a row, the table count for bridge play in ACBL-sanctioned games topped 3 million. That's a lot of bridge.

With all those games going on around the clock, it's easy to find one for yourself. If you are shy about mixing it up with real people right off the bat, go to one of the Internet bridge sites and play at a table with three robots.

You can find a club in or near your home town by visiting the ACBL web site.

CHAPTER 2

Getting Started

In This Chapter

➤ The object of the game

➤ The mechanics of bidding and play

➤ What is a contract?

➤ Tricks and trumps

In this chapter you will learn how to get the most from this book, which is aimed at helping you become a bridge player even if you have never turned a card in any game. You will also learn the basic requirements to get started on your goal of learning the best card game in the world.

They may seem mysterious at first, but you will find out all about those elusive tricks and why you will be going after them so enthusiastically in this new game you have discovered.

Bidding is considered by many to be the most important element of the game. We will cover bidding in the discussions of a game of bridge from start to finish.

Finally, you will find out about the all-important contract that you will undertake to fulfill every time you win the bidding.

Getting the Most from Your Smart Guide

You will take in the information in this book most effectively by going slowly. If you do not have much experience playing cards, you will need to learn your way around a deck.

First of all, get your hands on a couple decks of bridge playing cards. Note that they are different from poker cards, which are wider. You will be holding thirteen cards at a time, which would be difficult with poker cards.

Need to Know

The game of bridge is all about tricks, so it's important to know what a trick is. Cards are played among four people in a clockwise rotation, and when four cards, one from each player, have been played, that constitutes a trick. The rules say all players must follow suit, so if the first person to play puts a spade on the table, all the other players must play spades if they have them. The player with the highest-ranking card of the four is the winner of the trick. The ace is the top card in each suit, followed by the king, queen, jack, and on down to the 2.

To get an idea of how the play will go, shuffle the cards five times, then deal them one by one into four distinct piles. In a typical home game, you would distribute the cards one at a time to each of the other three players, starting with the person to your left.

Pick up your hand and sort the cards into suits. Players usually alternate red (hearts and diamonds) and black (spades and clubs) so that their suits don't get mixed up. Many an embarrassing moment has occurred because a player thought he had a certain number of hearts, only to find out that some of them were diamonds.

Knowing how many cards you have in each suit is important, as you will discover when the discussion turns to bidding later on.

Hands On

You might as well learn right from the start that how you hold your cards is important. If you hold them low or way out in front of you, your opponents can see them—and nothing is more helpful to an opponent than getting a glimpse of your hand.

Bridge Lingo

The bridge game has two phases: the bidding and the play. The bidding part is known as the auction, during which players take turns in clockwise rotation making various bids, mostly involving the four suits, which represent the cards they have been dealt.

Why is it so helpful if an opponent can see your cards? Because each player at the table can see two hands—his own and the one placed on the table as the dummy.

The word *dummy*, by the way, is not used in a negative sense; it is simply the term describing the hand of the player whose partner has won the right to play the cards.

At any rate, if a player can see his hand, the dummy, and your hand, there are only thirteen cards left that he hasn't seen, and it would be easy to reconstruct the entire deal from one quick glance at your cards.

Bridge Lingo

When you and your partner win the bidding, one of you will control the play of the cards for your side. That person is known as the declarer. The two opponents are known as defenders. After a defender leads, the partner of the declarer puts his hand on the table, and the declarer decides which card to play whenever it is the dummy's turn to play.

What's the Point?

Bridge is a game of tricks, and there are thirteen tricks available on every deal. Sometimes you will try for slightly more than half of the tricks, sometimes as many as nine or ten, and on rare occasions you will commit yourself to winning all thirteen. The number of tricks you need to win will be determined by the bidding.

Bridge Basics

When you play, the person sitting across from you is your partner. The people to your left and right are each other's partners. More important, they are your opponents.

Simply put, the bidding is the language by which the two partnerships communicate about their assets, the hands that they hold.

All hands are evaluated based on so-called high-card points (HCP). Through the years, other evaluation methods have been advanced, but most players stick to the simplest and easiest to remember. Counting high-card points as the way of evaluating a hand dates back to the Twenties and is virtually unchanged from that time.

The high cards on which the points are based are aces, kings, queens, and jacks.

➤ Ace: 4 points

➤ King: 3 points

➤ Queen: 2 points

➤ Jack: 1 point

That's 10 high-card points per suit, so a total of 40 high-card points in each deck.

Pointed Question

So, why bother to evaluate a hand? Who cares how many points my hand has?

Well, remembering that bridge is a game of tricks, you and your partner will be competing with your opponents during the bidding—and the winner of the auction will have to take a certain number of tricks to fulfill the contract.

Need to Know

The relative strength of your bridge hand is determined in large measure by the number of high-card points it holds. A hand with 13 high-card points is considered to have modest strength, and hands with 20 or more high-card points are considered strong. Your objective in the bidding is to convey the relative strength—or lack thereof—to your partner.

You will recall that the deck of cards is divided into four distinct suits: spades, hearts, diamonds, and clubs. Each card is marked with a symbol to help identify it:

➤ Spades: ♠

➤ Hearts: ♥

➤ Diamonds: ♦

➤ Clubs: ♣

The suits are listed in that order because they are ranked, which is necessary because of the way the bidding works. Spades have the highest rank, clubs the lowest.

Bridge Lingo

The two highest-ranked suits in bridge—spades and hearts—are known as major suits. The two lowest-ranked—diamonds and clubs—are known as minor suits. The distinction might seem unimportant, but it can have a significant bearing on your bidding decisions.

Trumps, Anyone?

To this point, only the concept of taking tricks has been advanced. So how do you actually do it?

There are two ways to win tricks. The first is by playing the highest card of the suit led. Remember, each of the four players must contribute a card to each trick. The second way to win a trick is by playing a trump.

A what?

In bridge, a trump card is essentially a wild card. The lowest trump card can beat the highest nontrump card.

Bridge Facts

In the game of whist, the precursor to bridge, the trump suit was determined by turning over the last card of the deck at the end of the deal. In bridge, the trump suit is determined by the last suit bid by the partnership that wins the auction.

One of the key goals of bidding for each partnership is to identify a suit that can be trumps, and it is axiomatic that you strive to select a trump suit for which you and your partner have more cards than your opponents.

Trumps provide an advantage in their ability to win tricks against higher cards of other suits, so you don't want to select a suit that opponents have more of than you. That's why you work on your bidding accuracy.

How the Game of Bridge Works

The first part of the process is the shuffle, followed by the deal. The dealer distributes the cards one at a time in clockwise rotation, starting with the player on his left.

When the dealing is completed, players take a brief moment to look over their hands, putting their cards into suits, and counting their high-card points.

The dealer gets the first chance to speak.

Bridge Lingo

In bridge parlance, any time you open your mouth during the auction, you are going to be making a call. Even in an informal game, your vocabulary for the auction is limited to fifteen words: *pass*, the numbers 1 through 7, *double*, *redouble*, *spades*, *hearts*, *diamonds*, *clubs*, and *notrump*. The significance of these terms will soon come clear. Any of these is a call. A bid, on the other hand, names a number and a denomination (suit or notrump). All bids are calls, but not all calls are bids.

If the dealer starts with a bid, he names a number and a suit or notrump (meaning he does not intend for there to be a trump suit), as in "one spade."

The auction then proceeds to the player at the dealer's left, and this is where the ranking of the suits comes into play.

Remember, clubs is the lowest-ranking suit, followed in ascending order by diamonds, hearts, and spades. Notrump has only just come into the conversation, but it is one of the denominations in the lexicon of bidding, and notrump outranks even spades.

Climbing the Ladder

Once a bid has been made, all subsequent bids must be at a higher denomination or at a higher level. For example, if a player bids 1♣, the lowest ranking suit, the next player may bid as low as 1♦.

If, however, the opener had started with 1♠, the next player would have to bid at least two of any of the other suits because they rank lower than spades. That same player, however, would be permitted to bid 1NT because notrump outranks spades.

Need to Know

The significance of the number in front of each bid comes down to the principle of the book. The first six tricks taken by the side that wins the auction do not count in the scoring. Those tricks are known as the book. So the number attached to any bid means that you plan to take that number of tricks—plus six. A bid of 1♠ means you plan to take seven tricks with spades as trumps; a bid of 7♠ means you plan to take all thirteen tricks (six for the book plus seven).

No Passing Fancy

The dealer always starts the auction, but he doesn't have to bid. If the dealer passes, it is the next player's turn to call, and he can pass or bid. If the bidding starts with four consecutive passes, the deal passes to the next player in clockwise rotation. That person collects and shuffles the cards and deals again.

If there is a bid, the auction continues until there are three consecutive passes. What follows is a bidding diagram along with an auction from beginning to end. The compass points each represent one of the four players in a diagram. You will see a lot of these in this book:

West	North	East	South
	Pass	Pass	1♠
Pass	2♠	Pass	Pass
Pass			

This diagram indicates that North passed as dealer, East also passed, and South opened the bidding with 1♠. West passed, and North bid 2♠. No one had anything else to say, and after three consecutive passes, the auction was over.

North-South (a partnership) won the bidding with a bid of 2♠, meaning that they expect to take eight tricks (six for the book plus two odd, meaning two more than the book).

Spoken or Silent?

At virtually every bridge club and at all tournaments nowadays, there is no spoken bidding. Players use devices known as bidding boxes. These are small plastic containers (one for each player) that have cards representing all the possible calls, including every possible bid—from 1 ♣ to 7 NT—plus cards for pass, double, and redouble (more on the latter two later).

Instead of saying, pass, a player will pull one of the green pass cards out of the box and put it on the table in front of him. Instead of speaking the words *one spade*, a player will pull the appropriate card from the box and place it on the table.

As the auction progresses, a complete record of the bidding is available for all to see— players place their bidding cards in such a way that previous calls are not covered.

Bridge Basics

One reason bidding boxes have become popular, even in social games, is that their use precludes, at least to an extent, inappropriate conveyance of information by means of voice intonations. A very firm "four spades" can be meant to alert a partner that there is to be no more bidding. This is a serious violation of the proprieties. Inappropriate communication can still take place, but to a much lesser degree with silent bidding.

Mixing It Up

The opponents are not always silent, however, and it behooves each player to try to compete during the auction, as in this case:

West	North	East	South
			1 ♦
2 ♣	2 ♥	3 ♣	3 ♥
Pass	Pass	Pass	

Note that North and South have bid up to 3 ♥, meaning they must take nine tricks in order to make the contract.

Bridge Basics

You know that the trump suit (or notrump) is determined by the last bid during the auction. One member of the partnership that wins the auction becomes declarer, and the other's hand is laid down as the dummy. What you might not know is the declarer is the first member of the partnership to name the suit that ultimately becomes the trump suit. No matter how many bids have been taken in the auction, the first person to name the suit plays it.

The Play's the Thing

So how does play proceed?

Once the declarer is determined, the player to the declarer's left will make what is known as the opening lead. The partner of the declarer waits until the lead is made before exposing his hand as the dummy.

The cards are laid out in suits, arranged in order vertically from highest to lowest with the trump suit, if there is one, to the dummy's right. For example, this is what the dummy might look like if one player had opened 1 ♠ and his partner had bid 2 ♠, followed by three passes:

♠	♥	♦	♣
A	Q	J	5
10	7	10	4
4	5	9	
8			

The cards are displayed this way only to provide a glimpse of what will actually be on the table. Just about every other diagram in this book will display hands—or full deals—the way you would see the cards in a newspaper bridge column.

Our example auction started with 1 ♠ and ended with 2 ♠. The declarer's hand might be:

♠ K Q 7 6 5

♥ A 4

♦ A 5 4

♣ 1 0 8 7

Note that the spades in the dummy as displayed in the first diagram are to the declarer's left, the dummy's right. When there is a trump suit, it is always placed on the table with the trumps on the left-hand side. The dummy also usually puts down the cards with colors alternating left to right.

Bridge Lingo

If you find yourself in the company of experienced bridge players, you may hear them use the term *lefty* or *righty* and wonder what they're talking about. Those are references to left-hand opponent and right-hand opponent, also known in the vernacular as LHO and RHO.

Always Follow Suit

Suppose in the given example you are the declarer, which means your left-hand opponent will fire the first shot. Say that person starts with the ♣A. That's the highest card of the suit, and you have clubs in both hands—in your own and in dummy—so you cannot win this trick.

In this case, you would reach over and play the ♣4 from the dummy, then wait for your right-hand opponent to play. It would then be your turn, so you would probably play the ♣7.

Note that in naming a card, the denomination (suit or notrump) comes before the card, as with ♣4, which indicates the four of clubs. With bids, the number comes first, so that there is no confusion between the bid of 4♣ and the four of clubs card, which would be ♣4.

Need to Know

When you are playing with a trump suit, any card of the trump suit will beat any card of a non-trump suit, but there is a significant condition attached to the use of trumps in this way. You must be out of the suit that is being played before you can use a trump on that suit. The laws of the game are pretty strict about failing to follow suit when you actually can, especially when you fail to follow suit and win the trick with a trump. The penalty for breaking this rule is severe.

After the first trick has been played, the player who makes the next play will be the one who won the first trick—in this case your LHO. If the opening lead had been a different club, one that was taken by your right-hand opponent, then RHO would lead to the second trick.

Similarly, if the opening leader had started with a spade instead of a club and you had won it in the dummy with the king, as declarer you would have picked a card from the dummy to play to the second trick.

This continues through until all the cards are played. The winner of each trick is the leader to the next trick.

Bridge Lingo

When you play a trump to win a trick against a non-trump suit, you are said to be winning a trick by ruffing. Note that *ruff* can be a verb, as in "I ruffed the heart with my last trump," and it can be a noun, as in "I took two ruffs in the dummy to make my bid."

In rubber and party bridge, whenever one side wins a trick, all the cards of that trick are gathered together and placed in front of one of the players of the winning side. The piles of four cards are kept separated so that the number of tricks won can be determined with a glance at any time during the play.

In duplicate bridge, the deals are played multiple times, so the cards are not mixed together during play as with rubber bridge. The cards arrive in trays—known as boards—with pockets for the cards designated North, South, East, and West.

The declarer does not touch the dummy's cards during play but instead designates the card to be played by the dummy. Each player keeps his own cards in front of him, placed vertically for tricks that have been won and horizontally for tricks lost. At the end of play, each player's cards are returned to the pocket of the tray they came from, and when the round is called, the tray is moved to another table.

It is outside the scope of this chapter to offer advice on how to play the cards in a contract of 2 ♠. Suffice it to say that there is much more to it than simply following suit.

Card play technique will come later, but you can see that the basics of play are easy to follow.

It's a Contract

Now that the word *contract* has been mentioned, it's time to explain what it is. After all, the name of the game is contract bridge.

Before Harold Vanderbilt invented contract bridge in 1925, the game was known as auction bridge. The bidding was rudimentary, of course, by today's standards, but in every case an auction preceded play.

In auction bridge, your score was determined by how many tricks you took.

Extra Points

In the game of bridge as it is played now, there are certain bonuses for taking a certain number of tricks. If you take nine tricks in notrump and have bid to the "game" level (3NT), you get a bonus. The same goes for ten tricks in spades or hearts (major suits) and for eleven tricks in diamonds or clubs (minor suits), assuming you have bid at least 4♥ or 4♠ or to the five level in clubs or diamonds. For those who are really ambitious, there are even bigger bonuses for taking twelve and thirteen tricks. Taking all but one trick is called a small slam; taking them all is known as a grand slam.

In auction bridge, you can bid 1♥, and if you take all thirteen tricks, you get the grand slam bonus. Similarly, if you bid 1♦ and take eleven tricks, you get the game bonus.

Vanderbilt's innovation changed the landscape with a simple new requirement: To earn a game or slam bonus, you had to bid it. If you want the extra points for a major suit game, you had to bid at least 4♠ or 4♥.

Bridge Basics

After you sign a contract to buy a house, you pay a penalty if you back out. Similarly, when you contract to make a certain number of tricks in bridge, there is a penalty for not achieving your goal. There are ways for your opponents to make that penalty significant.

The creative railroad tycoon also introduced the idea of vulnerability.

In rubber and party bridge, a game is typically played in three sets—a rubber. The first to win two sets is the winner. You win a set by being the first to get enough points to win a game—100 points.

When you have won a game, you are considered to be vulnerable, meaning certain bonuses increase—as do penalties if you fail to make your contract.

In rubber and party bridge, you have two ways of scoring: below the line and above the line on the score pad. The objective is to get to 100 points below the line, which is what you need for game. The way to score points below the line is to win the auction and make your contract.

Bridge Basics

Each trick you score in bridge carries a certain point value. For every odd trick—a trick in excess of the book of six—you score 20 if it's a minor suit or 30 if it's a major suit. For notrump, the first odd trick scores 40 points, and subsequent tricks score 30. All of these are below the line and count toward the 100 you need for game.

You can score a game in one fell swoop by bidding and making 3 NT, 4♠ or 4♥ or 5♦ or 5♣. The notrump game will come out to 100 points by virtue of the first odd trick scoring 40 points. Two more tricks at 30 points each gives you 100 points. Game in a major suit takes ten tricks: four tricks in excess of book at 30 points each for 120 points. Game in a minor suit requires eleven tricks: five tricks in excess of book at 20 points apiece.

You don't have to bid it all at once, however. If you bid and make two of a major suit on consecutive deals, that will score 60 points below the line twice, which will give you a game score.

Whoever reaches the game score of 100 points twice wins the rubber.

Pay the Piper

Auction bridge rules included penalties for failing to achieve the number of tricks that were supposed to be taken, but the scoring took a whole new direction with Vanderbilt's introduction of the concept of vulnerability.

If your side has won one game of a rubber, you are now considered vulnerable. If the other side wins a game, they are vulnerable also. But what does that mean?

Bridge Lingo

When you fail to make your contract by not taking the number of tricks you needed, you "go down" or "go set." The opponents might say, "We beat him in four spades" or "We set him in four spades" or "We set his contract." There are other, more colorful ways of describing an unsuccessful attempt. "He put it on the floor" describes an inept attempt, as does "He butchered that contract." They all add up to the same meaning: not enough tricks taken.

When an opponent senses—or can tell from his own hand—that you have bid too much, he can try to increase your penalty for going down. The opponent does this by saying double, or by pulling the red double card from the bidding box.

Adding Up Fast

When you are not vulnerable, the penalty for not making your contract is 50 points per undertrick, or tricks short of the contract target. If you bid 4♠ and take eight tricks, the two undertricks will cost you 100 points. If you were vulnerable and missed your mark in 4♠ by two tricks, it's 100 points per undertrick, or 200 points.

When you are doubled, the numbers escalate quickly. When not vulnerable, the first doubled undertrick costs 100 points, the second and third trick cost 200 points each. Beginning with the fourth undertrick, it's 300 points a pop.

If you are vulnerable and doubled, the first undertrick is 200 points. Subsequent undertricks are 300 points each.

In rubber and party bridge, the penalties for failing to make your contract are written above the line on your opponents' side of the score pad. These points do not count toward game. In duplicate bridge, penalties for going down show up as minus scores for you and plus scores for the opponents.

PART TWO

All About Bidding

CHAPTER 3

13 +13 = GAME **ABCs of Bidding**

> ### In This Chapter
>
> ➤ Counting points—what makes an opening bid?
>
> ➤ Opening at the one level
>
> ➤ Hand evaluation and reevaluation
>
> ➤ Opening at the two level and higher

In this chapter, you will learn the rudiments of communicating with your partner about your assets, the cards you hold in your hand. You will also learn the difference between hands with "body" and hands that are not as strong as they might seem. You will learn how the auction can cause you to revise your opinion of a hand, and you will see the difference between a sound opening bid and one that is sketchy at best.

Most of your opening bids will be at the one level—for example, 1♥ —but not all. You will see what it means to open at higher levels—and it's not what you think.

Finally, there will be a recap of the main principles in this chapter.

The "Points" of It All

The dealer has distributed the cards to all players. You waited until all the cards were dealt before picking up your cards, and you have counted to make sure you have thirteen. You carefully arranged your hand into suits, alternating reds and blacks.

Now what?

Well, you are waiting for the dealer to make the first call.

Bridge Basics

In bridge, the dealer is always first to act by passing or making a bid. This is easy to understand in party bridge, where a player actually distributed the cards. It is also true in duplicate, where there is but one shuffle and deal—at the outset of the game—and the position of the dealer is marked on the tray in which the cards are stored and moved from table to table.

While you wait for the dealer to act, you should be counting your points. That is the first step in the process of evaluating your hand. More about evaluation in just a bit.

High-card points (HCP), you will remember from Chapter 2, are assigned to aces, kings, queens, and jacks: 4 points for the ace, 3 for the king, 2 for the queen, and 1 for the jack.

You might be asking yourself why high-card points are important. This was covered briefly in Chapter 2, but a bit more detail is appropriate here.

Counting points is important basically for two reasons:

1. Bridge is a game of tricks.

2. A trick, four cards played in clockwise order, is won by the highest card played.

Look at this example:

North

♠ 9 8 7

West   East

♠ A 4 3 2   ♠ K Q J

South

♠ 1 0 6 5

This is just one suit. In a typical hand, you will have some of all four suits. The diagram is presented in this way to make a point.

Counting the high-card points, West has 4 for the ace. East has 6: 3 for the king, 2 for the queen, and 1 for the jack. North and South have no high-card points. When this suit is led, North-South will take no tricks. If West starts with the ace, that will win the trick because it is the highest card in the suit. If West leads another spade, East remains with the king and queen, both of which are higher than any card in the North or South hands.

Bridge Lingo

In bridge, the ace and the face cards are known as honors. The nomenclature originated with the rubber bridge practice of awarding points to any player who holds honors in the trump suit or, when the contract is notrump, all four aces. In that setting, the 10 is technically an honor as well, so any player holding A K Q J 10 in the trump suit is awarded 150 points, and the same is true for holding four aces at notrump. For holding four of the top five honors, the award is 100 points. The lucky player with A K Q J 10 in trumps is said to hold 150 honors.

Even after winning a trick with one of his honors, East will have another honor that also will take a trick. Move the high cards around a bit and it's a different story for North-South.

North

♠K 8 7

West   East

♠10 4 3 2   ♠Q J 9

South

♠A 6 5

Now when West leads a spade, the North-South hands have the top two cards in the suit and can take two tricks.

It's easy to construct a full deal where one side can take all or most of the tricks with very few high-card points. Don't hold your breath waiting for one of those. In general, you need high cards to take tricks, especially when you are playing without a trump suit.

Bridge Lingo

Every now and then you will pick up a hand with six cards of one suit, seven of another and no cards in the other two suits, or perhaps two six-card suits. Hands with such wild distribution are known in bridge parlance as freaks. They occur so rarely that there is not much in bridge literature about what to do when one of them comes along. Experience and intuition will help in those situations.

Adding Them Up

Now that you have your hand separated into suits, it's time to count up your high-card points. With 40 high-card points in the deck, it's not hard to imagine that the average hand has about 10. Of course, you will pick up hands with no high-card points, and some with 20 or more, but over the long haul you will average about 10.

Counting points has different objectives depending on your position at the table in relation to the dealer, including when the dealer is you. Here's a typical hand:

♠ Q J 8

♥ A J 6 5 3

♦ 1 0 6

♣ Q 1 0 4

The spade suit has 3 points (2 for the queen, 1 for the jack), and there are 5 points in hearts (4 for the ace, 1 for the jack), 0 points in diamonds, and 2 in clubs. This is an okay but undistinguished hand. If you were dealer, you would not consider it for an opening bid. On the other hand, should your partner open the bidding with 1♠ or 1♥, your outlook for those thirteen cards will improve considerably. More about responding to an opening bid in the next chapter.

Players count their points in part because through the information exchanged in the bidding, they want to know whether they have enough assets to bid game or even slam. Not counting adjustments for distribution, here are the high-card point requirements for games and slams:

Game

3NT (nine tricks): 25 HCP

4♠ or 4♥ (10 tricks): 25 HCP

5♦ or 5♣ (11 tricks): 29 HCP

Slam

Small slam in any suit (12 tricks): 33 HCP

Grand slam in any suit (13 tricks): 36 HCP

As stated, it is possible to make enough tricks for game or slam without so many high-card points, and you will learn more about how to identify the elements that make up for the lack of high-card points later on. For now, remember that to get credit for the bonuses that apply to games and slams, you must actually bid to the appropriate contract.

The First Step

So what makes an opening bid?

In the days when Charles Goren was the leading authority on bridge, players opened the bidding with four-card major suits—if they had at least a good thirteen high-card points hand. That has changed. Today's players prefer five-card major suits, where an opening bid of 1♠ or 1♥ promises at least five cards in the suit and the minimum standard for opening bids has been lowered to 12 HCP.

Bridge Facts

The vast majority of hands fall into five distinct "patterns"—that is, the way in which the suits are distributed. Slightly more than 71 percent of all hands you will see will have one of five different "shapes": 4-4-3-2 (21.5 percent), 5-3-3-2 (15.5 percent), 5-4-3-1 (12.9 percent), 4-3-3-3 and 5-4-2-2 (both about 10.5 percent). To clarify: 4-4-3-2 means two four-card suits, one three-card suit and one two-card suit in any combination.

Here is a chart to help you decide whether your hand is good enough in high-card points to open the bidding. For now, the topic is mostly about normal opening bids at the one level. Responder's first bid and opener's rebid will be discussed in the next chapter.

HCP	Action
0–11	Pass
12–20	Open one of a suit
15–17	Open 1NT if balanced
18–19	Open one of a suit, planning to rebid 2NT if balanced

Need to Know

It is important to distinguish between hands that are balanced and those that are not. In bridge terms, *balanced* means the four suits are more or less evenly distributed with no more than one two-card suit. Technically, there are only three hand patterns that fit the definition of balanced: 4-4-3-2, 4-3-3-3, and 5-3-3-2. Many players, however, include 5-4-2-2, especially when considering whether to open 1NT.

A couple of opening bids at the two-level warrant inclusion in this discussion:

20–21   Open 2NT if balanced

21+   Open 2♣, strong and artificial, with a long suit and unbalanced hand

Note that "strong and artificial" means that the 2♣ opener is showing a hand with lots of high-card points (strong) and that he does not necessarily have clubs (artificial). It is important to remember that you cannot pass when partner opens a strong 2♣.

With balanced hands that are stronger than 21 HCP, open 2♣, planning to rebid in notrump.

So far, the discussion has centered on high cards and what is necessary in general to open the bidding. Remember, every call you make sends a message to your partner—and, of course, to the opponents.

Strive For Five

The bidding system you will learn in this book is based on five-card majors. As stated previously, when you open the bidding with 1♠ or 1♥, almost invariably this promises at least five cards in the suit opened.

This is a typical opening bid in the five-card major system:

♠Q J 10 7 6

♥A K 6 3

♦6

♣Q J 4

This is an easy 1♠ opener: you have five of them and you have 13 high-card points.

Suppose, however, that this was your hand:

♠Q J 10 7

♥A K 6

♦8 5

♣Q J 4 3

You have the same 13 high-card points, but you don't have a five-card major. What should you do? On this deal, it's easy: you start with 1♣. That tells your partner that you have enough high-card strength to open the bidding and you have at least three clubs.

Open the bidding on a three-card suit? Really?

Well, in the five-card major bidding system, occasionally you have no choice.

Say for example, that you have this hand:

♠ Q J 10 7

♥ A K 6 4

♦ 8 5

♣ Q J 4

You have four cards each in spades and hearts—not enough to open one of those suits. What should you do?

You could go ahead and open one of a major, but partnership trust, as you will discover later in this book, is very important, so it's a good idea not to violate the agreements you made when you and your partner decided on the five-card major system.

So what does that leave? With the given hand, you must open 1♣. At least you have a couple of honors in the suit.

Bridge Basics

In the language of bridge, agreeing to play five-card major suit openings requires you to also use the so-called convenient minor opening. It comes up mostly when you have two four-card majors and 3-2 distribution in the minor suits. In practice, when you open a minor—especially when it's 1♦, you have at least four in the suit most of the time. Why does it make a difference for 1♦? The only time you have to open on a three-card diamond suit is when you are specifically 4-4 in the majors with only two clubs.

On rare occasions, you might decide to open a major with only four cards. The following hand is one such case:

♠ K J 10 7

♥ A K Q 4

♦ 8 5

♣ 7 6 2

hen you open the bidding, your partner tends to lead the suit you started with in the event
t the opponents outbid you in the auction. With this hand, you must open, but you have
a decided preference between clubs and hearts. Although your partner will expect a five-
card suit when you open 1♥, any anxiety he feels about your being short one heart will be
neutralized by gratitude to you for getting him off to the right lead.

Bridge Basics

When you have an opening hand and two suits of five cards each, open the higher-ranking suit,
planning to rebid the lower-ranking suit at your next turn to bid if it's appropriate. Do not let
the difference in quality of the two suits persuade you to make a poor choice. Suppose you
pick up this hand:

> ♠ 10 8 7 6 4

> ♥ A K J 6 4

> ♦ 8 5

> ♣ A J 4

That's an opener for sure, and many inexperienced players will naturally want to start with the
stronger suit, hearts. That is wrong, wrong, wrong. What if your partner bids 1NT? You don't
want to rebid a five-card suit, and introducing spades at the two level shows a much stronger
hand than you have. It's a lot easier if you start with 1♠. Over 1NT, you have an easy rebid of
2♥. Always start with the higher-ranking suit.

Riding the Range

So far, the examples presented for opening bids at the one level have been modest hands.
You probably remember, however, that the upper limit for your one-level opener is 20 high-
card points. From 12 to 20 is a wide range, but the bidding system is set up to allow you to
start at a low level with a really powerful hand, planning to express that strength at your
second turn to speak.

The topic of opener's rebid—his second time to make a call during the auction—will be
covered in depth later in this book. A couple of examples will give you a preview of how to
manage those very strong hands while relieving your anxiety about starting with a puny-
sounding bid of one when you have, in the vernacular, a rock crusher.

Bridge Lingo

Bridge jargon can be colorful, and it is often descriptive. The terms *singleton*, *doubleton* and *tripleton*, as you might expect, describe holdings in a suit of one, two, and three cards, respectively. Quadrupleton, if it were ever in the jargon pipeline, has not caught on. Another way to describe a solitary card in a suit is *stiff,* perhaps indicating that the card is considered dead, with no way to escape capture when a higher card is played.

Suppose you are dealt this hand:

♠ A K Q 7 6 3

♥ A K Q 5 4

♦ 8

♣ 7

Some players might open with a strong 2 ♣, but two-suited hands are difficult to bid starting at the two level. Experienced players would start with 1 ♠, planning to rebid strongly in hearts should their partner find a bid. Say your partner responded to your 1 ♠ bid with 1NT. Your second bid would be 3 ♥, showing a very strong hand, although the bid would not promise more than four hearts. Partner is not allowed to pass 3 ♥, so you will get another chance to bid hearts to show more than four.

Here's another:

♠ A K 1 0

♥ A K J 4

♦ K 1 0 8 5

♣ 7 6

You counted your points and came up with 18. That's too many to open 1NT, which has an upper limit of 17 high-card points. You don't have a five-card major, so you have to open 1 ♦. If your partner responds 1 ♥, you will bid 4 ♥, which shows the power of your hand (you will see why in the next chapter). If your partner bids 1 ♠, you will rebid 2NT, which shows a balanced hand too strong to open 1NT (15–17) but not strong enough to open 2NT (20–21).

Are you getting the idea about how you and your partner exchange information? Once the auction starts, everything you do—even passing—conveys information.

Asset Management

The point-count method of hand evaluation is tried and true, and it is used by most players because it is simple to remember and easy to apply.

Some care must be taken, however, in using points to determine your actions. Not all points are created equal, and their value is often determined by their location.

Need to Know

Most expert players believe the ace is undervalued at 4 points, and the same players view the jack as overvalued at 1 point. Some experienced players actually add value to a hand that contains no jacks and devalue hands with no aces. When assessing your hand and making decisions about bidding or passing, give more weight to hands with aces and kings rather than those with queens and jacks.

It is a good general principle to give higher value to hands with high cards—especially aces—in long suits. Consider this situation

Dummy

♦A 7 6 5 4

You

♦9 8 2

There are five missing cards in the suit. If you play low from your hand and the dummy two times, there is a good chance that when you play the third round of the suit, the ace will pick up the last outstanding diamond, and the 7 and 6 will be good. In fact, from a statistical standpoint it is more likely that the outstanding cards in the suit will divide 3-2 than 4-1 or 5-0. So you have a fine chance to take three diamond tricks by using correct technique.

Now what if you had the same diamonds in your hand but instead of five to the ace in the dummy, you had AK7. How many tricks do you think you would be able to take? Right— two is your maximum. There is no alignment of the opponents' diamonds that would allow you to take more than two tricks. You have more high-card points between the two hands, but the shortness of the suit limits your tricks.

Do you see the advantage of having that ace in a long suit? You don't even need the king most of the time to get three tricks.

Bridge Lingo

One of the key elements of hand evaluation is the number of so-called quick tricks that a hand possesses. A quick trick is what it sounds like—a card that will take a trick when the declarer wants to take it. Translation: aces and kings. Queens and jacks can take tricks, but only after you lead the suit two or three times. Queens and jacks, therefore, represent slow tricks, which are better for defense than for offense.

In deciding whether to open a hand, consider how many quick tricks the hand contains. You have one quick trick for every ace you hold and half a quick trick for every guarded king—guarded meaning that it has at least one other card with it. It is considered as half a trick because half of the time the ace will be in front of the king—held by the right-hand opponent—and half of the time the ace will be behind the king—held by the left-hand opponent.

With these ideas in mind, consider these two hands:

1. ♠ A J 10 9 7

   ♥ K J 10

   ♦ A 10 9 8 5

   ♣ 7

2. ♠ Q J 2

   ♥ K Q

   ♦ Q J 8 7 6

   ♣ Q 6

Both hands have 13 high-card points, but there are major differences between the two.

Hand 1 has two aces, a king and two jacks. The high cards are in the long suits. Hand 2 has no aces and only one quick trick—the ♥ K Q, which will almost always produce a trick with one lead of the suit.

Although there are 13 high-card points present in Hand 2, they are not what you would call quality points. The ♣ Q, for example, has only one card with it, so it is not guarded. If an opponent has the ♣ A and ♣ K—or even if the two cards are split between the two opponents—when they play them, the queen will be taken. The ♣ Q might be worthless.

Similarly, the ♥KQ are not pulling their full weight, as they would be if there was one low card to go with them. An opponent can cash the ♥A and capture one of your honors with no effort.

In sum, Hand 2 may have 13 HCP, but it is a poor collection and not worthy of an opening bid because of all the flaws.

Bridge Basics

One of the key elements of hand evaluation is the presence—or lack—of a fit with your partner in a suit that can be trumps. You have a so-called golden fit when each of you has at least four of the same suit—and it's best if the fit is in spades or hearts. One reason most players like five-card major openings is that after a 1♠ or 1♥ opener, it is much easier to discover those eight-card fits.

Here are some hand-evaluation tips that can help you distinguish between good points and bad points.

Add value if:

> ➤ You have your high-card points in long suits

> ➤ You have two suits of at least five cards each headed by honors

> ➤ Most of your high-card points are made up of aces and kings

> ➤ You have a singleton or void—one or no cards in some suit—and a fit with partner

> ➤ Your partner has shown a singleton or void along with a fit for your suit

Subtract value if:

> ➤ Your hand has no aces

> ➤ Your hand is flat"—balanced—especially when you have only one four-card suit, as with 4-3-3-3 shape

> ➤ Your high cards are in short suits

> ➤ Your high-card points are made up mostly of queens and jacks

➤ Your partner bids and/or rebids a suit in which you are short

➤ You have poor spot cards (non-face cards) in your long suits. For example, ♣A 10 9 8 7 has much more trick-taking potential than ♣A 5 4 3 2. With the former, you have a good chance to survive even with a bad split if your partner has any help at all in the suit.

What this all means is that you might find yourself opening some good 11-point hands and declining to open some 13-pointers.

Thinking Cap

It is critical in hand evaluation not to be bound by rules that say all 13-point hands should be opened and all 11-point hands should be passed. Experience will help improve your judgment.

You have already seen an example of a very poor 13-point hand. How about the following?

   ♠A K 10 9 6 5

   ♥3

   ♦A 9 8 5 3

   ♣7

It's only 11 high-card points, but any red-blooded bridge player holding that hand would open 1♠ without thinking twice. First, your high cards are in your long suits. Second, your best suit is the "boss" suit—spades. It's much tougher for the opponents to outbid you when you have the highest-ranking suit. Third, if you find a fit with your partner, you will take a lot of tricks, as when your partner turns up with

   ♠Q 7 3

   ♥6 5 4

   ♦K 1 0 6 2

   ♣A 8 2

Your partner has only 9 high-card points but with the double fit in spades and diamonds, it would not be surprising to see you take 12 tricks. It might not be that easy to get to 6♠ or 6♦, but game in spades is virtually impregnable.

Bridge Facts

Many players add points to their hands for extra cards in their long suits: 1 point for a six-card suit, 2 for a seven-card suit. On that basis, an 11-point hand with a six-card suit can be boosted to 12 points, good enough to open.

More than One

At one time, the higher you bid to start the auction, the more high-card strength you showed. That method went the way of the dinosaurs long ago. Players found that starting at high levels robbed them of what is known as bidding space, a precious commodity when you think a slam might be possible.

Nowadays, with just a few exceptions, opening bids higher than the one level usually show weakness and a long suit. Such a bid does not show high-card strength.

Here are some higher-level bids and their meanings:

> ➤ 2♦ / 2♥ / 2♠: A weak two bid, usually showing a six-card suit and 6–10 high-card points and limited defensive values (aces and kings), especially outside of the long suit. The 2♣ is not included because that is a strong artificial bid showing a very strong hand. Similarly, a 2NT opening shows 20–21 high-card points in a balanced hand.

> ➤ 3♣ / 3♦ / 3♥ / 3♠: Typically a seven-card suit with no specific range in high-card points, but nothing near an opening bid. The bid usually delivers at least a decent playing suit. A minimum would be a seven-card suit headed by the QJ10.

> ➤ 3NT: You have one of two choices, which are 24–25 balanced or a specialized bid usually based on a long, strong minor suit.

> ➤ 4♣ / 4♦ / 4♥ / 4♠: For majors, at least a seven-card suit; for minors, more likely an eight-card suit. There are tactical considerations that will be covered in later chapters.

> ➤ 5♣ / 5♦: This is usually an eight-card suit.

> ➤ 5♥ / 5♠: Specialized opening bids—perhaps the rarest in the game—that show very strong hands. The partner of the opener is invited to raise to six with the ace or king of the suit, to seven with both.

Bridge Basics

Most opening bids at levels of two and higher are made with the expectation that they will interfere with the opponents' constructive bidding. In that sense, they are known as preemptive bids—that is, taking bidding space away from the opponents. Players who make weak preemptive bids do not expect to make their contracts unless their partners come through with considerable strength.

There are certain considerations when deciding whether to open the bidding with a weak hand.

Vulnerability is the primary concern. When you are vulnerable, opening at a high level with a weak hand invites a big penalty if the opponents can maneuver to double you—and experienced opponents will do just that.

It is best to apply the Rule of Two and Three when considering whether to make a weak preemptive bid. If you are vulnerable, you should be within two tricks of your contract, assuming your partner has no help for you in terms of high cards. If you are not vulnerable, you can be a bit frisky, getting to within three of the level that you bid to.

For example, even vulnerable, you might try 2♠ with:

> ♠ A K J 10 9 6
>
> ♥ 3 2
>
> ♦ J 9 8 5
>
> ♣ 7

With such a good suit, you have some protection against foul trump splits. You would be very unlucky not to take at least five tricks with this hand in a spade contract, even if your partner were "broke."

It's a different story with:

> ♠ K J 6 5 3 2
>
> ♥ 7 6 3
>
> ♦ K 9 8
>
> ♣ 6

This would be acceptable as a weak two-bid at favorable vulnerability—they are, you are not—but it courts disaster at unfavorable vulnerability—you are, they are not.

There will be more about preemptive bidding—also known as defensive bidding—later on.

That said, if you prefer an aggressive style and don't mind "going for a number" occasionally—the number being minus 1100 or worse—get in there and mix it up whenever you have a long suit. Just make sure your partner is understanding. After all, he will also be writing the big minus on his scorecard, not just you. Experience will guide you in this area—if aggressive preemption wins out two out of three times, you are well ahead of the game. That's a success rate of 67 percent, good enough to win most pairs games you may play in.

Recap

Here is a recap of what you have learned so far.

➤ How to count points:

Ace: 4

King: 3

Queen: 2

Jack: 1

➤ What you need to open the bidding: 12 HCP or a good 11 HCP; How to tell good points from poor points

➤ How many points you need to bid a game:

Contract	HCP required
3NT	25 HCP
4♥ / 4♠	25 HCP
5♣ / 5♦	29 HCP
Small slam	33 HCP
Grand slam	36 HCP

➤ What it means to open the bidding higher than the one level:

2♣ and 2NT: Strong bids

Other two-level: 6-10 HCP, decent suit, limited defensive values

Three level suit: decent seven-card suits and not much else

3NT: Very strong balance or based on a long, strong minor suit

Four level: Eight-card suit and not much else

 **Better Bidding for All**

In This Chapter

➤ Losing trick count
➤ Sound versus light
➤ Responder's first bid
➤ Opener's first rebid

In this chapter, you will read a review of what you have learned so far about the language of bidding and different features of a hand that can affect its value. You will learn about your responsibilities—and how best to tell your story—when your partner opens the bidding. You will find out why you will sometimes mention a poor suit ahead of a strong one. And you will learn about a nifty trick for determining how high you and your partner should bid. You will also read about light and sound opening bids and the popular Rule of Twenty and how you might apply it—if at all.

Other important questions will be answered: When you open and your partner finds a response, how do you continue to paint an accurate picture of your hand?

Targets

At all times, you are mindful of the point of conducting an auction in the game of bridge, and your first objective is to try to determine how high you should go.

There are bonuses for bidding games and slams, and you want to reach the maximum potential of your assets combined with those of your partner. Bidding is designed to help you reach that potential.

Here's another reminder of the benchmarks to keep in mind as the auction unfolds:

> ➤ 25 points: Game in notrump or four of a major

> ➤ 29 points: Game in a minor suit

> ➤ 33 points: Small slam (12 tricks)

> ➤ 36 points: Grand slam (all 13 tricks)

Falling short of these standards doesn't necessarily mean you can't bid game. You will see how to make use of distributional factors that can greatly improve your chances for lots of tricks.

Points, by the way, are not necessarily of the high-card variety. You will learn in this chapter how to reevaluate a hand upward when certain conditions are met.

Bridge Facts

It's an old saying, but a true one: points don't take tricks—trumps do. That usually applies to a defender who mistakenly thinks a large collection of high-card points can make up for the opponents' extreme distribution. It can also apply it situations where the card gods bestow lots of high-card points on a partnership—with no way for the partners to make more than a few tricks.

In general, however, the benchmarks are accurate, especially when you have chosen a contract without a trump suit (notrump). When you don't have trumps to slow the opponents down, you need high cards.

Shape Up

A common mistake among inexperienced players is to count points for distribution at the wrong time. What does that mean?

First, the general rule for distributional points is as follows:

> ➤ 1 point for a doubleton (two cards in a suit)

> ➤ 3 points for a singleton (one card in a suit)

> ➤ 5 points for a void (no cards in a suit)

That's accurate, but only when a fit is found. Say that out loud; then say it again. It is vital that you remember this aspect of distributional points.

It bears repeating that a fit means you and your partner have eight or more cards in a suit between you—and, yes, it can matter how those cards are distributed between the two hands.

Here's a look at two hands to illustrate how distributional points can help you with your hand evaluation. The declarer's hand and the dummy are displayed as West (declarer) and East (dummy), instead of North and South, so you can easily see how they match up.

West	East
♠ A K 1 0 5 4	♠ Q J 9 8
♥ 7 6 3	♥ 4
♦ K Q 1 0 6 3	♦ A 9 5 4
♣ –	♣ 1 0 9 8 7

There are only 19 high-card points between the two hands, but East-West would be very unlucky not to be able to take twelve tricks. Few pairs would actually get to slam with these two hands, but if they did, they would make it most of the time, thanks to the singleton heart with East and the void in clubs with West.

Count the tricks in a spade contract. West would be playing it and could take five spade tricks in his hand along with five diamond tricks. That's ten tricks just to start. To get two more, it would be necessary only to play a heart from the West hand. Declarer could take two heart ruffs in the East hand to get up to twelve tricks.

Even if the opponent on lead started with a trump and played a second trump when in with a heart winner, there would still be two trumps in the East hand to deal with the two losing hearts.

Distribution plays a major role in this situation from both sides. West has two good five-card suits, plus a void in clubs. The opponents cannot take even one trick in clubs because West can ruff the first round of the suit.

Bridge Lingo

When you have a void in a suit in one hand and your partner has low cards in the same suit, the opponents have all the high cards, but as long as you have trumps, the opponents can take no tricks in the suit. That means that with 10 high-card points—the ace, king, queen, and jack— no tricks are available. In such cases, you are said to be playing with a 30-point deck.

This is jumping the gun a bit, but here's how to evaluate the East hand: 7 high-card points for the ♦A and the ♠QJ, plus 3 points for the singleton heart. That's 10 points. If East had three spades instead of four, the singleton would not have the same value. Think about it. If an opponent led a trump, as suggested previously, then played another on getting in with a heart, East would have only one trump to deal with West's two heart losers. Twelve tricks would be impossible.

Do you see where this is going? Yes, when you have extra cards in the suit your partner opens, you can count extra points for your distributional features.

Bridge Basics

When your partner opens a major suit and you have three-card support, that is adequate to offer support—that is, you can raise to a level indicating how strong your hand is (e.g., 1♥ to 2♥). With four or more cards in the major suit your partner opens, your hand improves dramatically, and any distributional feature your hand possesses is magnified.

Change the hands a bit, and the number of tricks available can change dramatically:

West	East
♠AK109854	♠QJ
♥764	♥A9
♦KQ	♦854
♣8	♣Q76543

The two hands still have nine spades between them, but the layout is not so friendly. With only two trumps in the East hand, if an opponent starts with a trump, it's possible only nine tricks will be available: seven spades, one heart, and one diamond. The hands don't fit so well, and although East has a doubleton, with only two trumps he can't count any distributional points for that feature. The singleton club does not generate any tricks for West, so it doesn't count in the equation either.

As you have probably noticed, the art of bidding is aimed at uncovering the attributes of your hand and your partner's that maximize trick-taking prospects.

Losing Trick Count

Counting high-card points is a tried and true method of determining how high you and your partner should bid. Distribution, of course, is also very important, as you have seen already in this chapter.

There is another way of evaluating the playing potential of hands. It is a method used by many experts, but that fact should not discourage casual or less-experienced players. Losing trick count (LTC) works for anyone who applies it correctly. The key to using the tool is to remember that it applies only when a trump fit has been found.

Here are the basics: A loser is a missing ace, king, or queen in a suit of three cards or longer. No suit has more than three losers. A suit of two low cards counts as two losers. A low singleton counts as one loser. A suit with a doubleton ace or king counts as one loser, a doubleton queen counts as two.

Here are some examples:

➤ ♠ A K Q 7 6: No losers

➤ ♠ A Q 7 6 4 : One loser

➤ ♠ K J 7 6 4 : Two losers

➤ ♠ A 7 6 5 4 : Two losers

➤ ♠ 1 0 9 6 5 4 : Three losers

➤ ♠ 1 0 8 : Two losers

➤ ♠ A 7 : One loser

➤ ♠ K Q : One loser

➤ ♠ K Q 7 : One loser

➤ ♠ 7 : One loser

➤ ♠ A : No losers

➤ ♠ void : No losers

So how does all this come into play?

No suit can have more than three losers, so no hand can have more than twelve losers. The same goes for your partner's hand. There are, therefore, a maximum of twenty-four losers between the two hands.

Using twenty-four as a base, when you add your losers to your partner's losers, the sum should be the number of tricks the combined hands can take. That is, if you have seven losers and your partner's bidding has shown at most seven losers, that's fourteen. Subtract that number from twenty-four and you find that ten is the likely number of tricks your side can take in your trump fit of at least eight cards.

Remember that LTC is applied only when your side has a fit. You have probably worked out that LTC is most useful when applied to major suit openings or when your partner opens one of a minor suit and raises your major suit response.

To further the equation, there are numbers to consider for the opening bidder and his partner—the responder.

For the opener:

> ➤ Minimum opening bid: Seven losers

> ➤ Enough to invite game over a simple raise: Six losers

> ➤ Enough to insist on game over a simple raise: Five losers

For the responder:

> ➤ Simple raise of opener's suit: Nine losers

> ➤ Invitational raise of opener's suit: Eight losers

> ➤ Opening hand plus a fit for opener: Seven losers

> ➤ A hand with at least mild slam interest: Six losers

> ➤ A hand with serious slam interest: Five losers

Examples:

West	East
♠ A K 10 9 8	♠ Q J 2
♥ 7 6 3	♥ A 9
♦ K Q	♦ 8 5 4
♣ 8 5	♣ J 7 6 5 4 3

West (seven losers) opens 1♠. East (nine losers) makes a simple raise to 2♠. West adds his seven losers to the expected nine in East's hand and comes up with sixteen. When West does the math (24 – 16 = 8), he has no further ambitions, happily passing.

Suppose, however, that the West hand was a bit different:

West	East
♠ A K 10 9 8	♠ Q J 2
♥ 7 6	♥ A 9
♦ A K Q	♦ 8 5 4
♣ 8 5	♣ J 7 6 5 4 3

Now West has only five losers. Add them to East's expected nine losers and the answer is fourteen, enough for West to sail right into 4 ♠. The combined hands have only 24 high-card points, but using LTC, the good game would be reached.

Turn Off the Light

Al Roth, one of the all-time greats of bridge, was famous for advocating super-sound opening bids. When the world was opening all 13-point hands, Roth and his followers were passing unless a hand contained 14 points. Roth was a great player and superior bidding theorist—he invented several bidding tools still in use—but today there are few adherents to the conservative approach to opening bids.

Sometimes it seems that today's players, especially those in high-level competition, are inclined to open the bidding on any hand with thirteen cards. Hyperbole aside, opening bids have grown lighter and lighter over the years—to the detriment of players ill-equipped to handle that style of bidding.

For many inexperienced players, the dubious Rule of Twenty has been a negative influence and the cause of a lot of bad results.

One reason for the popularity of the Rule of Twenty is that it is pretty simple: you can open the bidding on any hand in which the number of high-card points and the number of cards in your two longest suits total 20.

On the surface, that sounds reasonable. Shapely hands—5-5 or 6-5 in two suits—can have impressive playing strength. Unfortunately, when the Rule of Twenty is applied inappropriately, the result can be disaster.

For starters, not all hands that technically meet the Rule of Twenty standard are the same. Look at these two:

Hand 1	Hand 2
♠ A J 10 9 8	♠ Q J
♥ A J 10 7 6	♥ J 6 5 4 3
♦ 5 4	♦ A
♣ 3	♣ Q 6 5 4 2

Both hands have 10 high-card points, and both have ten cards in their two long suits. The difference between the two is vast, however.

Hand 1 has two quick tricks—the ♠A and the ♥A—and good spot cards in the two long suits. Your prospects on defense are reasonable, and you have an easy rebid after opening 1♠.

Bridge Basics

A hand is said to have body when the spot cards that go with the honors are 10s, 9s, and 8s rather than 4s, 3s, and 2s. The higher so-called intermediate cards can be promoted rather quickly into tricks, whereas promotion of lower spot cards takes much more effort and usually involves losing the lead multiple times.

Hand 2 is a disaster waiting to happen. If you apply the Rule of Twenty and open that mess, it would not be surprising to find yourself or your partner playing a doubled contract at the three level or higher. The two long suits are poor, and you have exactly one trick on defense. What will you do if you open and your partner, believing you have a decent hand, doubles the opponents at some low level?

Common sense is paramount when considering the Rule of Twenty. In fact, some experienced players prefer to use an adaptation called the Rule of Twenty-Two. You still apply the standard of 20 points in the same fashion, but you pass unless the hand also has two quick tricks. That is a reasonable compromise for those who find the Rule of Twenty irresistible.

The "Sound" of Bidding

All in all, beginners will be better off adopting a style of sound opening bids, favoring hands with high cards in long suits, quick tricks for defense (in case the opponents outbid you), and good intermediate cards. Hands with dubious values such as doubleton QJs are devalued, as are hands without aces or with flat shape (e.g., 4-3-3-3).

At some point, especially if you take up duplicate, you will probably want to learn the most popular bidding style, known as 2/1 Game Force (articulated as "two over one game force.") That means that if you open the bidding at the one level and your partner bids something at the two level, as in 1♠—Pass—2♦, with rare exceptions you and your partner must bid game in some denomination.

The 2/1 approach, which will be covered in more depth later in this book, works much better when openers are sound rather than light.

The recommendation that you stick with sound openers does not mean you have to adapt Al Roth's ultraconservative approach. It does mean that you should make an effort to learn hand evaluation so that you can identify features that make hands good, bad, and in between.

Partner Opened—Now What?

When your partner has opened the bidding, the conversation has begun. Opening bids tell different stories, so it's worth recapping what your partner is saying with each of the common opening bids at the one level and two level. For this discussion, the opening bid comes from the dealer.

> ➤ 1♣, 1♦: 12 to 20 HCP, at least three cards in the suit

> ➤ 1♥, 1♠: 12 to 20 HCP, at least five cards in the suit

> ➤ 1NT: 15 to 17 HCP, balanced distribution

> ➤ 2♣: A strong hand (21+ HCP) and at least one long suit; if balanced, 22 to 23 HCP

> ➤ 2♦, 2♥, 2♠: Six-card suit, 6 to 11 HCP

> ➤ 2NT: 20 to 21 HCP, balanced distribution

Talking to Partner

No matter whether your partner's opener is in a major suit or a minor suit, your first obligation after the opening is to decide whether you can respond. It is important to note that of the opening bids on the list you just read, only one—2♣—absolutely requires a response. For all the others, you can pass.

Why would you pass your partner's opening bid?

Remember the statement that every bid sends a message? Well, the message you send when you respond to your partner's opening is that you have at least 6 high-card points. With fewer high-card points, you would pass, also sending a message to your partner that unless he opened with a rock crusher, the deal probably belongs to the opponents.

Why do you need 6 HCP to respond?

In some cases you can get by with 5 high-card points, but you must have some values to respond or your side would routinely get too high. If you could respond with 0 high-card points, it would hamper the exchange of information with your partner.

For example, suppose your partner opened the bidding with this hand:

♠ A K 3

♥ K 10

♦ K Q J 9

♣ Q 10 9 8

Bridge Lingo

When you respond to your partner's opening bid, you are said to be keeping the bidding open. What that means is that if you pass, the next player can close things out by also passing. Remember, once someone has bid, if there are ever three consecutive passes, the auction is over.

This is what would be called a chunky 18 high-card points because of the 10s and 9s. There are too many high-card points for a 1NT opener, so the plan is to open 1♦ and rebid 2NT if your partner bids a major suit. When your partner's response guarantees at least 6 high-card points, you would feel safe rebidding 2NT. With at least 24 high-card points, your side would have the clear majority of the points, and your partner would probably produce at least one useful card.

But suppose you could respond with no points. Now your partner would be leery of a jump rebid because 2NT opposite a very poor dummy would be a disaster, even with the opener's good hand. You can see that communication would short-circuit quickly.

Minor Matters

When your partner opens with a minor suit and you have enough high-card points to respond, most of the time you will check your hand for major suits and respond accordingly.

Why majors? You focus on major suits because if your side has a game, it is more likely to be in a major suit (4♥ or 4♠) or 3NT. Game in a minor requires all but two tricks, and in tournament or club play, 5♣ or 5♦ scores poorly as a rule.

After your partner opens 1♣ or 1♦, here are your priorities, in order:

➤ Bid a major suit of at least four cards.

> ➤ Bid notrump with a balanced hand and no four-card major.

> ➤ Raise your partner's minor suit with an unbalanced hand and no four-card major.

These will apply in the vast majority of hands you will hold when partner opens.

There are some rules for responding in a major, and one of them is very important: with four cards in both majors, bid hearts first. This is in line with the principle of bidding "up

Bridge Basics

Some players get excited when their partner opens the bidding and they have an opening hand also. Some want to go jumping around to make sure the opener doesn't pass. Here is a hard-and-fast rule that will ease your anxiety: if your partner opens and you make a response in a different suit, even at the one level, it is 100 percent forcing if it is your first chance to speak. "Forcing" means the opener is not allowed to pass your response, which could be based on 20 points or more!

the line" when responding to your partner's minor suit opening.

Why does it matter? Well suppose you and your partner have these two hands (your partner is West, you are East):

West	East
♠ 9 5 2	♠ K Q 10 3
♥ A Q 10 7	♥ 6 5 4 3
♦ K J 7 6	♦ 8 2
♣ K 7	♣ A 6 5

Your partner opens 1♦ and the next player passes. You have enough to respond, but your spade suit is much stronger than your heart suit, so you might instinctively want to respond 1♠ instead of 1♥. Wrong!

If you respond 1♠, your partner will surely rebid 1NT. Your partner can't show him heart suit because if you hate hearts and have to go back to your partner's first suit, you would have to do so at the three level, which could make for an awkward, even disastrous, contract. Moreover, bidding that forces the responder to prefer the first suit at the level of three shows a much better hand than West holds in this case. You will learn more about this type of bid, known as a reverse, later in the book.

The bottom line is that with the two example hands, bypassing your heart suit because it is weak would result in your missing out on your 4-4 heart fit (your hand is definitely not strong enough to do anything but pass if your partner rebids 1NT). If you rebid 2 ♥ over 1NT, you show five spades, which you don't have.

So here is how it goes when responding with a major to an opening of a minor:

➤ With 4-4 in the majors, bid hearts first.

➤ With 5-4 in spades and hearts, bid 1♠. If the opener raises spades, you have found your trump suit. If the opener rebids 1NT, a 2 ♥ bid describes a hand with five spades and at least four hearts.

➤ With 5-5 in the majors, bid 1♠. You will rebid hearts, twice if necessary, to show this hand.

If you don't have a major suit and your hand is balanced, bid notrump at the appropriate level. After 1♣ or 1♦:

➤ 1NT: 6–10 HCP

➤ 2NT: 11–12 HCP (invitational—opener can pass)

➤ 3NT: 13–15 HCP

In all cases, the notrump bid denies holding a four-card major. In most cases, the hand will be balanced, but occasionally you will have to bid 1NT with an unbalanced hand, such as:

♠ Q J 4

♥ J 10

♦ Q 7

♣ Q 10 7 6 5 4

If your partner opens 1♦, you are stuck. You must respond, but you can't bid a major without four, you can't raise diamonds with only two and you don't have enough high-card points to bid 2 ♣. That shows at least 10 high-card points. Your bid, therefore, is 1NT.

When your partner opens 1♣, here are responses and their meanings by an unpassed hand:

➤ 1♦: Four or more in the suit, 6+

Bridge Basics

When you bid a suit in response to your partner's opener, you could have as little as 6 high-card points, but you could have up to 20 or more. When you respond in notrump, you describe your hand within certain limits, which is very helpful to your partner in determining how high the bidding should go.

HCP, might have a major, unlimited

➤ 1♥ or 1♠: Four or more in the suit, 6+ HCP, unlimited

➤ 1NT: 6–10 HCP, balanced hand, no four-card major

➤ 2♣: 6–9 HCP, four-card support, no four-card major

➤ 2NT: 11–12 HCP, balanced hand, no four-card major

➤ 3♣: 10–11 HCP, usually 5+ clubs, no four-card major

➤ 3NT: 13–15 HCP, balanced hand, no four-card major

Here are some responses when the opening bid is 1♦:

➤ 1♥ or 1♠: Four or more in the suit, 6+ HCP, unlimited

➤ 1NT: 6–10 HCP, balanced hand, no four-card major

➤ 2♣: 10 or more HCP, often five cards in the suit, no four-card major

➤ 2♦: 6–9 HCP, four-card support, no four-card major

➤ 2NT: 11–12 HCP, balanced hand, no four-card major

➤ 3♦: 10–11 HCP, usually 5+ diamonds, no four-card major

➤ 3NT: 13–15 HCP, balanced hand, no four-card major

Many players feel they must keep the bidding open with a poor hand when they are short in their partner's minor suit openings. No matter how poor the responding hand, it goes

Bridge Basics

When one player responds to his partner's opener with a jump bid in a different suit—for example, a response of 2♥ to an opening bid of 1♣—the responder has made a jump shift, a bid that is one level higher than necessary and "shifted" to a different suit. It is important to discuss the meanings of these bids with your partner. Some play the jump shift as a very strong hand with slam interest. Others go the opposite way, using jump shift responses to show long suits with weak hands. Either method is appropriate, as long as you and your partner are in agreement.

against the grain to pass with two low cards, or even one, in the partner's suit, knowing that the opening bid might be based on a three-card suit.

When the urge to bid with nothing strikes you, remember that the rare gain you achieve by bidding with nothing will not compensate for the erosion of your partner's confidence. In the long run, bidding without values is losing strategy. Besides, your pass will not necessarily end the auction, and there are mechanisms for escaping if your partner finds himself doubled with only three trumps opposite one-card support.

Major Issues

In many ways the auction is much easier when the opening bid is one of a major—for those who play five-card majors, that is. Having a system built around five-card majors, gives you much more information when your partner opens the bidding with 1♥ or 1♠.

As the responder, your first obligation is to offer support for your partner's suit, the minimum being three cards in your partner's suit. The sooner you establish that you have help for your partner's major, the smoother the auction will go.

As with minor suit openings, you must have some values to keep the bidding open. There is a bit more comfort, after all, in passing with two-card support for your partner's major suit opener. At the very least, you have seven cards between the two hands—that's more than the opponents have.

As you will see when the discussion turns to captaincy in the next chapter, optimum strategy is for one member of the partnership to limit his hand as soon a possible. When you are responding to a major suit, you have the first chance to do that.

Accurate Descriptions

When your partner opens a major suit, your first priority is to show support. Bridge teachers spend hours and hours drilling this principle into the heads of their students: support with support. A big question, of course, is how high you should go. Here is the basic scheme:

A single raise of your partner's major suit opener—from 1♥ to 2♥ or from 1♠ to 2♠— shows 6–9 high-card point and at least three cards in the major.

With more high-card points—10 or 11—raise to three of the opener's major. This is known as a limit raise. In some partnerships, a limit jump raise of a major guarantees at least four-card support. On those partnerships, it is necessary to improvise with limit-raise values but only three-card support for the partner's major.

For example, suppose your partner opens 1♠ and you hold the following:

♠ Q J 4

♥ A J 10

♦ K 7 6 5 2

♣ 8 6

If you don't guarantee four trumps by bidding 3♠, you can make that bid with this hand. In some partnerships, you would have to bid 2♦, showing a diamond suit and 10 or more high-card points. Over your partner's response, perhaps 2NT, you would bid 3♠ to show this hand type.

Some partnerships use a raise of a major to the three level as the equivalent of an opening hand, so 1♠—3♠ would be forcing to game – that is, the bidding could not end until the partnership was in 4♠ or higher. This scheme at least allows room to explore for slam if either hand is strong enough.

Other partnerships agree that a response of 1NT to an opening bid of 1♥ or 1♠ is forcing for one round. Using that method, if your partner opened 1♠ and rebid 2♣ over your 1NT bid, 3♠ by you would show limit-raise values with three-card support.

Helpful Gadgets

There are many ways to show strength after an opening of one of a major. Some of them will be covered in the chapter addressing conventions.

One popular method for conveying the strength of an opening bid opposite a major suit opening was invented by one of the all-time great players—Oswald Jacoby. In his method, a response of 2NT to a major suit opening showed at least four-card support and the equivalent of an opening hand. The specialized bid asked the opener to describe his hand further, paying particular attention to short suits. Here are the responses after 1♥—2NT:

> ➤ 3♣, 3♦, 3♠: Singleton in the suit bid
> ➤ 3♥: No singleton, but more than a minimum opening hand
> ➤ 4♥: No singleton, minimum opener

Here are the responses after 1♠—2NT:

> ➤ 3♣, 3♦, 3♥: Singleton in the suit bid
> ➤ 3♠: No singleton, but more than a minimum opening hand
> ➤ 4♠: No singleton, minimum opener

This is the basic scheme. There are wrinkles that will be explained in the section on conventions. The main purpose of introducing the convention is to illustrate the importance of finding a method to show game-forcing values opposite a major suit opening that allow for some exploration for slam.

for some exploration for slam.

Opener Speaks Again

Need to Know

If one of a major—three of a major shows an invitational hand, would one of a major—four of a major show even more? It does not. A direct jump to game in the major your partner opens shows a weak hand, usually with five-card trump support and some distributional feature, such as a singleton. The jump to four is strictly aimed at taking up the opponents' bidding space. It is not a strong bid.

Suppose you are the dealer and pick up this hand:

> ♠ A K Q J 4
>
> ♥ A J 10
>
> ♦ K J 10 5
>
> ♣ 8

Bridge would be a lot easier if you could start things off with, "Partner, I have a good 19-point hand with five excellent spades and a pretty good four-card diamond suit. What do you have to say to that?"

Yes, that would be convenient, but bridge doesn't work that way. Remember, you have strict limits about the words that can be spoken at the table.

Remembering that the auction is a process of communication between partners, on the given hand, you would start with 1♠. Your hand is much more than a minimum, but you can't convey that in your first bid.

As noted previously, opening with a bid of one of a suit shows a hand of 12 to 20 high-card points. Because that range is so wide, it is important for you to provide information to your partner about how good your hand is as quickly as possible.

After an opening bid of one of a suit, your plan is to describe your hand further, indicating whether you have minimum, intermediate, or strong hand. Here are the ranges:

Bridge Basics

If your partner opens with a bid of one of a suit and makes a jump bid in another suit (not the one you bid) after you respond, you are not allowed to pass until you and your partner reach at least game. If you have enough to respond (6 points) and your partner shows at least 19, that's 25—enough for game.

➤ Minimum: 12–15 points

➤ Intermediate: 16–18 points

➤ Maximum: 19–21 points

So how do you express these different hand strengths? A lot depends on what you opened and what your partner bid. In general, your options when you open a minor depend on whether you're working with a minimum, intermediate or maximum hand.

A Minimum Hand (12–15)

You opened 1♣ and your partner bid 1♦:

➤ If you have a four-card major, bid it. If you have two four-card majors, bid 1♥. A bid of 1♠ would deny four hearts.

➤ If you have a balanced hand and no four-card major, rebid 1NT. This will indicate 12–14 points. If you had 15 with a balanced hand, you would have opened 1NT.

➤ If you have an unbalanced hand and six or more clubs, bid 2♣.

➤ If you are unbalanced with four diamonds, raise your partner's bid to 2♦.

You opened 1♣ and your partner bid one of a major:

➤ If you have four of your partner's major, raise to the two level.

➤ If your partner bid 1♥ and you have four spades but not four hearts, rebid 1♠. Don't bother with hearts if your partner responded 1♠. If your partner has four hearts, he will bid them next, showing five spades and four or more hearts.

➤ If you do not have four of either major, rebid 1NT with a balanced hand.

➤ If you have an unbalanced hand with six or more clubs, rebid 2♣. Do not rebid a five-card club suit.

On occasion, when you have doubletons in the majors with four diamonds and five clubs, you will have to rebid 1NT, although technically it does not qualify as a balanced hand. With a minimum, you are not strong enough to rebid 2♦ over a major suit response.

You opened 1♣ and your partner bid 1NT or 2♣:

> ➤ In almost all cases, you will pass. If, however, you have club length and a singleton in another suit, it will be better to bid 2♣ over 1NT.

You opened 1♦ and your partner bid one of a major:

> ➤ Raise with support if your partner bid 1♥; without four-card heart support but with four spades, bid 1♠.

> ➤ Bid 1NT over partner's 1♥ to show a hand with neither four-card heart support nor four spades.

> ➤ Without major suits and with extra length in diamonds, rebid 2♦.

You opened 1♦ and your partner bid 1NT or 2♦:

> ➤ In almost all cases you will pass. If, however, you have diamond length and a singleton in another suit, it will be better to bid 2♦ over 1NT.

You opened one of a major and your partner bid 1NT:

> ➤ If you have a second suit of at least four cards, mention it at the cheapest level. There is one exception: a minimum opener with five hearts and four spades. If you rebid 2♠ over 1NT, that shows much better than a minimum hand.

> ➤ If you have extra length in the suit you opened, bid it again at the cheapest level. Do not rebid a five-card suit.

You opened 1♥ and your partner bid 1♠:

> ➤ If you have four-card support, bid 2♠.

> ➤ If you have a second suit, bid it at the cheapest level.

> ➤ If you cannot support your partner's suit and have no second suit to mention, bid 1NT.

> ➤ If you have extra heart length without support for your partner's suit, bid 2♥.

You opened one of a major and your partner bid two of a minor:

> ➤ If you have extra length in your suit, bid it at the cheapest level.

> ➤ Support your partner's suit with four or more cards.

You opened 1♠ and your partner bid 2♥:

> ➤ Your partner's bid shows at least five cards, so raise if you have three or more hearts.

> ➤ Rebid your suit if you have extra length.

> ➤ Bid notrump if you cannot support your partner or rebid your suit. You may have to improvise if you have a minimum opener and four or more of a minor suit. Over 2♥, you would have to rebid three of a minor, but doing so shows extra values. With a dead minimum (12 high-card points), this would be a gross distortion of your hand. On this one occasion, you might have to rebid 2♠ with only five of them.

An Intermediate Hand (16–18)

You open one of a suit and your partner responds:

> ➤ If your partner responds with one of a suit and you have four-card support, make a jump raise of his suit. For example: 1♦—1♥; 3 ♥. The semicolon in this sequence indicates that the opener is bidding for the second time. Note that with four-card support for your partner's suit and shortness in another suit, you do not have to have 16 actual high-card points. In the sample auction, you might have:

> > ♠A Q 9
> >
> > ♥A J 5 4
> >
> > ♦K 10 9 7 2
> >
> > ♣3

> ➤ If you open 1♦ and your partner bids 1 ♥, your hand is much too good to make a simple raise to 2 ♥. Your hand reevaluates to 17 high-card points—counting full value for the singleton club. Let your partner in on the secret with a raise to 3 ♥. With a balanced hand and 18 high-card points, rebid 2NT over a response at the one level.

> ➤ If your partner's response is 1NT and you have a balanced hand, rebid 2NT, inviting your partner to bid 3NT with the upper part (8–9) of his range (6–9).

> ➤ Make a jump rebid in your suit with extra length (at least six). Do not do this with a five-card suit.

If you open one of a suit and your partner responds at the one level, a rebid at the one level by you leaves the strength of your hand in doubt. Let's use this hand as an example:

> ♠A K J 4
>
> ♥A 10
>
> ♦K J 10 5 3
>
> ♣8

You open 1♦ and your partner bids 1♥. You are not strong enough to rebid 2♠, a jump shift showing 19–21 high-card points. You must rebid 1♠ with your nice 16 points. Your partner will not pass because your strength is still unknown at this point. As far as your partner is concerned, you might have a hand exactly as strong as the one you actually hold. Also, your partner's 1♥ bid did not deny four spades. Your partner might well be poised to raise to 2♠.

A Maximum Hand (19–21)

You open at the one level and your partner responds at the one level:

➤ If you opened one of a minor, your partner responded one of a major, and you have support for the major, raise to game—four of partner's major.

➤ If you opened one of a minor, your partner bid 1♥, and you have four spades but fewer than four hearts, rebid 2♠. This is called a jump shift.

➤ If you opened one of a minor, your partner responded one of a major, and you cannot support either major but have 18–19 high-card points, rebid 2NT. With a balanced hand and 20–21, you would have opened 2NT.

➤ If you opened one of a major and your partner bid 1NT, raise to game with 18 and a five-card suit or any 19-point balanced hand. With a second suit, make a jump rebid in that suit. For example:

♠ A K Q 8 4

♥ K 10

♦ A K 10 7

♣ 5

You open 1♠ and your partner responds 1NT. You have 19 high-card points, enough for game even if your partner has only 6 high-card points. Show your strength by bidding 3♦ at your second turn. This is another jump shift. If you had three diamonds and two clubs, making your hand balanced, you would raise to 3NT directly.

➤ If you opened one of a major and your partner raised you to two of your major, bid game or whatever bid in your system would be appropriate for slam exploration (more about that in later chapters).

➤ If you opened one of a major and your partner bid a new suit at the two level, make a forcing bid, perhaps jump raising a minor (e.g., 1♠—2♦; 4♦).

Messages Sent

You should be getting the picture about how the language of bidding works. You can't just blurt out what you have, but the bids you make describe your hand within narrow limits, at least as you get deeper into the auction.

Each bid—or failure to bid—tells a story, and it is important for each member of the partnership to tell the truth, as it were, in selecting bids. Nothing is more frustrating for your partner than making choices based on your bids and then finding that you had nowhere near the values your bids expressed.

When you put your hand down as the dummy, you never want to hear your partner ask, "Say, Partner, where is the hand you held during the auction?"

CHAPTER 5

Constructive Auctions

> ## In This Chapter
>
> ➤ More exchanges of information
> ➤ 1NT—the ultimate limit bid
> ➤ The principle of captaincy
> ➤ Dealing with misfits

In this chapter, you will read more about how your conversation with your partner should go after the opener has had a second chance to speak. You will learn about the 1NT bid: when to use it and how it works. And when you read about some of the tools that come with 1NT, you will be a more formidable foe.

You will find out what to do when you and your partner can't find a fit. And your introduction to one of bridge's most important principles—captaincy—will give you another weapon in your fight against those pesky opponents.

Keep Talking

So far, you have learned what a normal opening bid looks like, what it takes to make a response when your partner opens, and how most of the time the opener's second bid clarifies the strength of his hand—minimum, intermediate, or strong.

The opener's second bid also clarifies whether the opener has a balanced hand, a second suit, or perhaps extra cards in the suit that was opened, as with 1♠-1NT; 2♠. That auction should always show at least six spades, but not enough high-card strength for an intermediate bid. If the opener had started with six or more spades and 16–18 high-card points, his second bid would be 3♠.

To review, here are some sample auctions, with their meanings:

1. West	East		2. West	East
1♣	1♥		1♦	1♥
1♠			1NT	

3. West	East		4. West	East
1♠	1NT		1♥	1♠
2♠			3♠	

5. West	East		6. West	East
1♣	1♠		1♦	1♥
2NT			4♥	

7. West	East		8. West	East
1♠	1NT		1♣	1♠
3♦			2♥	

1. West shows 12–17 high-card points with four spades and fewer than three hearts. With four hearts, West would raise East's bid of 1♥ to 2♥.

2. West shows 12–14 high-card points with fewer than four hearts and without four spades.

3. West shows a minimum opener (12–15 high-card points) with six or more spades.

4. West shows an intermediate hand (16–18) with four-card spade support.

5. West shows 18–19 high-card points, a balanced hand with fewer than four spades. If West had four spades, the bid would be 3♠ or 4♠.

6. West shows four-card support for hearts and a hand that reevaluates—via high-card points and/or distributional points—to at least 19 support points.

7. West shows a strong hand with 19–21 high-card points with probably five spades and at least four diamonds. This bid forces the partnership to bid to game.

8. West shows a strong hand—at least 17 high-card points —with five or more clubs and probably four hearts.

Bridge Basics

When you and your partner find a fit in a suit, your hand often improves. The presence of a fit makes your distributional points—especially singletons and voids—come to life. The newly valued hand is then considered in the light of support points, the combination of high-card points and distributional points.

Setting Limits

When you open the bidding with one of a suit, the high-card strength of your hand is covered in a relatively wide range—from a good 12-pointer up to 20 or so high card points. That's a lot of territory, so to speak. If the responder has, say, 7 or 8 high-card points, the two hands could belong anywhere from the one level to game.

Similarly, when a player opens the bidding and his partner responds at the one level, as in 1♦—1♠, the responder is known to have at least 6 high-card points, but he might have significantly more than that, up to 20 or more. Now we are talking about a high-card point range of 6–20. Yikes!

So how do the partners manage to sort this out?

You do it this way: At some point—and earlier is better than later—one member of the partnership will limit his hand.

Bridge Facts

The concept of support points—high-card points plus points for singletons and voids—is valid only when you plan on playing in a suit contract, that is, when you plan to have trumps. A singleton or void is useless for notrump play because when you play notrump, there is no trump suit to stop the enemies from cashing their winners.

You may be wondering what *limit* means in a bridge context. Well, consider this auction:

1♠—2♠

The 2♠ bid is a limit bid. It describes a hand with spade support—at least three cards in spades—and 6–9 support points. In other words, the limit of the hand is 9 support points. Now, suppose the opener is sitting there with a bare minimum opening bid. From his partner's response, the opener knows that the two hands should go no higher than they already are, so he will pass with full confidence that they are in the right spot.

Now consider how the opener would view things if 2♠ could be based on a much stronger hand. It would create an unsolvable dilemma for the opener, who would be fearful of getting too high by trying for more or missing a game by passing. That kind of guessing game would make accurate bidding impossible.

Here's another example:

1♣—1♥; 1NT

The opener's 1NT shows a balanced hand with 12–14 high-card points—with 15, 16, or 17 the opener would have opened 1NT—with three or fewer hearts but at least two (the hand would not be balanced if it contained a singleton or void). A 1NT rebid also denies four spades because the responder's 1♥ did not deny four of that suit.

From there, the responder has an excellent idea what to do next. If he has a balanced minimum without extra length in the suit he just bid, passing will be the choice nearly all the time. If the responder has a minimum-strength hand with extra length in hearts, he might make the signoff bid of 2♥. If the hand is unbalanced and does not seem suitable for notrump play, perhaps with a hand such as

♠ 4

♥ K J 6 4

♦ Q 5 4 3

♣ Q 1 0 9 8

the responder might bid 2♣. This bid is not a constructive move forward. It says to the partner, "I heard your bid, so I know what you have, and on that basis I think we are better off playing in a suit. I have good support for your opening bid, so let's play there."

Ear to the Ground

The auction has actually been rather informative for the responder, who knows from the 1NT rebid that his side probably has about 21 high-card points, barely more than half the deck. The responder also knows that the opponents have at least nine spades between them because his partner's 1NT response after the 1♥ bid denied holding four spades, so the opener has a maximum of three. The responder has only one, so the opponents must have at least nine of them, possibly ten.

The opponents will almost surely lead spades, and even if the partner has a decent holding in the suit, perhaps AJ10, the lead against 1NT would almost surely be a spade, and it's likely their suit would end up taking a lot of tricks in notrump.

Efficiency

One of the most efficient bids you will have in your arsenal of "weapons" is the 1NT opener. Whereas an opening bid of one of a suit can show anywhere from 12 to 20 high-card points, the narrow range of the 1NT opener makes for much smoother auctions.

In the days of Charles Goren, a 1NT opener described a hand with 16 to 18 high-card points, balanced distribution, and at least three of the four suits "stopped."

Bridge Lingo

As you learn more about bidding, you will often be searching for so-called suit stoppers. So what exactly is needed to stop a suit? A stopper is a holding that will keep the opponents from cashing all the cards in their long suit at notrump. Examples are an ace, which will always win a trick at notrump; a king with at least one other card, such as ♠K 1 0 9 ; in some cases three or more to the queen; sequences such as QJ10, KQ, and J1098. AK is known as a double stopper.

Most modern players today use a range of 15 to 17 high-card points, which seems to work better. Many players found that starting an auction with one of a suit holding a balanced hand of 15 high-card points made the bidding a bit awkward. Consider this sequence:

> 1♣—1♠; 1NT (12–15 HCP, balanced hand)

If the responder has a 10-point hand, he might be thinking, "If the opener has 15 high-card points, I should bid 2NT to invite a game. We don't want to stop in 1NT if we can make 3NT, and with 25 high-card points, we would have enough. Then again, what if the opener has a bare minimum 12 points? If I invite game by bidding 2NT, we might get too high."

That kind of thought process can weigh you down and force you to use mental energy best spent on other matters. When a 1NT rebid shows 12–14 high-card points, a responder with 10 high-card points knows that the maximum between the two hands is 24, usually not enough for game, so it's easy to pass or make some other bid that ends the auction.

Need to Know

When one partner has limited his hand in the bidding, the other partner can make a so-called sign-off bid. Some refer to it as a drop-dead bid, meaning there is to be no further bidding from the opener. An example is:

> 1♣ — 1♥; 1NT— 2♥

The 2♥ bid is not forward going, it is a signal that the auction is at an end. If the responder had bid a new suit, the opener would have to keep bidding. When a responder bids his suit a second time, that's a sign-off.

Some partnerships agree on a range that is described as 14+ to 17 for their 1NT openers. That means that the opener has judged that the 14-point hand he is looking at has one or more attributes that enhance its playing strength.

Here are some examples of features that make a 14-point hand seem more like 15:

In a five-card suit, these hands would probably qualify for 14+ rank:

♠ A J 7	♠ K J 4	♠ Q J 5
♥ Q J 6	♥ A 8 2	♥ Q 10 7
♦ A Q 7 6 5	♦ 6 2	♦ A K Q 8 6
♣ 8 6	♣ K Q J 5 4	♣ 5 4

Suits with good body, meaning 10s and 9s such as:

♠ A J 10	♠ K J 4	♠ Q J 10
♥ K J 6	♥ A 10 7	♥ Q 9 7
♦ A J 10 9 8	♦ 10 9	♦ A K Q 10 9
♣ 8 6	♣ K Q J 9 8	♣ 5 4

All of these hands are worth upgrading to 14+ status—or just call them 15 if you want to.

The advantage of using a 14+ to 17 range is that when the opener starts with one of a suit and rebids 1NT, the responder with 10 high-card points doesn't have to worry about missing game because the 14-point maximum that the opener is showing will be a "lesser" 14, and game probably will not be possible.

This treatment is, of course, strictly up to the partnership. Most simply require at least 15 high-card points for a 1NT opener.

Knowing and Going

It is an axiom of bridge that "he who knows, goes."

That means that if you know from your hand and your partner's bidding that you belong in game, you must do something to get there. That's why the 1NT opener, with its narrow range, is such a good bid.

When your partner opens 1NT, showing 15–17 high-card points in a balanced hand, all you have to do is look at your own hand and you can tell right off the bat what to do.

Useful Conventions

Before we get into your actions after your partner opens 1NT, it's time to learn about some of the bidding tools you will need to further communication with your partner.

First on the list is a little number called Stayman, which is somewhat of a curiosity in the world of bridge. The convention called Stayman gets its name from a famous player of the Fifties and Sixties—Sam Stayman. What's curious about the fact that his name is on one of the most common conventions in bridge history is that he didn't invent it.

Bridge Facts

In bridge, a convention is a bidding tool. Common conventions are Stayman over notrump openings, and Blackwood 4NT to ask for aces. The Stayman bid of 2 ♣ and the Blackwood bid of 4NT are known as conventions because when you bid one of them, you are not proposing to play in the denomination named.

The Stayman convention was actually invented by George Rapee, another fine player of Stayman's era, and actually beyond. In fact, the two were partners in some tournaments. Rapee was a very smart man and a great bridge player, but he wasn't much of a self-promoter. Stayman actually ended up writing about the convention in a major bridge publication, so the convention was named after him.

Enough history—no doubt you want to know how one of the most common conventions actually works.

Suppose your partner opens 1NT and you have this hand:

♠ A J 9 7

♥ 8 2

♦ K Q 6 5

♣ 6 5 4

You have 11 high-card points. Combine them with your partner's minimum of 15 high-card points, and you have at least 26, more than enough to bid game. If you don't play Stayman, you would probably just go straight to 3NT. That's all well and good, but suppose this is your partner's hand:

♠ K Q 8 6

♥ 6 5 4

♦ A J 3

♣ K Q J

It is very likely that the opponents will start off leading hearts, and no matter how the suit is divided, they will almost surely take at least five tricks and defeat 3NT, possibly by more than two tricks. This might be the full deal:

```
                    ♠ A J 9 7
                    ♥ 8 2
                    ♦ K Q 6 5
                    ♣ 6 5 4
    ♠ 1 0 4 3                      ♠ 5 2
    ♥ K Q 7                        ♥ A J 1 0 9 3
    ♦ 1 0 9 4                      ♦ 8 7 2
    ♣ A 1 0 8 7                    ♣ 9 3 2
                    ♠ K Q 8 6
                    ♥ 6 5 4
                    ♦ A J 3
                    ♣ K Q J
```

East will be on lead against 3NT and will start with a heart—in later chapters you will find out why it would be the ♥ J—and the opponents would quickly take five heart tricks, followed by the ♣ A. Declarer would be down two, when ten tricks in spades would be trivial.

So how do you get to spades—your 4-4 fit? Easy: just bid Stayman 2 ♣.

When your partner opens 1NT and you bid 2 ♣, you are not saying that you want to play a club contract. Rather 2 ♣ is a conventional bid, asking your partner if he has a four-card major.

Here are the parameters for using Stayman:

At least 8 high-card points

At least one four-card major

When you bid Stayman, partner:

> ➤ Must bid a four-card major if he has one

> ➤ Should bid hearts first if he has two four-card majors

> ➤ Must bid 2 ♦ if his hand does not contain a four-card major

> ➤ Can never, ever pass your 2 ♣ bid

Why do you need 8 high-card points? Because if your partner bids 2 ♦ to deny a major or a major you do not have, you will have to counter with a bid of 2NT. If you bid Stayman with a lesser hand, you could be way too high in the bidding at 2NT.

Need to Know

The one time you can bid Stayman without at least 8 high-card points is when you have a very weak hand with shortness in clubs. You might have:

♠ J 6 5 4

♥ Q 4 3

♦ 10 9 8 7 6

♣ 3

If you pass 1NT, your partner will go down, maybe a lot. The good thing about bidding Stayman with such a train wreck is that you know your partner is going to bid one of your suits. After all, he can't pass and isn't going to bid 3 ♣ over your 2 ♣. Playing in a suit will be much better than notrump. This tactic is known as Garbage Stayman for obvious reasons.

The reason you bid hearts before spades if you have two four-card majors is mostly about safety and preserving your plus score.

If you open 1NT, your partner responds 2 ♣, and you have both majors, bidding 2 ♥ does not deny having four spades. If, over your 2 ♥, your partner bids 2 ♠, he is showing the equivalent of a raise to 2NT with four spades, just in case you also have four of that suit. Here are your responses:

> ➤ With four spades but a minimum 1NT, simply pass and stop comfortably in 2 ♠

> ➤ With four spades and sufficient values to accept the invitation, bid 4 ♠

> ➤ Without four spades but with enough to accept the game invitation, bid 3NT

> ➤ Without four spades but without a maximum for your opener, sign off in 2NT

Bridge Lingo

When you use Stayman to uncover a fit in a major suit, you are aiming for what is known as the golden fit. A 4-4 fit is considered superior to a 5-3 fit in many cases, especially when both fits are present in the partnership hands. Consider that if the suits in both fits are strong, you can get discards on the long suit in the 5-3 fit if your trump suit is the 4-4 fit. If, however, your trump suit is the 5-3 fit, there are no discards available in the other eight-card fit because both hands have the same number of cards.

Stay Low

If you bid spades first with both majors, your partner would have to bid 2NT if he didn't have spades with you, and in order to play in hearts—your obvious fit—you would have to bid at the three level even with a minimum 1NT opener. It's better to be able to sign off at the lower level.

Here are some hands for practice. What do you bid with each one after your partner opens 1NT?

Hand 1	Hand 2	Hand 3
♠ A J 10 9	♠ K J 4 3	♠ 10 7 3
♥ 7 6	♥ A 10 7 5	♥ K Q 9
♦ Q J 10 9 8	♦ 2	♦ A K Q 10
♣ 8 6	♣ K Q J 9	♣ 8 5 4

Hand 1 is ideal for Stayman; bid 2♣. If your partner bids 2♠, raise to 3♠. This is invitational, asking your partner to bid 4♠ with a maximum 1NT opener. If your partner bids 2♥, bid 2♠. Your partner has not denied four spades, and you want to show your invitational hand with four spades. If your partner declines the invitation by bidding 2NT, you must pass. If your partner bids 2♦ (no major), bid 2NT.

Hand 2 is also a good candidate for Stayman, but this time you plan to bid game over whatever partner responds. If he bids one of your majors, you will raise to four of that major. If your partner responds 2♦, you will bid 3NT. You don't like your singleton diamond, but there is a reasonable chance that your partner has something decent in the suit. After all, he doesn't have a major, and you have most of the high-card points in clubs.

Hand 3 is a ringer. There's only one bid for you to make: 3NT. You don't have a major, but you do have 13 high-card points, giving your side at least 28 high-card points. That's more than enough for game, and not enough to consider slam.

Over to You

The next handy gadget is one that should be considered a must for any player who wants to get the most out of the bidding when a partner opens 1NT. It is the transfer bid.

Consider this hand:

> ♠ A J 6 5 4
>
> ♥ K 4 3
>
> ♦ 10 9 8
>
> ♣ 7 6

Your partner opens 1NT, showing 15–17 high-card points. You immediately start thinking about bidding your spade suit, but you have a dilemma. If your partner has 17 high-card points, you want to be in game because you would have 25 high-card points between you. If your partner has just 15, you want to stop at a low level.

If you don't play transfers, you have to guess what to do, making a sign-off bid of 2♠ or a game-forcing bid of 3♠, which shows enough high-card points to be in game and giving your partner the choice between 3NT (if he doesn't have at least three spades with you) and 4♠ (if he does have a fit with you).

Guessing with hands like this means you will be wrong part of the time, and you could get on an unlucky streak and be wrong just about every time. Even worse, you will be having your run of bad luck without involving your partner at all.

Bridge Facts

Bridge players can thank the late Oswald (Ozzie) Jacoby for the wonderful convention known as the transfer bid. Jacoby was one of the all-time great players, a former code breaker during World War II, and a great bidding theorist. Because of his gift to the game, the transfers are technically known as Jacoby Transfer Bids.

The solution to the problem is to put Jacoby Transfer Bids in your bidding tool kit. Here's how they work:

When your partner opens 1NT, a bid of 2♦ tells your partner to bid 2 ♥. A bid of 2 ♥ tells your partner to bid 2♠. From there, you have a much better chance of communicating effectively with your partner.

With the example hand that started this discussion, you would bid this way:

Partner	You
1NT	2 ♥
2♠	2NT

That tells your partner that you have only five spades and only invitational values. Here is how your partner will respond:

> ➤ With a minimum and fewer than three spades, the opener passes.

> ➤ With a minimum and three or more spades, the opener signs off in 3♠.

> ➤ With a maximum and fewer than three spades, the opener bids 3NT.

> ➤ With a maximum and three or more spades, the opener bids 4♠.

Isn't that much better than having to guess and not get your partner into the discussion?

What if you have more than five of your major? No problem. Here's an example:

♠ A J 6

♥ K J 10 9 4 3

♦ 5 3

♣ 7 6

You have 9 high-card points and a reasonable suit but not enough to commit to game.

You do know, however, that your side has at least eight hearts between the two hands. Remember, a balanced hand contains no singletons or voids.

The proper bidding in this case is:

Partner	You
1NT	2 ♦
2 ♥	3 ♥

This tells your partner that you have at least six hearts and 8–9 high-card points. Your partner's response will be based mostly on his high-card points, and your partner will upgrade his hand if it's a really good fit with you in hearts.

Need to Know

The Jacoby Transfer Bid does not necessarily begin and end with the major suits. Some partnerships agree that a bid of 2 ♠ is a transfer to 3 ♣ and that a bid of 3 ♣ is a transfer to 3 ♦. That is worth a discussion to make sure both players in a partnership are on the same page.

Besides making the auctions much better, transfer bids have a tactical advantage in the play. Suppose you are not playing transfers and hold

♠ Q 7

♥ K J 6 5

♦ A Q 5

♣ A J 3

You open 1NT and your partner bids 2 ♠. Without transfer bids, this is to play. You have no choice but to pass. You will be putting this hand down as the dummy—and the opening lead will be going through your good holdings rather than up to them. Further, your partner's weakness bid limits his hand, so it will be easier for the opponents to figure out what to do as play progresses.

Playing transfers, your good hand will remain concealed, and the opening lead against you is more likely to be favorable—a diamond away from the king, for example. This concept can be critically important in slam bidding. Consider this situation:

♠KJ10965

♥AQ

♦Q32

♣84

♠A3   ♠742

♥109876   ♥54

♦K765   ♦1098

♣102   ♣97653

♠Q8

♥KJ32

♦AJ4

♣AKQJ

South opens 2NT (20–21) and North knows slam is a good prospect. Eventually, the good slam in spades will be bid. If North-South are not playing transfers, however, the slam will be in jeopardy.

East will be on lead against the slam and will certainly lead the ♦10, the top of his only sequence. That will be it for the slam. If the declarer plays low, West will win the king and the trump ace will be good for down one. It doesn't work for North to go up with the ♦A and try for discards. East can ruff the third round of hearts, and West can ruff the second round of clubs.

If North-South are playing transfers, South will be declarer in 6♠, possibly even 6NT. In either case, West will be on lead against the slam and can do no harm. A diamond lead will be right into the AJ, and another lead allows South to win and knock out the ♠A to take twelve tricks in comfort.

Game Plan

When your partner opens 1NT, in most cases you will know what to do almost immediately. Here is your plan (assume you are playing transfers):

HCP	Action
0–7, five of a major	Transfer to your major and pass
0–7, no long major*	Pass**

8–9, five of a major	Transfer to the major and bid 2NT
8–9, six or more of a major	Transfer to the major and raise to three
8–9, four of at least one major	Bid Stayman 2 ♣, followed by a raise of the major or 2NT if no major fit is found
8–9, no major	Bid 2NT, invitational
10–15, no major	Bid 3NT
10–15, four-card major(s)	Bid Stayman, then game if a major fit is found, 3NT with no major fit
10–15, five-card major	Transfer to the major and bid 3NT (choice of games)
10–15, six-card major	Transfer to the major and bid game in that suit
16–17, no major	Bid 4NT, inviting slam (opener goes with 17)
16–17, four- or five-card major	Bid Stayman or transfer as appropriate and invite slam
18+	Drive to slam via Stayman or transfer, or just bid it directly (1NT—6NT)

*A long suit in this context is one of five or more cards.

**With a minor suit of at least six cards, you can bid 2 ♠, which forces the opener to bid 3 ♣. You can then pass with six or more clubs or bid diamonds with six or more of that suit.

Who's in Charge?

Earlier in this chapter, you learned about the concept of limiting your hand—that is, making a bid that shows a certain range. You learned that 1NT is the ultimate limit bid because the range is relatively narrow (15–17). An important adjunct to the principle of limit bids is one known as captaincy. It's pretty simple: When one player in the partnership makes a limit bid, the other player is captain of the auction. When you limit your hand, you might or might not know how good your partner's hand is, but your partner—by virtue of your bid—knows within a certain range the total assets of both hands.

Because your partner knows more than you do, your partner is captain for this deal, and what he says goes.

This concept is vitally important in competitive bidding. That topic will be covered in depth in a later chapter, but an example will help reinforce the concept of captaincy.

West	North	East	South
1 ♣	1 ♠	Pass	2 ♠
3 ♣	Pass	Pass	?

Suppose you hold:

♠ K Q 5

♥ K 8 7 6

♦ J 1 0 9 8

♣ 5 2

You might be tempted to take another bid, raising to 3 ♠. After all, you have two honors in the suit your partner bid and you do have a maximum for your raise to 2 ♠. If you value your partner and wish to be a good partner yourself, you will pass and respect your partner's decision.

Decision? Yes, your partner heard your raise to 2 ♠ and chose not to compete over 3 ♣. You told your story, your partner knows you might have as good a hand as you actually do—and he still chose to pass. You limited your hand to 6–9 support points with your raise to 2 ♠. You have the maximum, but you don't have any more than you said you did, and your partner chose to bow out.

Bridge Basics

One of the most important concepts of bridge is that of avoiding a common trap for inexperienced players—taking a second bid on a hand worth only one bid. Wise players counsel beginners against bidding the same cards twice. Once you have told your story, unless your partner forces you to bid again, you must refrain from further bidding.

Partnership communication and trust are keys to success in bridge. If you do not understand the concept of captaincy, or if you willfully ignore it to bid as you please, you will not reach your potential as a player.

Fighting It Out

As we have seen, discipline is important in the game of bridge, especially so in certain awkward situations—namely the handling of misfit hands.

Sometimes it is obvious that your hand and partner's do not fit well at all, as in this case:

You	Partner
♠ A 9 7 5 4 3	♠ Q
♥ K Q 5 4 3	♥ 7
♦ 3	♦ K Q 7 6 5 4
♣ A	♣ K J 6 5 2

You have a clear-cut 1♠ opener, and your partner has a normal, if minimum, 2♦ response. When you rebid 2♥, your partner should already be starting to feel queasy about this one. He doesn't have enough to change suits by bidding 3♣—that would be forcing to game, and the hand is nowhere near strong enough for that—so your partner probably would rebid 3♦.

Note also that both hands have poor spot cards. With 10s and 9s to accompany the long suits, either hand would have more trick-taking potential.

If you are wise, you will resign from the auction at that point before doubling by the opponents starts—and it will. It is almost certainly obvious to the opponents that you are struggling, and they may already be licking their chops. Bidding notrump with this obvious misfit is unthinkable, and you don't want to compound the problem by bidding out your pattern with a 3♥ bid. Pass 3♦ and hope your pass came soon enough.

You and partner have high-card points, but they are not well placed. Sometimes you just have to give up and hope the next deal works out better.

The example provided might seem extreme, but it's not that unusual. Sometimes the card gods like to have fun at your expense. You can minimize the damage if you get out of these auctions as soon as you diagnose the misfit.

CHAPTER 6

Power Management

In This Chapter

➤ Bidding with strong hands

➤ The strong 2♣ opener

➤ Weak and strong bids at the two level and higher

➤ Responding to weak two-bids

In this chapter, you will learn what to do when you have been dealt a proverbial rock crusher. You will be introduced to one of the most popular options for bidding very strong hands—the 2 ♣ opener. You will also discover that not all superstrong hands should be opened with 2 ♣.

You will learn how to respond to your side's powerhouse opening bids. And there will be more discussion of opening bids at the two level and higher—weak and strong.

Finally, you will find information about slam bidding—when to go and making sure you get to the right slam.

Hands on Steroids

It is safe to say you will never be dealt a perfect hand—one that will take all the tricks in the highest possible contract—7NT—no matter what. Such a hand would be something like this:

♠ A K Q J

♥ A K Q

♦ A K Q

♣ A K Q

The odds against being dealt that hand are more than 158 billion to 1. If you could deal an entire hand in one second, you could crank them out at that rate twenty-four hours a day for more than 300,000 years before you would be likely to see that hand, so don't even think about it. And anyway, what fun would it be? You would open 7NT and claim when the opening lead was made. The real fun of bridge is figuring out problems and solving them.

That said, you will be dealt some very strong hands if you play enough, and it's worth the effort to prepare yourself for getting the most out of them.

Bridge Facts

In the old days of bridge, the more a player bid as opener, the stronger his hand, and all opening two-bids were strong (21 high-card points or more). Gradually, players came around to the view that based on frequency, starting at a higher level made more sense as a weak bid to take up the bidding space of the opponents, so most players switched to weak two-bids for all suits except clubs. That one suit is reserved for the really strong hands.

High Means Low

You may be tempted at times to start off by bidding what you think you can make—for example, just going straight to 4 ♠ with a hand such as this:

♠ K Q J 1 0 9 6 5 2

♥ A

♦ A 1 0 9 8

♣ —

Opening 4 ♠ with that hand would be very wrong—and if you are wondering why this situation is even mentioned, you are showing potential as a bridge player. An opening bid of 4 ♠ would look more like this:

♠ K Q J 1 0 9 6 5 3

♥ 4

♦ 7

♣ J 4 2

When you open at a high level, your objective is to take bidding space from the opponents. You don't really expect to make your contract. What you want to do is force the opponents to start communicating and guessing at a very high level.

Bridge Basics

A tried-and-true principle of competitive bidding is to force your opponents to make the last guess. That applies particularly in the area of preemptive bidding. For example, if you open the bidding with 5 ♣ and the next player has a decent hand without a clear-cut action, you force him to guess what to do. Bidding could be right or it could be a disaster, but that also applies to doubling or passing. The one player at the table not guessing is your partner. By bidding 5 ♣, you have described a hand with a long, decent suit and the expectation of taking nine or ten tricks.

Suppose you open the first example hand with 4♠ and your partner holds

♠ A 4

♥ 8 7 6

♦ Q J 5 4 3

♣ 5 4 3

Your partner will never dream there's a slam in the offing. He will be looking at all those losers and hoping you don't end up doubled. Your partner will never expect you to have an ace on the side—and a void. In fact, you might easily take all thirteen tricks.

Remember, opening at the two level (except for 2 ♣ and 2NT), three level, and higher shows weakness, not strength.

Serving Notice

When you open 2♣, you are telling your partner—and the opponents—that you have a strong hand based on high-card points or trick-taking ability—possibly both.

So what, you may wonder, do you need for a strong 2 ♣ opener? In general, the more balanced you are, the more high-card points you need.

Here are some examples of hands with which you open 2 ♣:

Hand 1	Hand 2	Hand 3
♠ A K Q J 7	♠ K 4	♠ A K Q J
♥ A Q	♥ A K J 10 9 6 4	♥ K Q 10 7
♦ A J 10	♦ A 4	♦ A K Q 8
♣ 9 8 6	♣ A 7	♣ 5

Hand 4	Hand 5	Hand 6
♠ A 3	♠ A K Q J 10 7 6 5	♠ A Q J 5
♥ A Q J	♥ A 8 2	♥ A K 10 9
♦ A K Q 7 6 5	♦ 3	♦ A Q 8
♣ K 4	♣ 5	♣ K 4

These are all 2 ♣ openers for the reasons explained below:

➤ Hand 1: This hand is balanced with 21 high-card points, but the hefty five-card spade suit makes it too good to open 2NT, which shows a balanced 20–21. You plan to open 2 ♣ and rebid 2 ♠, perhaps even 2NT to show the true strength.

➤ Hand 2: With the long, strong heart suit and two aces, you have at least eight tricks in your own hand. It won't take much from your partner for you to make game in hearts—and you might be on for a slam.

➤ Hand 3: Hands with 4-4-4-1 shape are difficult to bid, especially starting at the two level, but you have no choice with 24 high-card points. You plan to open 2 ♣ and rebid 2♠, treating that good suit as a five-carder. The problem with "cheating" a bit and planning to open 2 ♣ followed by a high-card points–showing bid of 3NT (24–25) is that you might miss out on a major suit fit (your partner won't be able to check for a major if your second bid is 3NT). If your partner has nothing in clubs, you could go down in 3NT while being on for 4 ♥ or 4 ♠.

➤ Hand 4: This is one of those hands that you will call balanced even if it doesn't technically fit the definition of a balanced hand. Open 2 ♣ and rebid 2NT, avoiding the difficult bidding sequence of 2 ♣—2 ♦; 3 ♦. Your partner will be sorely tempted to bid 3NT over 3 ♦, and if he does, the wrong hand will be playing the contract.

Need to Know

Going strictly by the book, a hand must have one of the following patterns to be considered balanced: 4-3-3-3, 4-4-3-2 or 5-3-3-2. There are times, however, when judgment must prevail. Suppose you are the dealer and you have the following:

♠ A Q

♥ K 5

♦ Q J 10 8

♣ A 10 7 6 5

If you open this hand one of a minor and your partner bids a major, you can't rebid 1NT because that shows 12–14. You can't rebid 2NT because that shows 18–19. So you have to bid something else, and your partner will likely play notrump if that is where you belong—and that's poor. This is a hand you want led up to not through. Just open 1NT and tell your partner you had a diamond in with your hearts.

> ➤ Hand 5: This hand doesn't have a lot of high-card points—just a lot of tricks. With eight solid spades and an ace on the side, you have nine tricks in your hand. There's an excellent chance your partner will provide something useful for you. The one caution with this kind of hand is that it would be wrong to open 2♣, planning to rebid 2♠, which typically shows 21 or more high-card points. To describe this hand, open 2♣ and rebid 4♠. That bid says you don't have a lot of high-card points, but you do have playing strength equal to eight or so tricks. Do not open this hand with a bid of 4♠. That describes a weak hand without much defensive strength.

> ➤ Hand 6: Open 2♣ and rebid 2NT, describing a balanced hand with 23–24 high-card points.

It is worth noting about Hand 5 that there are varying interpretations of the "legality" of opening that hand with a bid of 2♣ at a tournament. With only 14 high-card points, it is far short of the expected 21+ most 2♣ openers deliver. The hand has so many tricks, however, that it would be dangerous to open 1♠. All your partner needs is the ♥K, and there are an easy ten tricks. If your partner's only high-card points were represented by the ♥K, however, he would probably pass and a game would be missed.

The key issue is your intention of opening 2♣ with a hand that is light on high-card points but heavy on tricks. It is wrong to open 2♣ with the sole intention of keeping the opponents out of the auction. You can protect yourself when you open 2♣ with light high-card strength by jumping to game in your long suit at your second turn, which shows that kind of hand.

Need to Know

When your partner opens with a non-forcing bid (i.e., a one-level opener), conventional wisdom is that a response of any kind delivers at least 6 high-card points. That is a reasonable standard, but it's not etched in stone. If your partner opens the bidding and you have an ace, even if that represents the only high-card points in your hand, you should strain to keep the bidding open, especially if you have a fit for your partner's suit. With no fit and really poor distribution, you probably should just pass. Bear in mind that in general, a

Tricks of the Trade

On most occasions when you open 2♣ and rebid in a suit rather than notrump, you are describing a single-suited hand. When your suit is very powerful—good enough to play for one or no losers opposite a void—you want your partner to know that so the two of you don't waste bidding space trying to find another suit to play in.

Suppose you are dealt this hand:

♠ Q 3

♥ A K Q J 10 7 6 3

♦ A K Q

♣ —

You will open 2♣, planning to rebid in hearts—but don't bid just 2—your partner most likely will bid 2♦ as a negative, or "waiting," bid. If so, you should rebid 3♥. This bid shows a powerful, one-suited hand with a suit that has at most one loser no matter what your partner holds. It tells the responder not to worry about trumps. You are interested in what he can say about the other suits.

Note that this applies mainly when the opening 2♣ bidder has a major. When opener has a strong hand with a long minor, if you don't play in slam, your most likely contract will be in notrump. If you jump to 4♣ or 4♦, you have bypassed the likely best contract.

Take Your Cue

When your partner shows a strong hand with a superstrong trump suit, he is interested in whether you have controls in the other suits.

Bridge Lingo

In many auctions, you will be called upon to describe controls—or lack of them— in your hand so it's important to know what a control is. Basically, a control is the ability to win the first or second round of a suit that the opponents might lead. Confining the discussion to suit contracts, first-round control can be an ace or a void. Second-round control can be a guarded king (a king and one or more cards) or a singleton. Third-round controls—doubletons or guarded queens—are not usually shown.

It's worth taking another look at that hand.

♠ Q 3

♥ A K Q J 10 7 6 3

♦ A K Q

♣ —

What do you need to start thinking about bidding a slam? Right—something from your partner in spades. You can't use Blackwood 4NT convention (asking for aces) because if your partner shows one ace, you don't know which one it is. If it's the ♠A, great. If it's the ♣A, the opponents might well be able to cash two spade tricks if you land in a slam.

Do you need the ♠A? Not necessarily. Your partner might have the king, and that would be good enough for you to take twelve tricks. You already have eleven tricks—eight hearts and three diamonds. Even if the opponents have the ♠A, they can't take two fast tricks in the suit if your partner has the king.

So how do you find out? Your bid of 3♥ tells your partner unequivocally that hearts are trumps, and it asks your partner to bid the cheapest suit in which he has a control. What does *cheapest* mean? It means the bid with the fewest steps from 3♥, a step being the next bid up. From 3♥, the next step is 3♠, then 3NT, then 4♣, etc. When you have been asked to bid your controls up the line and you skip one of them, it means you don't have a control in that suit.

Suppose your second bid is 3♥ and your partner's next bid is 4♣. That means two things:

1. Your partner has a club control—ace, guarded king, singleton, or void

2. Your partner has no control in spades. Remember, your partner skipped over that suit to bid 4♣.

You will sign off in 4♥, knowing that you are not missing a slam. Likewise, if the bid over 3♥ is 4♦, it denies controls in spades and clubs.

If your partner bids 4♥ over your 3♥, it means he has no controls in spades, diamonds, or clubs. This method of showing controls in side suits after a trump suit has been agreed upon is called cue-bidding.

Holding Back

Most very strong hands should be opened 2♣ to make sure at least game is reached, but with a strong two-suited hand—5-5 or better in the two suits—sometimes it's better to start at the one level to give yourself maximum room for finding the best fit.

Many players holding the following hand might, in their excitement, start proceedings with a strong 2♣.

♠ A K J 5 4 3

♥ —

♦ A Q

♣ A K 5 4 3

It is better to begin with 1♠. If your partner raises to 2♠, it would not be unreasonable to jump to 6♠. That's an auction that gives little information to the opponents, making the opening lead somewhat of a crapshoot for the defenders.

If you start with 2♣ and your partner bids the predictable 2♦, you will rebid 2♠. If your partner cannot raise your spade suit, just about anything he bids will force you to the four level to show your second suit.

A much cleaner auction would be 1♠—1NT; 3♣, establishing a game force and showing your second suit. If your partner bids 3NT over 3♣, you will bid 4♣ to show your distribution and a hand that is not suited for play in notrump. Your bid of 3♣ is called a jump-shift. It always shows a very strong hand with two suits.

Note that if you open 1♠ and your partner passes out of weakness, it's unlikely you will have missed a game. If your partner does not have a fit with you in spades or clubs and is too weak to bid over 1♠, you might well be poised to avoid a minus score.

Remember, too, that your partner's pass does not end the auction. There's a good chance the player in the pass out seat will decide to balance. For all he knows, his side has more high-card strength than yours.

If your right-hand opponent takes some action, you will be right there with a club bid, jumping to 3♣ if the auction permits. This would just about guarantee a five-card suit and a very unbalanced hand—not to mention strong. You would hardly take that action opposite a partner who couldn't keep the bidding open unless you had the goods.

Suppose your partner had as little as the following hand:

♠ 6 2

♥ 9 4 3 2

♦ 5 4

♣ Q J 9 8 7

If you get to bid your second suit at the three level, your partner will easily picture you with at least ten cards in the black suits, possibly eleven. That leaves you with at most three red cards, so your partner knows you will ruff all but two or three of them. It would be trivial for your partner to go to game with a bid of 5 ♣, and you would follow with 6 ♣. You know your partner has good trumps—otherwise, why would he get so excited?—and your partner has at most two spades, which are covered by your ace and king in that suit.

Talking Back

When your partner opens 2 ♣, you have several options, but you may not pass. Your partner's bid is 100 percent forcing.

There are many schemes for responding to the forcing 2 ♣ opening. Some partnerships agree to bid suits in which they have aces, if any. Some respond in steps to show controls on the formula of an ace equaling two controls, a king one. First step shows no controls, second step shows one, third two, etc.

For newer players, the best system for responding to 2 ♣ is the simplest. This is the recommended method.

After an opening bid of 2 ♣:

➤ 2 ♦: Negative or "waiting"

➤ 2 ♥: A suit of at least five hearts with at least two of the top three honors in the suit

➤ 2 ♠: A suit of at least five spades with at least two of the top three honors in the suit

➤ 2NT: A balanced hand of at least 8–10 high-card points in the form of card combinations known as tenaces (e.g., AQ, KJ) that are better led up to

➤ 3 ♣: A suit of at least five clubs with at least two of the top three honors in the suit

➤ 3 ♦: A suit of at least five diamonds with at least two of the top three honors in the suit

There are no other bids you will make on the first round.

Bridge Basics

You are allowed to bid 2NT in response to a strong 2♣ opener, but it will be a rare bid for you. The main reason is that it will wrongside the contract. What that means is that the strong hand will be in the dummy, and the opening lead will go through that strength. With the strong hand as declarer, any lead will come up to that hand. This can be a huge tactical advantage. The other reason 2NT is a rare bid is that you will not have the requisite holding all that often.

The bid you will make most often is 2♦, which some partnerships describe as negative to indicate a poor hand.

A better method is to use the 2♦ response as a waiting bid. *Waiting* means that you have a hand that you cannot describe with your first bid. You do not necessarily have a bad hand, but you do not have a hand with a suit of at least five cards with two of the top three honors, nor do you have a hand suitable for a bid of 2NT (which you sort of want to avoid anyway).

You might, for example, have the following:

♠ Q 7 6 5 4 3

♥ A 5

♦ 1 0 9 8 7

♣ 4

Your natural impulse is to bid 2♠ because you have six of them, but if you have agreed that a 2♠ bid shows a suit with two of the top three honors, you must wait until you get another chance to speak before you mention your long suit.

For example, if your partner rebids 2♥, you will then bid 2♠. Your partner will know you have at least five of them, and he will know that the suit is not as good as five to the AK, AQ or KQ—otherwise you would have bid 2♠ at your first turn. Your partner will take that into account in selecting the next bid.

What if you do have a truly dreadful hand? There's an app—that is, a bid—for that. It's called the second negative bid of 3♣.

Here is a bidding sequence followed by interpretations to help sort this out:

Partner	You
2♣	2♦
2♥	3♣
3♦	3♥
Pass	

➤ 2♣: "I have a rock, Partner."

➤ 2♦: "I don't have a descriptive bid for you just now."

➤ 2♥: "I have at least five hearts. What do you think of that?"

➤ 3♣: "I have a miserable hand and I cannot raise hearts."

➤ 3♦: "Maybe you like my other suit better."

➤ 3♥: "I prefer hearts and I still have a lousy hand."

➤ Pass: "I get it. We probably don't have a game."

Now, what if you had a poor hand but you did have some support for the suit your partner names when he makes the second bid?

There is a very useful scheme for the responder's second bid when he can support the opener's suit, especially when it is a major.

Here is your hand, followed by a sample auction:

♠ J 10 7 6

♥ 7 3

♦ K 8 7 3 2

♣ 8 4

Partner	You
2♣	2♦
2♠	?

What should you bid?

The answer is 3♠. If you bid 4♠, you are telling your partner that you have spade support but no other noteworthy "feature"—no ace, no king, no singleton, no void.

Do you see why it's important to allow room for more exploration? Suppose this is your partner's hand:

♠ A K Q 9 8 2

♥ A 4

♦ A Q J 4

♣ 6

If your 3♠ promises at least one feature, your partner will envision a possible slam and continue the auction with a bid of 4♣, showing first- or second-round control of that suit. You will show where your outside strength lies by bidding 4♦. Your partner will then probably bid 4NT to ask about your aces (your bidding has not denied the ♣ A). When your partner learns that you have no aces, he will settle for 6♥.

Had you bid directly to 4♠, your partner would have passed. There would be no point, of course, in bidding Blackwood. You already said you don't have an ace.

Bridge Basics

The Blackwood convention is the world's most popular bidding tool—and it's also the most abused convention. Here are some requirements you must meet before bidding 4NT to ask your partner how many aces he has:

➤ You must have no suit with more than one quick loser

➤ You must have no void in a side suit

Suppose you have two fast losers in one suit and a singleton in another. If you bid 4NT and your partner shows one ace, it could be the wrong one. If you bid slam, the opponents might cash two winners in your doubleton suit. If you sign off at five, your partner's ace might be in your doubleton, causing you to miss a cold slam. Guessing in these situations is losing bridge. Similarly, if you have a void and your partner shows one ace, it could be in your void suit—just where you don't need it.

More Power

If you are playing Standard American or one of its cousins, the only opening bid other than 2♣ you are likely to use that shows an extra-strong hand is 2NT. In most bidding systems, an opening bid of 2NT shows a balanced hand of 20–21 high-card points. In the early days of bridge, players were taught that a 2NT opener guaranteed a stopper in all the suits. Similarly, a 1NT opener showed a hand with no more than one unstopped suit.

That philosophy went the way of the dinosaur long ago. The chance to make a descriptive bid with a narrow range far outweighs such concerns as stoppers. Bidding accuracy is more important.

For every time the opponents run a suit against you because your partner can't cover for the weakness in your hand, there will be many other occasions when you right-side the contract because of your 1NT or 2NT opener. In the long run, you will come out ahead of the game by keeping the strong hand concealed—and the way to do that is to get the notrump bid in first.

Made to Be Broken

Earlier in this chapter, you learned that the strict definition of a balanced hand allows for only three patterns: 4-3-3-3, 4-4-3-2, and 5-3-3-2.

For your 2NT openers, it will behoove you to be more creative, especially when you have a long, strong minor suit. Suppose, for example, that you pick up

♠ A Q

♥ K Q 7

♦ A K Q 1 0 7 2

♣ 1 0 9

If you start with 1♦ and your partner responds 1♠, you will be poorly placed in the auction. A rebid of 3♦ is grossly inadequate, showing 16–18 high-card points. You have 20 high-card points and a very strong six-card suit, a circumstance that should dissuade you from rebidding 2NT, showing 18–19 high-card points. Some players would give strong consideration to opening 2♣ and rebidding 2NT to show 22–24 high-card points. There are a lot of tricks in this hand.

Need to Know

When your partner opens 2NT, the bidding tools you use after a 1NT opener are still there for you, just one level higher. After your partner opens 2NT, 3 ♣ is still Stayman, asking about four-card majors, 3 ♦ and 3 ♥ are still transfers to hearts and spades, respectively.

You aren't much better off if your partner's response is 1♥. You definitely want to be in game once your partner responds, but you don't want to jump to 4♥ with only three-card support. It would be tragic if you landed in 4♥ when your partner had some really weak holding in the suit and went down, only to find that 3NT was trivial because of your powerful diamond suit.

So what about rebidding 3NT over 1♥ or 1♠? Again, that shows a different hand—one with a long, strong minor and 17–18 high-card points—and usually a singleton in your partner's major.

Do you see where this is going? It's not unusual in bridge to be faced with a number of choices, none of which truly fits the situation. In such a case, it's best to select the smallest lie. In this case, it would be describing your almost-balanced hand as actually balanced. After all, you are one card away from having a balanced hand by the book.

When you open the hand under discussion with a bid of 2NT, your partner will be in charge and will be able to place the contract immediately. Here are some hands you might have and the action you should take with them. The strong hand (North) is repeated for convenience. You are South.

♠ A Q

♥ K Q 7

♦ A K Q 1 0 7 2

♣ 1 0 9

West	North	East	South
	2NT	·Pass	?

Hand 1	Hand 2	Hand 3
♠ J 1 0 8 7	♠ K J 9 8 7	♠ K J 5
♥ A 9 4 3	♥ J 1 0 9	♥ A 8 7 6 5 4
♦ 6 4	♦ 5 4	♦ 4 3
♣ Q J 6	♣ Q 8 7	♣ 8 7

Hand 4	Hand 5	Hand 6
♠ K 3 2	♠ K 1 0 9	♠ K 3 2
♥ 1 0 8 6	♥ A J	♥ A 1 0 9 6
♦ 4 3	♦ 9 8 3	♦ J 5 3
♣ A J 8 7 6	♣ K 8 6 5 4	♣ K Q 4

➤ Hand 1: Bid 3♣ (Stayman), asking your partner if he has a four-card major. As with 1NT, if North has both majors, he will bid hearts first. When North bids 3♦ (no major), you will bid 3NT. You have 8 high-card points, more than enough to commit to game when your partner shows 20–21.

➤ Hand 2: Bid 3♥, a transfer to spades. After your partner bids 3♠, you plan to bid 3NT, telling your partner you have enough to bid game but only five spades. If you had six spades, you would know that you and your partner have at least eight of them between your two hands, so you would just place the contract where you know it should be. That's the beauty of descriptive bids like 2NT. The responder can place the contract or give the opener a choice of contracts.

➤ Hand 3: Bid 3♦, a transfer to hearts. If you remember what you just read about hand 2, you will know what to do next. You have six hearts, so there's a guaranteed eight-card fit (maybe more), and you don't have enough to consider slam, so just transfer to hearts and raise your partner to 4♥.

Need to Know

Sometimes, when you open 1NT or 2NT and your partner makes a transfer bid, just knowing that your partner has at least five of the suit will improve your hand dramatically. Suppose you hold

♠ A K 10 9

♥ A J 9

♦ A 9 6 5

♣ 5 4

and you open 1NT. When your partner bids 2♥, a transfer to spades, you have reason to be excited about your hand. With four-card support and three aces, you have a fantastic hand for play in spades. So how to you let your partner in on the secret? Easy: bid 3♠. This is known as super acceptance of the transfer, describing a hand with near-maximum high-card points, mostly aces and kings, and at least four spades. Your partner can still pass if he has a truly lousy hand, but your partner might be able to bid game or even more if he knows about the great fit and your strong hand.

➤ Hand 4: Bid 3NT. You have no interest in your partner's major suit holdings, so just bid the only game that makes sense.

➤ Hand 6: Bid 4NT. No, you are not asking for aces in this situation. Bidding 4NT in response to your partner's opening of 1NT or 2NT tells him to go to 6NT if he likes his hand. With the hand under discussion, North will charge ahead to the twelve-trick contract. It's true that 6NT might go down if the ♣A sits over the king in your hand, but if the opening leader starts with anything but a club, you will most likely have twelve tricks in the other suits. Even a 4-0 split in diamonds won't beat 6NT if East has the void. The first round of the suit will reveal the bad break, and North will easily run home with twelve tricks. A bid of 4NT in this situation—directly over a 1NT or 2NT opener—is known as a quantitative raise and does not ask for aces as most 4NT bids would.

➤ Hand 6: Bid 6NT. You have 13 high-card points, your partner has at least 20, so you have 33 high-card points between you, theoretically enough to bid a slam (it's a workable formula in practical terms as well). Don't even think about bidding Stayman to try to find a major suit fit. Your totally flat shape suggests that notrump will be better than a suit contract.

Less Power

You have already learned about weak, preemptive opening bids at the two-level and higher. These are designed mainly to disrupt the opponents' communication by making them start their discussion at a higher level than they want to.

The most common of these preemptive bids is the weak two-bid: 2♦, 2♥, and 2♠. You gain the greatest advantage, of course, when you can open at the two level in the boss suit—spades. Unless the next bidder has a good enough hand to bid 2NT—which shows the equivalent of a 1NT opener and a spade stopper—he will have to bid at the three level, which can be uncomfortable in many situations.

That factor is a persuasive argument for those who prefer to play undisciplined weak two-bids. Making life difficult for the opponents more frequently is an adequate tradeoff for the occasional disaster that results from opening 2♥ with a poor hand and a poor suit, perhaps a hand such as this:

♠J 5

♥Q 7 6 5 4 3

♦Q 9

♣J 7 6

That is a truly dreadful hand, and opening 2♥ on that collection invites a big penalty. It will also put pressure on your partner, who will be in a quandary with a good hand and a modest fit for hearts. If your hand could be as bad as the one above, your partner will be worried that any move toward game could land you too high. There are conventions for finding out about hand strength and suit quality, but players just starting out are better off with a more disciplined approach.

Here's a suggestion: Agree with your partner that you will almost always have at least 5 high-card points in your suit when you open a weak two-bid in first or second seat.

Bridge Basics

When you are in third seat and the auction begins with two passes, if you have a subminimum hand yourself, you can bet that the player who will bid after you is counting his points and thinking of high-level contracts. It's up to you to throw a monkey wrench into your left-hand opponent's plans if you can. That means that when it comes to weak two-bids, the gloves are off. Any suit of five or six cards is fair game for a weak two regardless of quality. With a six-bagger, you might even consider opening at the three level. Your main objective, after all, is to take up bidding space before Mr. Rock Crusher on your left has a chance to speak.

If you take that approach, your auctions will be much easier when your partner opens a weak two-bid and you have a good hand yourself.

Here's a tip for when your partner opens with a weak two-bid in the first or second seat: don't think in terms of high-card points; think tricks. Here's an illustration of this concept at work:

Your partner opens 2♥ and you are looking at

♠ A K 7

♥ Q 6 5

♦ K Q 8 7 6 5

♣ 6

If your agreement about weak two-bids guarantees 5 high-card points in the suit, you know your partner has at worst six spades to the AJ. So think about how the play will go. Even if you have to lose a trick to the ♥K, your partner will have five heart tricks to go with two spade tricks and at least one diamond. That's eight tricks. The ninth and tenth tricks will most likely come from two club ruffs in your hand.

You have only 14 high-card points, but your trump support and possibilities for ruffing tricks in your hand make bidding 4♥ a good gamble.

There are ways, of course, of getting information about your partner's hand if you need it. Suppose, for example, your partner opens 2♠ and you hold

> ♠ K Q 6
>
> ♥ A Q 7 6 5 4
>
> ♦ 6 5
>
> ♣ A 4 3

Because of your agreement that your partner will have at least 5 high-card points in the spade suit (AJ in this case), you know you can count on six spade tricks. Your two aces bring the total to eight—but that's not enough. It's possible that your heart suit will produce some tricks, but you can't be sure.

One way to find out is to bid 2NT. This is not an offer to play in notrump. It is a special bid asking your partner two questions:

1. Are you at the top of your range for your weak two-bid?

2. If you are, do you have a feature you can show?

Most partnerships use a range of 6–10 high-card points for a weak two-bid, so when you bid 2NT, your partner will make his decision by reviewing points.

Bridge Lingo

In the world of weak two-bids, when you open a weak two-bid and your partner bids 2NT, he wants to know about features in your hand. In this context, a feature is usually an ace or king outside the trump suit. Some partnerships include outside queens as well. If you are at the top of your range for your weak two-bid and have an ace or king, simply bid the suit that contains your feature. It's that simple.

If the weak two-bidder has an ace or king, your partner bids the relevant suit. With no feature, your partner rebids his long suit.

Going back to the example hand:

♠ K Q 6

♥ A Q 7 6 5 4

♦ 6 5

♣ A 4 3

After your partner's 2♠ opener and 2NT from you, if your partner rebids 3 ♥, showing the ♥ K—it can't be the ace because you have it—you will bid 4 ♠ with confidence. Likewise, if your partner shows the ♣ K, you will consider bidding 4 ♠ because that brings your known trick total to nine—six spades, two clubs, and the ♥ A. If the ♥ K is to the declarer's left, he will be able to take ten tricks by playing a heart from his hand and putting in the queen if the left-hand opponent (LHO) plays low. That's a 50 percent proposition, making it worth a shot. If your partner has a singleton heart, he could play to the ace and ruff some hearts, hoping the king falls to establish the queen. Playing low to the ♥ Q if East plays low and hoping the king is in that hand – is known as a finesse. You will learn more about that in the chapter on card play.

If your partner bids 3 ♠, showing a minimum or no feature, you will pass and hope he doesn't go down.

There will be times when you have a good hand but no fit for your partner. On the occasions when you have a good suit of your own, you can bid it. If you have not already passed, bidding a new suit over a weak two-bid is 100 percent forcing. That means your partner is not allowed to pass.

Suppose your partner opens 2 ♦ and you have

♠ A Q J 10 7 6 5

♥ 5

♦ K Q J

♣ A 4

You should bid 2 ♠. Your partner must take another bid. His choices are to raise your suit with any three cards or two to an honor. If your partner has a singleton in your suit and a second suit of at least four cards, he can bid that suit. Otherwise, your partner should rebid his suit—3 ♦ in this case. You will rebid your spade suit, which probably will end the auction.

Note that in the example hand, your suit is strong. With a weaker suit tread carefully, especially if you do not have a fit in the suit your partner opens.

One other tip about weak two-bids: when you have support for your partner's suit, give him a raise no matter how weak your hand is. This bid is not invitational—it is meant only to further the preempt and make life harder for the opponents.

Bridge Basics

It is axiomatic in bridge that high-card points do not take tricks—trumps do. When you have an abundance of trumps—for example, a known ten-card fit—you can bid a lot to put pressure on the opponents without fear of going for a number. You can take a lot of tricks with a big trump fit and distributional features such as singletons and voids. Even if the opponents defeat your contract, in most cases they can make some contract that would score better than the plus they get for beating you.

Say partner opens 2 ♥ and you hold

♠ 6 5

♥ K 8 4 3

♦ Q J 6

♣ J 5 3 2

If your right-hand opponent (RHO) bids or makes a takeout double, bid 3 ♥. This is in no way constructive. You simply want to make it tougher for the opponents to exchange information.

To sum up the recommended weak two-bid structure:

➤ Play a disciplined style in first and second seat: promise 5 high-card points in the suit or three of the top five honors—e.g., KJ10876 or AQ10652.

➤ As responder, count known tricks in determining whether to bid game or slam or to ask for more information.

➤ To gain more information, bid 2NT, asking whether your partner has an outside ace or king.

➤ No matter how weak your hand, raise your partner's suit whenever you have three-card or better support.

CHAPTER 7

 **Competitive Bidding**

In This Chapter

➤ Getting into your opponents' auctions

➤ The takeout double

➤ Doubler's second turn

➤ Overcalls

In this chapter, you will learn about some of the more competitive aspects of bridge. You will discover why it's important to be active even when your opponents get in the first lick. You will be introduced to one of the oldest conventions in bridge—the takeout double—and you will learn what you need to make a takeout double and how to respond when your partner makes one. To complete the lesson on takeout doubles, you will find out what the doubler should do at his second chance to bid.

You will also learn about overcalls—what you need to bid when your opponents open first, and how to manage the auction from that point.

Busy, Busy

Bridge is a game for ladies and gentlemen to be sure, but that's more of a reference to decorum, sportsmanship, and ethical behavior at the table. When it comes to going for tricks and making life difficult for the opposition in legal ways, the gloves are off.

The greatest difference between the bridge of today and that of your grandfather is that way back when, the side that opened the bidding pretty much had the auction to themselves.

That was especially true if the opener was 1NT, played in the old days as showing 16–18 high-card points.

Nowadays, everyone is in there, seemingly all the time and often on what the British would call tram tickets. Bidding with poor hands is not recommended, but active opponents are a lot more difficult to play against even if you nail them with a big penalty now and then.

Whoever opens the bidding has an advantage in having fired the first shot. The opening partners have taken a big step in exchanging information. It's easier, for example, to make competitive decisions knowing that your partner has at least 12 or more high-card points.

There are two ways for you to counteract the advantage that your opponents have when they open in front of you. The first is the takeout double. The second is the overcall.

Double Your Pleasure

When the player to your right opens the bidding and you double, you are using one of the oldest conventions in bridge.

In many settings, a double means you think the opponents have bid too much, and you want to increase the penalty. When you double an opening bid by your right-hand opponent, you are telling your partner a couple of things:

> ➤ You have approximately an opening hand.

> ➤ You have at least three-card support for the unbid suits. (There is one major exception to this rule. You will read about it in this chapter.)

The takeout double is a highly effective tool for neutralizing the advantage the opponents have by opening the bidding.

Your double is a request for your partner to bid his best suit—and sometimes *best* means longest, not necessarily strongest in terms of high cards.

Suppose your right-hand opponent opens 1 ♣. Here's what a takeout double by you should look like:

♠ A 1 0 8 6

♥ K J 6 5

♦ K J 3

♣ 4 3

You have 12 high-card points and at least three cards in the unbid suits. This is almost a textbook takeout double because of the major suit holdings. Your partner will always strain to bid a major, so having four of each is just what the doctor ordered.

If you have the ideal shape, you can shade the high-card points slightly, as with this hand when your right-hand opponent opens 1 ♣:

♠ A J 9 6

♥ K 1 0 7 6

♦ K 7 4 3

♣ 2

You have only 11 high-card points, but you have excellent support for any suit your partner might mention, and the singleton in clubs means that your partner might be able to ruff some of his club losers in your hand.

Bridge Lingo

When your partner overcalls in a suit and you bid one of the other two suits, you are said to be crossing suits with your partner. There are a couple of reasons why you would do this:

➤ You hate your partner's suit (you have a singleton or void) and you have a decent suit of your own to mention, usually at least six cards long

➤ You have a very strong suit that you believe should be the trump suit if your side wins the auction. If your hand, for example, consists mostly of a suit headed by KQJ109 and two or three others, your hand might take no tricks unless your suit is trump. If it is trump, it will take a lot of tricks.

Following are some hands for your consideration. Your right-hand opponent has opened 1♦. What action, if any, do you take with the following:

1. ♠ 5 2
   ♥ A J 4 3
   ♦ Q 3
   ♣ K Q 7 6 5

2. ♠ A K 7 6 5
   ♥ Q J 9 8
   ♦ 7
   ♣ K 4 2

3. ♠ A 1 0 9 8
   ♥ K 1 0 8 7
   ♦ 3
   ♣ K 1 0 9 4

4. ♠ J 1 0 9 8
   ♥ A K J
   ♦ A Q 9
   ♣ J 9 7

5. ♠ A Q J 9
   ♥ K J 1 0 7
   ♦ 4
   ♣ A K 7 6

Here are the answers

1. Pass: You have 12 high-card points, but with only two spades a takeout double should not be on your list of possible actions. What will you do if the opener's partner passes and your partner bids 1♠? Are you going to leave your partner with a possible 4-2 spade fit? Are you going to bid 2♣? That shows a much stronger hand than you have, as you will see later in this chapter. If you cannot resist getting into the bidding, the only possible choice is an overcall of 2♣, which could work out very badly for you if your partner is broke and your left-hand opponent has a club stack. Note also that the doubleton ♦Q is a poor holding in the suit opened by an opponent. No experienced player would ever overcall 2♣ with that hand when vulnerable.

2. Double for takeout: You could overcall 1♠—you do have a nice suit—but in the long run it will pay off for you to keep hearts in the picture by making a takeout double instead. Suppose your partner's hand is

♠ 4 3

♥ A 10 7 6 5

♦ 6 4

♣ Q J 6 5

If you overcall 1♠ and the next player passes, your partner almost surely will also pass. What can he bid with a smattering of values, but not enough to make a move over your 1♠ bid—plus a doubleton spade? It's usually bad practice to run from a partner's bid holding a doubleton. The time to worry is when you have one or none. With a strong suit, perhaps ♠AKJ109, an overcall would be reasonable. With that hand, your partner will certainly bid hearts if you make a takeout double, and he actually has enough to bid if the opener's partner has something to say. Game might be called in hearts but unlikely in spades.

3. Double: Yes, you have only 10 high-card points, but you have perfect shape, hard values in your ace and two kings, plus good intermediate cards. This is aggressive but not crazy. Most experienced players would happily double 1♦ with this hand, although they might have a bit of trepidation about unfavorable vulnerability.

Bridge Basics

One of the most common errors among new players is making a takeout double with the wrong shape—that is, without support for all unbid suits. These are commonly referred to as off-shape takeout doubles. Many players mistakenly believe that a takeout double shows only an opening hand—and who cares about support for unbid suits? That is bad bridge, sure to create lots of lousy results.

4. Overcall 1NT—do not double: It's always a good idea to make the most descriptive bid possible the first chance you get. You have 16 high-card points and a double stopper in diamonds. If your partner has a little something over there, he can bid Stayman or perhaps transfer to hearts or spades.

5. Double: If your partner bids a major, you will make a strong move toward game—and it wouldn't be outlandish to simply bid four of whichever major your partner selects. This is a powerful hand.

Show Your Strength

There are a couple of cases in which you can double when you don't have support for all unbid suits. The first is when you have a powerful one-suited hand that needs very little from your partner to make a game. Here's an example: Say your right-hand opponent opens 1♦ and you hold

♠ A K Q 1 0 9 8

♥ 2

♦ K 7 6 4

♣ A Q

Say you overcall 1♠ and find your partner with a hand such as the following:

♠ J 5

♥ 7 6 5 4

♦ 8 2

♣ K J 1 0 5 3

With only doubleton support for spades and a total of 5 high-card points, your partner will pass—as he should opposite a simple overcall. You can see, of course, that game your way is on ice. So how should this be handled?

You can double first, and when your partner bids 2♣, you bid 2♠, showing a hand with a good spade suit and 17 or more high-card points.

As you might have guessed, the second exception to the rule about doubling without support for unbid suits also involves a powerful hand.

Suppose your right-hand opponent opens 1♥ and you are looking at this hand:

♠ A Q 10

♥ K Q J 9

♦ A K

♣ 1 0 9 8 4

A normal range for overcalling 1NT is the same as for opening 1NT—usually 15–17, although some prefer to increase the upper end by a point to make it 15–18. The hand in question, of course, does not qualify for a 1NT overcall because it is too strong. If you bid 1NT and your partner has a 6-point hand, he will never make a move toward game—why should he when your maximum as far as your partner knows is 23 high-card points?

You must make a bid that describes how strong your hand is, and the way to do that is to double. You have only two diamonds, but you plan to show your strength after your partner picks a suit. Say your partner bids 1♠. You have an easy bid of 1NT to show 18–20 high-card points, or 19–21 if your overcall range is 15–18.

Tell the Truth

When your partner makes a takeout double of an opening bid and the next player passes, your partner has some expectations:

> ➤ Your partner wants you to bid your best suit—and in most cases, *best* means longest.

> ➤ Your partner wants you to give him some idea of how high you should get in the bidding. One of the most common errors of the inexperienced player is failing to describe the strength of the responding hand.

Here is a general rule of thumb for responding to a takeout double:

With 0–8 high-card points, bid your suit at a minimum level, as in a response of 1♠ when your partner doubles an opening bid of 1♣, 1♦, or 1♥ for takeout. Similarly, if your partner doubles 1♠ for takeout and your best suit is clubs, bid 2♣—the lowest bid you can make in that suit.

With 9–11 high-card points, respond with a jump in your best suit. For example, if your partner doubles 1♥ for takeout and you have 10 high-card points and at least four spades, respond to the double with a bid of 2♠. With a club suit and 9–11 high-card points, you must jump to 3♣ when your partner doubles one of a major or 1♦.

There will be times when a bid in notrump seems more appropriate with your hand. Bear in mind that a bid of 1NT in response to a takeout double shows a couple of things:

> ➤ At least one stopper in the suit that was opened plus some values, something on the order of 8–10 high-card points. Remember, you need high-card points for taking tricks in notrump, so you won't be bidding notrump with 6 or 7 high-card points. With 11–12 and a stopper in the opponent's suit, you can bid 2NT.

> ➤ With 12 or more high-card points, bid opener's suit (a cue-bid). This simply says that you have an opening hand and that your side probably should be in game. Your partner will bid a four-card major if he has one or both, starting with hearts in that case, and you can raise to game if you find a 4-4 fit.

It is a common mistake among inexperienced players to want to pass their partner's takeout double when they have a really weak hand.

Write this down and keep it with you as a reminder: The weaker you are, the more important it is to respond to your partner's takeout double. For example, suppose your left-hand opponent opens 1♠ and your partner doubles for takeout. Both sides are vulnerable, and you hold

♠ 7 3 2

♥ J 7 6 3 2

♦ 6 5

♣ Q 9 2

Three high-card points—yikes! You're getting a sinking feeling and thinking that if you bid, the doubling will start and it will be bloody. Well, consider this: your partner is professing to be short in spades—typical for a takeout double—and you have just three "babies." With such a weak hand, how do you think you're going to defeat 1♠? It's likely that if you pass and find yourself defending 1♠ doubled, you will need a calculator to total up the score for the overtricks, which will cost you 200 points each.

Even worse, your partnership will suffer. Your partner will feel very aggrieved to make a normal takeout double and end up writing down a mammoth score for the other side.

Bridge Basics

Most of the time, when you cue-bid following your partner's takeout double, it's forcing to game. There is one exception: when your partner doubles one of a minor for takeout and you have two four-card majors to go with 9–11 high-card points, you cue-bid to get your partner to bid his better (or only) major, which you will raise as an invitation to game. With 4-4 in the majors and an opening hand yourself, cue-bid and go to game in whichever suit your partner selects.

Furthermore, just because you are weak, doesn't mean your side is in trouble—and you do have a fifth heart. Suppose your partner has something like this:

♠ A Q

♥ A 1 0 9 8

♦ K 8 6

♣ J 1 0 8 6

If you are extremely unlucky, you might go down with your weak hand and the above hand as the dummy, but if you do, your opponents will almost certainly have missed out on a better score, maybe even game.

There are other important points regarding your response to your partner's takeout double:

➤ You should be aggressive with shapely hands.

➤ Holdings of five- and six-card suits (other than the one your partner doubles) mean your side can take a lot of tricks, even without a lot of high-card points.

➤ You can pass your partner's takeout double, but only with a very strong holding in the opener's suit—e.g., ♠QJ10987 when the opening bid was 1♠. Your partner will lead a trump if he has one because you have said you prefer this suit as trumps, and pulling trumps is something you want to start in on right away.

➤ Every now and then, your partner will double for takeout and you will find yourself with a weak hand and only one four-card suit—the opener's. You can't pass with a weak hand, you can't bid the suit naturally (not that you would want to), so your best strategy is to bid one of your three-card suits without showing distress over your situation. Many players have finely tuned antennae, and if you let them know you are in trouble, the doubling will start. Make your bid cheerfully without overdoing it, and you might survive.

Here are some hands for you to bid after your partner has doubled 1♦ for takeout:

1. ♠Q J 9 6 3
   ♥A 4
   ♦Q 10 9 8
   ♣6 4

2. ♠K 8 4
   ♥Q 10 7
   ♦K J 7
   ♣10 9 6 3

3. ♠A J 10 9 8 7 6
   ♥A 5
   ♦8 7 6
   ♣4

4. ♠7
   ♥K Q 7 6 5
   ♦6 4 3
   ♣K 6 5 4

5. ♠A 5
   ♥Q J 4
   ♦A J 9 5
   ♣J 7 6 5

Here are the answers:

1. Bid 2♠: If one of your clubs was a heart instead, giving you a singleton club, you would be very close to just bidding game. You have a five-card spade suit (good chance you have a nine-card fit) a side ace, and a chunky four-card side suit.

2. Bid 1NT: You have a four-card club suit, but a bid of 2♣ tells your partner nothing about your hand, which is pretty good in context. A bid of 2♣ would be made on a hand with 0 high-card points, so your partner might not be able to make a move. You have a 9-point hand with good intermediates, a stopper in the opener's suit, and no four-card major. You should always strive to make the bid that gives your partner the maximum in useful information.

3. Bid 2♦: You know for sure that you are going to play in 4♠—your partner, after all, promised support for the unbid suits, so you know you have at least ten spades between you. That singleton club also looks valuable, as does the ♥A. Jumping to 4♠ has merit, but it wouldn't take much from your partner for you to have an easy slam, perhaps

> ♠K 5 4 3
>
> ♥K Q 7 6
>
> ♦2
>
> ♣A 8 7 6

That's just 12 high-card points, but it's a perfect takeout double. You might have to learn a few more bidding tricks to get to slam, but any experienced player would be delighted to be in 6♠ with hand 3 and the above hand as the dummy.

4. Bid 2♥: A good way to think about hands of this type is to imagine you are raising your partner. In effect, that's what you are doing. Your partner professes to have at least three cards in every suit except diamonds. You have only 8 high-card points, but the shapeliness of your hand argues for more than a 1♥ bid. You can count an extra point for the fifth heart, and a couple of playing points for the singleton spade. Bidding only 1♥ with this hand would be a serious underbid.

5. Bid 3NT: You have everything you need for this bid: a great stopper in diamonds, 13 high-card points and high cards that should fit with your partner's hand to help you take some tricks.

Bridge Lingo

If you play enough bridge, you may hear other players talking about working cards and wonder what that means. Basically, honor cards in your hand are much more valuable if your partner has honors in the same suit. For example, ♦ Q J 2 facing ♦ 5 4 3 might take no tricks, whereas ♦ Q J 2 facing ♦ K 8 7 6 will be good for at least two tricks once the ace is dislodged, and you will take three tricks in the suit if your opponents have three diamonds each. Add the ♦10 to the longer holding and you are guaranteed three tricks.

The discussion so far has assumed that your opponents have nothing to say after the opening bid. That, of course, will not be the case in many auctions. Players have learned that allowing you to proceed with your exchange of information unencumbered by their "noises" does not work out well for them.

When your partner doubles an opening bid of one of a suit, the most common interference you will encounter will be a raise of the opener's suit by the third hand, as in the auction 1♠—Dbl—2♠. A wise partner of the opening bidder will raise with almost any excuse. It helps the opener with his decision later in the auction if he wants to compete—and it makes it more difficult for your side to find your best spot.

Without intervention by the opening bidder's partner, you are obliged to bid something in response to the takeout double (except on the rare occasion when you are loaded in the opener's suit). When the third hand bids, you are no longer required to bid—your partner will have another chance to do something. If you speak when you are not required to, that is known as a free action—and you must remember that making a free bid indicates values.

Contrast these two auctions:

West	North	East	South
1♠	Dbl	Pass	2♥

West	North	East	South
1♦	Dbl	1♠	2♥

In the first auction, the bid of 2♥ could be made on a hand with no high-card points. South must bid, and hearts is the suit he picked. The bid does not promise anything beyond four or more hearts.

In the second auction, once East bid 1♠, South was no longer under any obligation as far as bidding. Therefore, the bid of 2♥ shows that South has something constructive to add to the conversation of the auction. South might have a hand such as

♠ 6 5 4

♥ Q 10 9 8 7

♦ 8

♣ K J 4 3

This is not a powerful hand, but the so-called playing points are promising. There is an extra heart, the suit has good intermediates, and there is a second suit with two honors. This is a clear-cut free bid of 2♥. It's worth noting that the opponents probably have a big fit in diamonds: South has a singleton, and North is likely to be short in that suit as well. South should help North cope with the bidding, which is probably about to heat up. There may not be another chance.

Bridge Lingo

When responding to a takeout double, especially when the auction becomes competitive, consider your hand in terms of playing points or support points rather than strictly high-card points. Add an extra point for every card in your prospective trump suit in excess of four, and add points for singletons and voids. Pretend that your partner opened the suit you are thinking of bidding, then decide what you would do to support that suit. A simple raise might not be sufficient.

Change that example hand just a bit, and South (you) would be even more aggressive. Here's the auction again, plus your hand: 1♦—Dbl—1♠ - ?

♠ 6

♥ A Q 10 9 8

♦ 8 5 4

♣ K J 4 3

You would not be out of line to jump to 4♥. Opposite a normal takeout double, this hand has enormous playing strength. Bidding only 2♥ would be timid, and that is not a characteristic of a winning bridge player.

Talking Back

You have learned that as the responder to a takeout double, your obligation is to select a suit to play in—and let your partner know how strong you are. To reiterate the parameters:

➤ 0–8 HCP: Make a minimum bid in your best suit

➤ 9–11 HCP: Jump in your best suit

➤ 12+: Cue-bid the opener's suit or jump to game

Pretty easy rules, but what about the doubler? What are the doubler's obligations once your partner has spoken?

There are two scenarios to consider when you have made a takeout double and your partner has selected his response:

1. Other than the opening bid, the opponents have been silent

2. The opener has something to say after your partner has made his choice.

When the opponents have made no more noise after the opener's bid, raising your partner's suit carries a special message.

Consider this auction:

West	North	East	South
		1♦	Dbl
Pass	1♥	Pass	2♥

What do you think South's 2♥ bid means?

Consider the information provided by North's 1♥ bid. North has said he probably has four hearts and up to 8 high-card points. Remember, if his hand evaluated to more than 8 playing points, he would have bid more than 1♥.

The raise to 2♥ by South, therefore, is an invitation to game, and it must show a hand much better than an average takeout double. Think about it: South is telling North to bid game if he is on the upper end of the range for the response of 1♥—7 or 8 points. So what must South's hand have to make this invitation? His hand should look something like this:

♠ Q J 10

♥ A K 10 7

♦ K 8

♣ A J 10 7

If South makes a jump raise, it shows even more—roughly 20 high-card points. In that case, South would be telling North to bid 4 ♥ with all but the very weakest hand he could have in the context of the auction.

This is sort of a corollary to the situation in which the responder to a takeout double does not express the strength of his hand correctly. When South raises with an ordinary takeout double in an uncontested auction, his action is just as inappropriate as that of the underbidder. It is vitally important for both parties in these auctions to know what the different bids mean. Being on different pages, so to speak, makes for inaccurate and unsuccessful auctions.

That takes care of the unimpeded auction, but consider the same scenario with a different situation:

West	North	East	South
		1♦	Dbl
Pass	1♥	2♣	2♥

Does South's 2 ♥ bid in this auction mean the same as in the other auction?

It does not. When the bidding becomes competitive, partners must do everything they can to provide useful information to each other, and in this case, the information provided by South can be vital in helping North decide whether to continue to compete or to bid on.

So what is South telling North when he raises hearts freely? South is saying that he has four-card heart support. Remember, South's takeout double promised only three-card support for unbid suits. Say South's hand was

♠ K 7 6 5

♥ A 10 9

♦ 4 3

♣ K Q J 7

In the scenario in which East (opener) takes another bid, this is a clear-cut pass. There is nothing about this hand that warrants a free bid. It is pretty much what was described by the takeout double. If South's partner, North, has a modest hand with only four hearts, North will probably pass because he knows that if he bids on, he will be playing a 4-3 heart fit—and he is limited to 8 playing points. Change the hand slightly, however, and it's a different story from South's perspective.

♠ K 9 8 6

♥ A 1 0 9 4

♦ 4 3

♣ K Q J

With this hand, you want to let your partner know that you have four-card heart support, which will be useful information should the opener's partner get into the mix, perhaps by raising the opener's second suit. That extra trump in your hand will make a huge difference in your partner's outlook on the situation.

Speak Up

Another way to compete is via the overcall, a bid made after an opponent has opened the bidding. For example, when your right-hand opponent opens 1♦ and you bid 1♠, your bid is an overcall. If the bidding goes, 1♣—Pass—1♥ and your partner bids 1♠, that is also an overcall.

In general, there are three reasons to overcall:

1. To get to play the contract (it helps your cause a lot if your suit is spades)

2. To get your partner off to the best lead

3. To interfere with the opponents' bidding

Reasons 1 and 2 accomplish reason 3 in many cases. If you have the boss suit—spades—and can find a fit in that suit by overcalling, you can often outbid your opponents, and even if they defeat you in your contract, you often find that the score they get from beating you isn't as good as the one they would have had if you had allowed them to buy it.

There are risks to entering the auction after the other side opens the bidding because the partner of the opening bidder has a pretty good idea of his side's assets at that point—the partner certainly knows the minimum his side can have—and he may be poised to exact a big penalty on you.

Bridge Lingo

If you play enough bridge, sooner or later you will encounter an opponent with a stack in your trump suit. What that means is that the opponent has as many trumps as you do, sometimes even more. Unlike when you overcall—which should promise at least a halfway decent suit—an opening bid of a suit does not come with any guarantees as to high-card strength, so it would not be unusual for a person to open 1♥ on five to the jack, and find that the next player had a holding such as ♥ A K Q 1 0 9. Now that's a stack.

That said, it is risky to pass because you might miss a game—sometimes even a slam. All things considered, if it's a close decision, it's usually best to get in there. If you are overcalling in second seat, there are still two unknown hands, and it pays to be optimistic that your partner has some help for you.

You may be wondering why it makes a difference if someone gets into the bidding after your side opens. Consider the following situation:

Your partner opens the bidding with 1 ♣ and you hold

♠ 8 7 4

♥ Q 6 5 4 3

♦ K J 5

♣ 6 2

You are all set to respond 1♥ when your right-hand opponent intervenes with a bid of 1♠. Now what?

You have enough to respond at the one level, but if you bid 2♥, that shows at least 10 high-card points, and you aren't close to that. If you make a habit of making bids that misrepresent your hand that grossly, your partner won't ever know what to do, and when you do have enough to bid 2♥ in that situation, your partner might pass, fearing you have the bad hand.

What about bidding 2 ♣? Don't even think about it with two-card support. In most situations, a bid of 2 ♣ in competition shows four or more. After all, the opener might have started with a three-card club suit.

Bridge Basics

In many competitive bidding situations, vulnerability is the key. When your side is vulnerable, you are subject to a larger penalty for failing to make your contract, and the opponents are more likely to double if you get too high—the payoff for them is worth the risk. When the vulnerability is favorable for you—meaning your opponents are vulnerable and you are not—the opponents are more likely to bid on because it's harder to get a big score by doubling non-vulnerable opponents. In other words, at favorable, you can be a lot friskier in the bidding.

With the example hand after your partner opens 1 ♣ and your right-hand opponent bids 1♠, you have just enough high-card points to bid 1NT, but you have no semblance of a stopper in spades, so 1NT is not a consideration either. In short, you are kind of stuck.

There is a tool you can use in this situation—and you can read about it in the next chapter—where the negative double is covered. The point is that when the opponents get into your auction, the bidding often becomes a lot more difficult.

Now, what if your right-hand opponent had overcalled your partner's 1 ♣ opener with 1 ♦ instead of 1♠? Well, that's an entirely different situation. In that case, you could bid 1♥ with a clear conscience. A bid of 1♥ over a 1♦ overcall is the same as if your right-hand opponent hadn't bid at all. It doesn't promise any more than 6 high-card points, enough to respond 1♥ without interference.

Bidding Space

The most effective overcalls, at least in terms of discomfiting your opponents, are those that take up the most bidding space. As in the previous discussion, if you overcall an opening bid of 1♣ with a bid of 1♦, you have used no bidding space. The opener's partner can bid 1♥ or 1♠ with no difficulty whatsoever.

When you overcall with a bid of 1♠, the opener's partner has no suit he can bid at the one level, which makes bidding with modest values somewhat problematic.

Bridge Lingo

There are simple overcalls, and there are jump overcalls—and it pays to know the difference. A simple overcall is one that is made without jumping a level of bidding. For example, a bid of 1♠ over an opening of 1♥ is a simple overcall. Similarly, a bid of 2♣ over an opening bid of 1♦ is a simple overcall because to bid clubs over any suit bid requires going to the next level. A jump overcall, on the other hand, skips a level of bidding, as in 1♥—2♠ or 1♦—3♣. Most partnerships agree that jump overcalls are weak in the same way that weak two-bids and opening three-bids are weak.

One of the most effective overcalls in terms of interfering with the opponents' bidding is 2 ♣ over an opening bid of 1♦. Most bidding systems are geared to finding a fit in a major suit, and that can be tough to do if the responder doesn't have a five-card major to mention or doesn't have the high-card strength to bid it directly.

Quality versus Quantity

So what should your typical overcall look like? More important, what should your partner expect when you stick your nose into the opponents' auction?

First, you overcall for one of the stated reasons, the first two of which are constructive. A simple overcall is made with the hope of finding a fit or finding your partner with enough assets that your side can buy the contract. On the other hand, a jump overcall showing a weak hand is meant to take up bidding space so that the opponents have to guess about their best spot—or guess whether to keep bidding or stop and double you.

As an example, say your right-hand opponent has opened 1♥. Here are some hands that would be appropriate overcalls:

Hand 1	Hand 2	Hand 3
♠ A Q J 8 9	♠ 4 3	♠ J 10 9 8 7
♥ K 4	♥ J 6	♥ A
♦ J 7 6 5	♦ A K J 6 5 4	♦ K 6
♣ 3 2	♣ A J 10	♣ K Q 10 8 3

➤ Hand 1: You have a textbook 1♠ overcall. Your shape is not great, but you have a good suit and your ♥K is likely to be a trick. Your side could take a lot of tricks if your partner has spades with you.

➤ Hand 2: You would overcall 2♦ at any vulnerability, but take away one of the diamonds, leaving you with only five, and it's a different story. You might still bid, but you would not be surprised to be doubled and go down a lot. Having an extra trump means one less for the opponents. That one little trump can make a huge difference.

➤ Hand 3: You should bid 1♠. Yes, the clubs are better than the spades, but with two suits of equal length you should almost always start with the higher-ranking of the two. If your opponents compete to 2♥ and it comes back to you, a bid of 3♣ would show your good distribution and reasonable high-card strength. If your partner comes up with a raise for your overcall, you would certainly make a game try by bidding your club suit, but it would not be out of line to simply jump to game over a raise. That undisclosed five-card suit could come in handy.

Just Four, Partner?

When you overcall, you normally promise at least five cards in your suit. Is there ever a time when you would overall with only four? Yes. It might be a rare occasion, but overcalling on a four-card suit can be productive. The key is for your partner not to hang you in the auction by bidding too much with too few trumps.

Suppose your right-hand opponent opens 1♥ and you hold

> ♠ A K Q 10
>
> ♥ 7 6 5 4
>
> ♦ A 5 4
>
> ♣ 10 3

You have an opening hand, but you can't make a takeout double because if your partner bids 2♣, you have nowhere to go. The benefits of overcalling 1♠ are many: you preempt the bidding and make the responder's job tougher because if he can't raise the opener's hearts or bid 1NT (no stopper), he will have to bid a minor at the two level. If the responder isn't strong enough, he will have to do something else. If the opponents have the balance of power, they may end up playing the contract, and if your partner is the opening leader, he already knows the best suit to start with thanks to your overcall. When you catch your partner with good trump support, you can take a lot of tricks—and you have the boss suit. You could easily make game if you hit your partner with

> ♠ J 9 8 7
>
> ♥ 3
>
> ♦ Q J 10 9 8
>
> ♣ A 9 5

All you would really need is the ♦K to be with the opening bidder—not an unreasonable assumption—and you could easily take ten tricks, maybe even eleven. If you decline to overcall, you could be shut out of the auction.

Even if you don't have a lot of high-card points, if you find a big trump fit with your partner, you could have a good save against the opponents making contract.

Many players employing five-card major suit openings would start with 1♠ on the hand in question because of the preemptive value of owning the highest-ranking suit—and to be sure their partner gets off to the best lead should the opponents buy the contract.

Bridge Basics

There are risks in overcalling. Your opponents might double and get you for a number such as 800 or 1100 or worse. That said, there are also risks in passing. You might miss a game or slam, and your opponents, given a free run, will almost always arrive at the right contract—bad for you. In the long run, you will profit with a mildly aggressive style of competitive bidding. If you get clobbered once in five deals, break even in two, and get top scores in two, your average is 60 percent, which will be profitable in the long run. Busy bidders make life tough for their opponents.

It is important to understand that overcalls are not created equal. Some are weak, some are strong, and some fall in between.

Most overcalls you make will be the in-between variety, and most players agree that a simple one-level overcall shows about 8–16 high-card points (with more high-card strength, remember, you will double first, then bid your suit).

Vulnerability will be a significant influence as you exercise your judgment in competitive bidding.

You would happily overcall 1♥ over a minor suit opening on

♠Q 7 2

♥A K 7 6 4

♦6 4 3

♣K 4

You don't promise the moon when you enter the bidding, and unless forced to, you don't plan on bidding again.

If the opening bid was 1♠ and your side was vulnerable, you would never consider bidding 2♥. You have poor shape, poor intermediate cards in your suit, only five of them, and a dubious holding in the opener's suit. It would be easy to construct layouts where 2♥ by you would be doubled and you would take only two or three tricks—a real massacre.

Change the hand just slightly, and most experts would enter the auction expecting good things to happen. Here's an adjusted hand:

♠K 3

♥A K 1 0 9 6 4

♦6 5

♣Q J 4

Now you have a chunky six-card suit, only a doubleton in spades, and if you end up playing a heart contract, that ♠K is almost surely going to be a trick. Players just about always lead their partners' suits.

Advancer Advances

In bridge parlance, the partner of the player who makes an overcall is known as the advancer, although that person will not always have anything to say. Here are three reasons why an advancer may remain silent:

1. A poor hand

2. Little or no support for the partner's suit and no good suit to bid instead

3. Acceleration of the auction to an uncomfortable level, as when the opener's partner makes a preemptive raise of the opener's suit

There are some general guidelines for an advancer who does have something to say. When a partner has overcalled:

➤ A simple raise represents the same hand you would have if your partner were the opening bidder—in other words, with three-card or better support and 6–9 support points.

➤ When the advancer's hand is too good for a simple raise, he must cue-bid the opener's suit. This shows at least a good 10 to a poor 12 playing points. With more, the advancer will continue to bid if the overcaller signs off.

➤ When the advancer has four-card or better support for the overcaller's suit and not many high-card points, in most cases a jump raise is advised. This is not a forward-going bid but simply an effort to jam the opponents' auction.

➤ If you have a long, strong suit that has not been mentioned and little or no support for the suit in which your partner overcalled, you should bid your suit. This sends the message that you think your hand will take more tricks with your suit as trumps than if it were not the trump suit. This a forward-going action, but it is not forcing (your partner can pass).

How would you bid the hands in the following auction?

West	North	East	South
1♣	1♥	Pass	?

1. ♠ A 7 6   2. ♠ 8 4
   ♥ Q J 4   ♥ A J 7 6 5
   ♦ J 10 9 8 7   ♦ 6
   ♣ 6 2   ♣ 10 6 5 4 3

3. ♠ A K   4. ♠ 6 2
   ♥ J 10 9   ♥ K 10 7 6
   ♦ K 6 5 4 2   ♦ A Q J 6
   ♣ 7 6 5   ♣ A 9 2

5. ♠ J 8 7   6. ♠ K 8 7 6
   ♥ 10 9 6 5   ♥ 5
   ♦ Q J 7 6   ♦ K Q J 10 9 7 6
   ♣ 4   ♣ 4

Here are the answers:

1. Bid 2♥: You would make the same bid if your partner opened 1♥. This is descriptive, and you have nothing more to say unless forced to by your partner.

2. Bid 4♥: You have enormous playing strength, and your five-card club suit could be facing a singleton in your partner's hand. Only at unfavorable vulnerability would you consider bidding less than 4♥.

3. Bid 2♣: Your hand is too strong for a simple raise to 2♥. If your partner signs off in 2♥ or passes when the auction gets competitive, you will respect your partner's wishes and also pass. You have told your story, so you have nothing more to say.

4. Bid 2♣: If your partner signs off, you will take one more stab, perhaps raising to 3♥ to show your extras.

5. Bid 3♥: This is a weakness-showing bid, guaranteeing at least four trumps and most likely a singleton or void.

6. Bid 2♦: Unless your partner has a self-sufficient suit of his own, diamonds is most likely the spot for your side. If you put your hand down as the dummy and your partner has a low singleton, your hand might take no tricks if you end up playing in your partner's suit.

Some partnerships have an agreement that a jump overcall shows a good suit along with intermediate strength—13–16 high-card points. This is playable if both partners agree to it and understand how it works. The main problem with this approach is the low frequency. You will have more opportunities for interfering with the opponents' bidding by jumping with weak hands and long suits.

A sort of hybrid approach is to agree that jump overcalls when not vulnerable are weak but are intermediate when you are vulnerable. When the vulnerability is unfavorable, a jump overcall will deliver the upper part of the overcall range.

Bridge Basics

An often-heard admonition in bridge cautions players against bidding the same cards twice. To be successful and appreciated by your partner, you must make this one of your guiding principles. Once you have made a bid that describes your hand, you must not voluntarily take another bid. Few things are more irritating than being put in a minus position by a partner who has told his story but keeps on bidding. Write this down and say it twenty times: "I will not bid the same cards twice."

CHAPTER 8

More Competitive Bidding

In This Chapter

➤ Two-suited hands

➤ Competing against preempts

➤ When your partner preempts

➤ Balancing

In this chapter, you will learn what to do when you are dealt the kind of hand that has the potential for a surprising number of tricks—the distributional two-suiter. You will read about how to respond when your partner gets into the bidding with a two-suited hand. You will also learn some rules for coping with your opponents' preemptive bids, and what to do when your partner preempts the opponents' auction.

The Law of Total Tricks, explained briefly, is introduced as a valuable tool for competing. It's not foolproof, but it's a helpful adjunct to your bidding arsenal.

Finally, one of the most important aspects of competitive bidding is covered—the rules for balancing—trying to get your opponents out of their comfort level.

The Shape of Things

You have heard a lot about high-card points, even losing trick count. These concepts are useful in improving the accuracy of your conversation with your partner—in other words, the bidding.

Bridge Facts

In the early days of bridge, if your opponent opened the bidding and you bid the same suit—a cue-bid—that showed a powerful hand with support for the unbid suits. It was like a supercharged takeout double. The problem with the convention is that it seldom comes up in actual play. In essence, it is a wasted bid. Enter Mike Michaels, creator of the convention that bears his name. Today, if your right-hand opponent opens one of a minor and you bid the same minor, it shows a hand with at least five cards in each major. If the opener starts with a major, the bid of the same suit shows the other major and an unspecified five-card minor suit in a relatively modest hand. As you can imagine, this comes up far more often than the strong takeout cue-bid.

Among the most accurate and effective tools for use in competitive bidding are the various ways of showing two-suited hands. In this context, *two-suited* means a hand with two suits of at least five cards each, perhaps

♠ Q 10 9 6 5

♥ K 7 6 5 4

♦ 6

♣ A 3

This hand is not good enough to open the bidding, even using the dubious Rule of Twenty that many inexperienced players rely upon.

Suppose, however, that your right-hand opponent opens one of a minor in first seat—that is, as dealer. Now you are in business. This hand is an automatic Michaels cue-bid (see the Bridge Facts entry, left) if the opponents are vulnerable and you are not, and it's reasonable when neither side is vulnerable.

Here are some example auctions:

West	North	East	South
		1♣	2♣

West	North	East	South
		Pass	Pass
1♦	2♦		

West	North	East	South
1♥	Pass	Pass	2♥

West	North	East	South
		1♠	2♠

In all examples, the bid of the opponent's suit is artificial, not natural. If you have a hand with length in the opponent's suit, you usually pass and await developments. For example, suppose you hold

♠ A 7 6

♥ K 9

♦ 6 4

♣ K Q J 9 8 7

Now you hear your right-hand opponent, the dealer, open 1 ♣. At your first turn to call, you have no option but to pass. You cannot double because that is for takeout, and you have doubletons in two unbid suits. You will be in a mess if your partner bids a red suit, and if you try to introduce your good club suit after doubling, you will be showing an extra-strong hand with support for the suit partner bids. You cannot overcall 1NT because you do not have sufficient high-card strength. If you and your partner are using the Michaels cue-bid—highly recommended—you cannot cue-bid because that would show at least 5-5 in the major suits.

Your only option, therefore, is to pass. Yes, you hate to pass with such a great suit, but wait: you will have your chance. Suppose you hear this auction (you are South):

West	North	East	South
		1 ♣	Pass
1 ♥	Pass	1 ♠	?

Now you can bid 2 ♣, which perfectly describes your hand: enough strength to bid at the two level and (almost certainly) a good six-card suit in clubs. Remember, East in this sequence might well have only three clubs, possibly even three low ones. In any case, you have the chance to make a descriptive bid at your second turn. If the bidding really takes off—say East rebids 2NT over West's one-level response, showing 18–19 high-card points—you will be glad you passed initially, and

Need to Know

There is an important point about Michaels cue-bids that many inexperienced players do not appreciate. When you use this convention, you are telling your partner that you have a hand with at least five cards in two suits, depending on what the opener's suit was. If you bid Michaels with five cards in one suit and four in another, you are violating the agreement and affecting partnership trust. Your partner will sometimes have to pick between three-card holdings in the two suits you advertise. If you bid with 5-4 in your two suits and your partner selects the wrong one, it could be a disaster. Stick to the agreement: have 5-5 or better in your suits or pass.

you might even double if they get to 3NT. Even more important, such bidding would tell you that your partner is dead broke, so your disciplined pass probably saved you from a big penalty.

Back to the Michaels discussion. There are a couple of rules most players use when adding the Michaels cue-bid to their agreements.

One rule is that vulnerability is an important factor in deciding whether to enter the auction to show a two-suiter, particularly if the opening bid was 1♠. Remember, if you make a Michaels cue-bid of 2♠ over the opener's 1♠, your partner will have to bid at the three level. That is dangerous territory when your side is vulnerable, even more so when you are vulnerable and your opponents are not. Non-vulnerable opponents will jump at the chance to double if you venture into the bidding with inadequate values.

The following hand has disaster written all over it if you force your side to the three level:

> ♠3
>
> ♥K 7 5 4 2
>
> ♦Q 6 5 4 3
>
> ♣A 3

Let's say both sides are vulnerable and your right-hand opponent opens 1♠. It would be suicide to bid Michaels—2♠, showing hearts and a minor—with this hand. Your long suits are anemic, and if you don't have a fit with your partner in either suit, it means your opponents are loaded with high cards and better spot cards in those same suits. They will kill you if you end up at the three level.

It's true that you might get lucky and find your partner with a big fit, which means lots of tricks, but while that one thing might occur, two others are more likely:

1. Your opponents will double you and collect a big number

2. Your opponents will end up winning the contract and, thanks to your informative bid, the declarer will play the hand as if they can see all fifty-two cards.

Another rule is that when you use a Michaels cue-bid, your hand should be weakish or very strong, not in between.

There is sound reasoning behind that rule. When you have a modest hand, you get your bid in and say no more unless forced to do so by your partner. You cede captaincy to your partner, who will understand by your passes that you have shape but not a lot of strength, perhaps a hand such as one of the following (after your right-hand opponent opens one of a minor):

♠ J 10 9 8 7	♠ K Q 9 8 4	♠ A J 9 6 5
♥ Q J 10 9 8	♥ Q 10 5 4 3	♥ Q J 8 7 6 4
♦ 2	♦ 7 6 5	♦ 6
♣ A 3	♣ --	♣ 3

Any of these would be acceptable Michaels cue-bids, even vulnerable, because of the good spots. Once you have bid Michaels with any of these hands, however, you do not have another voluntary bid.

So when can you bid again after using the Michaels convention? When you have such a strong hand that you feel game (or even slam) is a possibility. You just want your partner to pick a suit. You might have something like one of these (also after your right-hand opponent opens one of a minor):

♠ A K J 10 9	♠ A K Q 9 8	♠ A K 10 9 6 5
♥ A Q J 9 8	♥ K J 10 9 8	♥ A Q J 8 7 6
♦ A	♦ 5	♦ --
♣ 4 3	♣ A Q	♣ 3

With the first two, if your partner makes a minimum response, you will raise to show you have extras. With the last, you will take a shot at game when your partner makes his pick, and it would not be out of order to have an auction such as this:

West	North	East	South
		1♣	2♣
Pass	2♥	Pass	4♦

This is a specialized bid that shows a hand good enough to go to game and shortness in diamonds. It is called a splinter bid, which you will learn more about later. If your partnership is not using the bid, you can simply raise to game. You must have at least this much because your partner's bid does not promise a single high-card point. You forced him to bid, right? All your partner's 2♥ bid says is that he prefers hearts to spades.

Alternatives

There are other ways to show two-suited hands. The simplest is by using the takeout double in the correct situation. Your hand is as follows:

♠ Q J 8 7

♥ K 8

♦ A Q 6 5 4

♣ 3

Now here is the bidding (you are South):

West	North	East	South
1♣	Pass	1♥	?

You have a perfect takeout double. In this position, it shows spades and diamonds, the unbid suits.

Bridge Lingo

When you enter the unusual world of bridge, it won't be long before you pick up the jargon and learn how players communicate. It is not unusual for players to share stories of unusual events—or to pose problems, especially in bidding. When someone says, "you hold . . ." you know you are about to be asked what you would do in a certain situation with a set of thirteen cards. *You hold* is usually followed by a quick rundown of a hand, perhaps: ". . .five spades to the king-queen, singleton ace of hearts, five solid diamonds, and two low clubs. What's your bid?"

The two-suited double works just as well when you are in second seat (the person to bid right after the dealer). Your hand:

♠ A Q 10 6

♥ 8 7

♦ A Q J 7

♣ 6 5 2

The bidding (you are still South):

West	North	East	South
		1♣	Pass
1♥	Pass	2♥	?

When East opened 1♣, your hand was not suitable for any direct action. Overcalls usually show at least five cards in the bid suit, and you should never consider a takeout double of 1♣ with that hand. What if your partner bids hearts? You must bide your time. In this case, it pays off. With four-card support for both unbid suits plus opening-bid values, you have a textbook takeout double on your second turn to bid.

Out of the Ordinary

One of the most popular conventional bids to show two suits is called the Unusual 2NT. It acquired the *unusual* handle because in most cases when someone bids 2NT, it shows a good hand, sometimes a very strong hand.

For example, if your partner opens 1♣ and you respond, say, 1♥, and your partner rebids 2♣, a bid of 2NT by you is not an attempt to tell your partner you hate his suit. In that sequence, 2NT is inviting your partner to bid 3NT if he has a good hand. Your 2NT bid, therefore, shows roughly 11–12 high-card points. Opening with 2NT shows 20–21 high-card points, and if you open 2♣ and rebid 2NT, that shows 22–23 high-card points. The exception to the rule about 2NT showing strength is when it is bid directly over an opponent's one-level opening bid. A direct bid of 2NT shows the two lowest unbid suits.

Opening bid	Meaning of 2NT
1♣	Diamonds and hearts
1♦	Clubs and hearts
1♥/♠	Clubs and diamonds

In all cases, 2NT shows at least five cards in the suits that are shown. It is important for partnership harmony to avoid making this bid with fewer than five cards in either suit.

Jumping to 2NT over an opponent's one-bid does not guarantee a lot of high-card points. Remember, having good shape can compensate for a lack of strength, especially if the bid uncovers a big fit between the two hands. That does not mean, however, that you should use this convention with any old hand just because you have two five-card suits. Both suits should have some "texture," which means good spot cards.

A suit such as Q6543 is poor—you might take no tricks with that suit as trump—but QJ1098 will always take at least three tricks if it is the trump suit.

As mentioned previously, vulnerability is a factor. When you bid 2NT as a takeout—that means you are not offering to play in notrump—your partner will have to bid at the three level. If you jump into the auction with a collection of tram tickets, the result will usually be minus 1100 or worse.

The other factor is that when your side is vulnerable and your opponents are not, you must consider whether you have a reasonable chance to win the auction because if you don't, the declarer will have a big advantage in knowing ten of your cards before the opening lead is made. Such information helps the declarer play a lot better than if you kept your mouth shut and made him dig for information.

For example, at favorable vulnerability, you might consider bidding 2NT over 1 ♠ with

♠ 2

♥ 4 3

♦ Q J 8 7 5

♣ Q J 10 5 3

The payoff when you hit your partner with four of five of one of your minors can make bidding 2NT worth the risk of getting doubled and going down a lot. Your partner will bid his head off with a good fit just to jam the opponents' auction, and they will be reluctant to double because their vulnerable game usually pays more than they will get in a penalty. If your partner can jack the auction way up there, your opponents may misjudge and bid too much or too little.

At unfavorable vulnerability, you have no realistic hope of buying the bidding because your opponents won't worry about missing a non-vulnerable game. They will double you with alacrity and punish you for your folly. If they buy the contract, they will know exactly how to play it because your ill-considered bid will have given them so much information about your and your partner's hands. That could be the difference between making it and going down.

Go for It

Now that some general parameters for making two-suited bids have been established, it's time to consider the situation from the other side of the table—from the advancer's point of view. Remember, the advancer is the partner of a player who overcalls or makes a takeout double.

In general, when your partner shows a two-suited hand that has certain limitations, it's best to take your best shot right away.

Bridge Basics

When your partner enters the auction with a bid that shows at least ten cards in two suits, your major concern will be your holdings in those suits. The more cards you have in either or both suits, the more you will bid. Remember, if your partner has, say, ten cards in the majors, he won't have more than three cards in the minors, maybe fewer. If you have a big fit with one or both of your partner's suits, don't be timid. Having lots of trumps between the two hands can be insurance against a lack of high-card points.

Suppose the bidding has gone as follows (you are South):

West	North	East	South
1 ♣	2 ♣	3 ♣	?

Your hand is:

♠ J 8 7 6 5

♥ 3

♦ A 10 8 7 5

♣ 7 6

You have only 5 high-card points, but there are at least ten trumps between your hand and your partner's. Remember, your partner's 2 ♣ bid shows at least five cards in each major. At any vulnerability, you have a clear-cut bid of 4 ♠. Your partner doesn't need much more than the following for you to have a great shot at ten tricks.

♠ A 10 9 3 2

♥ A Q 9 6 4

♦ 4

♣ 5 2

Suppose, however, that your hand is more like this:

♠ 5 3

♥ J 7 2

♦ K Q 5 3 2

♣ Q J 3

You have more in high-card points, but your shape is dull, your spots in your partner's two suits are poor, and your best fit is probably just eight cards. The difference between an eight-card fit and a ten-card fit is enormous in terms of trick-taking power. On the given auction, if you're feeling frisky and the vulnerability is favorable, you might risk 3 ♥ over 3 ♣, but be prepared for it to work out badly on occasion. If East had passed in the given auction instead of bidding 3 ♣, you would never consider anything but 2 ♥.

Need to Know

Your decision about how high to bid when your partner shows a two-suiter will often include a consideration of context. For example, if your side is vulnerable and your opponents are not and your partner gets into the bidding in such a way the you could end up at the three level, it is reasonable to count on your partner for at least the equivalent of a better-than-minimum opener and two good suits. In such a case, you should consider that you are raising one of your partner's suits. It will pay in those instances to be more aggressive even without a super trump fit.

Consider this auction:

West	North	East	South
1♠	2NT	3♠	?

What would you bid with each of the following hands at favorable vulnerability and at unfavorable vulnerability.

Hand 1	Hand 2	Hand 3
♠532	♠10987	♠A876
♥7654	♥QJ9	♥J109
♦KQ753	♦Q108	♦KQ6
♣J	♣Q65	♣1094

➤ Hand 1: At either vulnerability, bid 5 ♦. At favorable, you probably won't make it, but this looks like a good save. At unfavorable, your partner should have enough for you to make your contract. One thing is for sure, as a defender you won't be taking many tricks in diamonds—and your partner is likely to have a singleton spade.

➤ Hand 2: Even at favorable vulnerability, you don't want to get into this auction. Your queen-oriented hand is more suited to defense, and your opponents may be too high already. Don't rescue them by bidding 4♣. This is a clear-cut pass either way.

➤ Hand 3: At favorable, bid 4♦ for the lead. You expect a plus if your opponents bid on to 4♠. At unfavorable, bid 5♦ to make.

Under Pressure

In the world of competitive bidding, the opponents will try to do to you what you try to do to them—foul up their auctions. That means lots of weak opening bids at the two-level and higher.

Coping with preemptive bidding requires judgment, and that comes from experience. In general, however, when the opponents open with a weak bid, entering the auction requires reasonable values, especially when vulnerable. Have you noticed, by the way, how often vulnerability comes up in competitive bidding? That's because it matters.

There is a handy rule that can help you when it comes to coping with your opponents' preemptive bidding—at least at the two level. It is called the Rule of Eight. Here's how it works:

When you are considering whether to bid over a weak 2♦, 2♥, or 2♠, figure that your partner has about 8 high-card points and make your bid on that basis. Ask yourself how you think you will do if your partner has the expected high-card points. Of course, your partner won't always have that much strength, and occasionally he will have more, but that's part of the equation. If you and your partner are on the same page regarding this rule, it will help with your competitive judgment.

Generally, when one player overcalls, the advancer is encouraged to raise with any hand that would be considered a raise of an opening bid. For example, if your partner overcalls 1♣ with 1♥, you would raise to 2♥ holding

♠ A 5 4

♥ Q 7 2

♦ 9 4

♣ Q 10 7 6 2

If you and your partner are in agreement about the Rule of Eight and your partner overcalled a weak two-bid in diamonds with a bid of 2♥, you would pass because you have what your partner expects. Put the ♦A in place of the ♦9 and you would have a raise to 3♥, which tells your partner you have at least a king more than the expected 8 high-card points.

But what if your partner has more than just a minimum overcall? You are worried that if his hand is too good, you might miss a game if you pass with your 8 high-card points.

The solution is that when your partner has extras, say a good 16 or more high-card points, he must jump—that is, over a weak 2♦, your partner must bid 3♥. That is not a weak bid. You don't preempt over a preempt.

The Rule of Eight, by the way, is still in play. Your partner's jump to 3♥ carries this message: "Partner, I'm playing you for about 8 high-card or support points. If you have them along with a fit for me, bid game. Otherwise you can pass."

Bridge Basics

When your opponent opens a weak two-bid, one of your competitive tools is the bid of 2NT. Do not confuse this with the Unusual 2NT described earlier in this chapter. A bid of 2NT over an opening of 2♦, 2♥, or 2♠ shows a balanced hand of 15–18 high-card points and at least one stopper in the opener's suit. Most pairs agree to use their normal 1NT structure over the bid of 2NT. In other words, 3♣ is Stayman and transfers are on.

When an opponent opens at the two or three level and the next player bids 3NT, that bid is usually based on a stopper in the opener's suit and a long, running side suit. For example, over a 2♠ opener, a typical 3NT overcall would look like this:

♠K J 8

♥A 10

♦A K Q J 7 6

♣J 9

A seventh diamond would be desirable, but no bid other than 3NT is conceivable.

Over other high-level opening bids, the general principle is that the higher you have to bid, the more you have and, you hope, the longer your suit. Sometimes, though, you just have to suck it up and bid even when you know the outcome could be a disaster.

For example, say your right-hand opponent opens 2♠ and your hand is as follows:

♠ 4

♥ A K J 7 2

♦ K Q 1 0 6 5

♣ 1 0 9

It could be dangerous to overcall with this hand—you would love to have a sixth heart—but how would you like to have the bidding go 3♠ on your left followed by two passes? Now you have to bid at the four level. Yikes!

It's true that you could be clobbered if you bid 3♥, but you know the saying about faint hearts and fair maidens. You can't double because your hand isn't strong enough to double and bid a suit, which shows a good 17 high-card points or more. Your only choice is to bid your heart suit. Even vulnerable, you must get in there and fight. Minus 800 hurts only for a minute.

Remember also that if your partner gives you a raise in hearts, you have a very nice playing hand. You would happily bid game and expect to make it if your partner can make a peep.

Bear in mind that passing has risks as well. Missing games can be very costly, and when you are playing in a duplicate game, you can take some comfort in knowing that other players will face the same dilemma. Most players tend to take an aggressive action when it's close between wimping out and bidding, so you might as well jump right in.

The other factor is that your opponents won't necessarily know that you are in trouble, and if you give them a free run by bidding only when you're rock solid, your opponents' bidding accuracy will increase measurably.

For the record, this is the kind of hand you would like to have for bidding over of a weak 2♠ bid:

♠ 5

♥ A K J 1 0 9 8

♦ A K 6 5

♣ J 9

It's not that much stronger in high cards than the hand before it, but there is an extra trump and good body in the long suit.

Double Trouble

At higher levels, takeout doubles lose some of their shape requirements, tending instead to show more in the way of high-card strength than adequate support for all suits. If you do make a takeout double of a high-level bid without something in every suit, you must have a fallback position. Say an opponent opens 3♠ and you hold

♠ A 2

♥ A K Q 10 7

♦ A Q J 7 6

♣ 9

You don't want to bid 4♥. That is what is known as a unilateral bid. In other words, you are not involving your partner in the decision. The best course of action with this hand is to double for takeout. If your partner bids 4♣, you can bid 4♦. That will get your message across, and you will be successful if your partner has a hand like this:

♠ 5 4

♥ J 9 6

♦ K 7 5

♣ J 10 8 5 3

Your partner will know when you bid 4♦ that you were under pressure because of the preemptive bid, and he will understand that you have a two-suited hand with the red suits. You will find your way to 4♥, where you belong (the major suit game requires only ten tricks, whereas 5♦ requires eleven).

It's different, however, if you have this hand:

♠ A

♥ A K Q 10 9 8 4

♦ A J 10

♣ J 9

There is only one place you want to play and it's in hearts. Just bid your long suit and hope your partner can provide a card or two for you. Even if your suit was not as good as the one shown—perhaps ♥ K J 1 0 9 8 7 5 —you would still get into the bidding. When push comes to shove, it's better to be a bit more aggressive.

Bridge Lingo

There's a term in competitive bidding called *staying fixed*. What that means is that sometimes your opponents will put you under pressure with an unusual bid, and you will feel as though you are being robbed. For example, an opponent opens 4 ♠ and the next player (your partner) makes a double for takeout. Once your partner shows a sign of life, your hand might be good enough that you would explore for slam if you had more bidding space. The fact is, however, that you don't have that space, and if you end up bidding too much and going down, your opponents will have succeeded in their goal of messing up your auction. In close cases, it's better to stay fixed.

Partner Jacks 'em Up

When it comes to disruptive bidding, turnabout is fair play. Your side can do the same to your opponents if you have the right ammunition.

There are two schools of thought on the subject of preemptive bidding, applied mostly to weak two-bids. It is a fact that an opening bid at the three level or higher takes away bidding space from your side in addition to disrupting your opponents' bidding.

Regarding weak two-bids, these are the predominant styles:

➤ Super-aggressive, where any five-card suit can become a weak two-bid

➤ Disciplined, semi-constructive

The risks associated with the aggressive style are as follows:

➤ When you open at the two level with a poor suit, you could end up being doubled and doing down a lot

➤ You will frequently get your partner off to a bad lead, say when you open a jack-high suit and your partner leads the king from a doubleton

➤ The partner of the weak two-bidder is often forced to guess, and if you get on an unlucky streak, you could have a series of bad results.

The risks associated with a more disciplined style are different but more palatable. For starters, you will preempt less frequently, making life easier for your opponents, and your opponents will often beat you to the punch with their preempts. These are negligible minuses compared to the benefits of a more disciplined style.

If you and your partner prefer a more disciplined style, consider these parameters:

Except for third seat—especially at favorable vulnerability—you will always have a six-card suit. Your first- and second-seat weak two-bids will promise at least 5 high-card points in the suit. At minimum, your suit would be headed by the A-J or K-Q. This will facilitate your constructive bidding. For example, suppose your partner opens a weak 2♠ and you are looking at this hand:

♠ K Q 4 3

♥ A K Q J 9

♦ A 1 0 9 8

♣ —

Playing the recommended style, your partner's spade holding cannot be worse than six to the A-J. The two of you have the top four cards in the suit with only three out, so you know you can take six spade tricks. You are also an odds-on favorite to take five heart tricks, so you are now up to eleven tricks, add in the ♦ A and you're up to twelve. All you need is a club ruff in the dummy and you're a lock for thirteen tricks. You could go straight to 7♠, confident of making it.

Now consider how you would approach this deal if your partner's opening 2♠ could be based on a five-card suit to the jack. You could be in jeopardy at 4♠, let alone slam. A slam might still be on, but it won't be so easy figuring out whether it's a good contract.

You won't always be dealt such a big hand when your partner opens a weak two-bid, but knowing the quality of the suit is a big plus. Here's another example to consider after your partner opens a weak 2♥:

♠ 5

♥ J 9 6 4

♦ A K 7 6

♣ K Q 1 0 8

Your partner's 2♥ promises 5–10 high-card points, so you might have only 18 high-card points between the two hands, but stop and count the potential tricks. Your partner must have at least K-Q or A-Q in his suit (but not a A-J because you have the jack). You have ten trumps between you, so your partner will almost surely take five tricks in hearts. Your opponents can't run your hand out of trumps because you have so many of them, so your partner should be able to ruff a couple of spades in your hand. That's five trumps in your partner's hand, two in yours for seven, plus the top diamonds for nine and at least one club trick for ten. Bidding 4♥ directly over 2♥ is clearly indicated.

Even if you have a lesser hand without a serious chance of game, it still pays to extend the preempt by raising your partner when you have a good trump fit, even with a hand such as this:

♠ 5 4

♥ J 9 6 4

♦ Q J 9 6

♣ A 1 0 4

At favorable vulnerability, it would not be out of line to jump to 4♥ as an advance save. You don't expect your partner to make it, but the damage can't be that bad because you know your partner's trumps are decent—and your opponents are surely on for some game. Even better, if your right-hand opponent passes and you jump straight to game, your left-hand opponent won't know if your bid is based on high-card strength or just a good trump fit.

Consider your dilemma if your partner's 2♥ could be based on a ratty five-card suit. Jumping to game could be a disaster.

Need to Know

You may have noticed that a good trump fit, especially one of nine cards or more, is a powerful offensive weapon. When you have lots of trumps and shortage (singletons or voids) in your hand and/or your partner's, you can take tricks without a lot of high-card points. There's an old saying, "Points don't take tricks, trumps do." That means that the more trumps you have between your hand and your partner's, the more you can bid even without a lot of high-card strength. This is an important aspect of competitive bidding that many new players do not appreciate. Don't be a point counter, but do count trumps.

The fewer the trumps you have in support of your partner, the more conservative you should be in the bidding. When you don't have so many trumps, you need more high-card points.

Higher and Higher

If you adopt a policy of disciplined weak two-bids, you may find yourself bucking a current trend. You should decide what you are comfortable with and stick to that philosophy.

Opening bids at the three level and higher may also call for a slightly different approach on your part. Whereas the trend nowadays is to open at the three level with six-card suits—as opposed to the traditional seven—newer players are probably better off sticking with the traditional agreements.

In the early days of bridge, the higher your opening bid, the more high-card strength you showed. It is well known, of course, that although there were many fine players back then, in general the bidding was atrocious.

Again, it is easier for the partner to judge what to do if he knows what to expect from, say, an opening bid of 3♥. If it could be a six-card suit, you don't necessarily want to further the preempt by raising with a weak hand and only two-card support, which you might do if you could be certain it's a seven-bagger. If you know it's at least seven and you have three trumps yourself, you would feel more comfortable giving your partner a boost. Having ten trumps can make up for the lack of high-card points.

When you are considering a weak opening bid, use the handy Rule of Two and Three, which says that when you are vulnerable, you should be within two tricks of your bid in your own hand; when non-vulnerable, you should be within three tricks. In other words, looking at your own hand and assuming your partner has a little something for you, when you open vulnerable at the three level, you should be able to take seven tricks (assuming you end up playing the contract). If you are not vulnerable, you should be able to take six tricks.

Here are some examples of reasonable vulnerable three-bids:

♠KQJ10987	♠74	♠6
♥K8	♥KJ106543	♥43
♦J107	♦A654	♦K65
♣4	♣---	♣AQJ9874

You can dial it back a bit when you are not vulnerable, as with these:

♠KQ85432	♠5	♠J10
♥8	♥KJ106543	♥432
♦J1072	♦54	♦AQ109875
♣4	♣QJ8	♣K

Be careful when you have a long suit headed by the AKQ. If you open three of that suit, you might easily miss a game, most often 3NT. A seven-card suit headed by the top three honors can take a lot of tricks.

Be careful, by the way, of having too much outside your long suit. When you open the bidding to show a long suit and a weak hand, your partner will start thinking about possibly taking a sacrifice against your opponents' best contract, especially if your partner has a good trump fit with you. You should have no more than one defensive trick outside your suit—one ace or possibly two kings but no more. The reason is simple: If you have defensive tricks and your partner takes a save against your opponents' contract, it might end up being a "phantom." That means your side saved against a game that wasn't making. Not good.

Guessing Game

When your partner opens the bidding at a high level and catches you with a pretty good hand, there is some guessing to do. A common mistake for new players is to bid 3NT over their partner's opening three-bid with the wrong kind of hand.

Suppose your partner opens 3♦ and this is your hand:

♠ A J 9 8

♥ K Q 7 3

♦ 3

♣ A K 10 4

You have a fine hand, but you must keep in mind that your partner is showing weakness, not strength, perhaps a hand such as this one:

♠ 7 5

♥ 10 6

♦ Q J 10 7 6 5 4

♣ Q 3

This would not be an unreasonable 3 ♦ opener if your side is not vulnerable. Looking at your hand and your partner's, you will have no chance for nine tricks. Your opponents will probably start with a major suit and will win the first diamond when you play the suit. You can reach the dummy with the ♣ Q, but an opponent will win the next diamond play and your dummy will be stone dead. You will be down at least a couple of tricks, probably more.

It's a different story if you have a different kind of hand, perhaps:

♠ A K 4

♥ A 9 4 3

♦ A 8 2

♣ 10 9 4 2

Now you have an excellent chance for nine tricks in notrump. You have ten diamonds between your hand and your partner's and three quick tricks. You would be very unlucky not to take six diamond tricks to go with your other three top tricks.

The point is that you need a fit to bid 3NT when your partner opens at the three level. Lots of high-card points won't help if you have to play the contract all out of your own hand.

Balancing Act

One of the key aspects of competitive bidding is the fine art of balancing. In England, it's called protecting.

In essence, to balance is to try to push the opponents up a level when the opponents' auction appears to be about to die out at a low level, as with the following:

West	North	East	South
		1♥	Pass
2♥	Pass	Pass	??

You, South, are said to be in the balancing seat. If you pass, the auction is over and the opponents will have a nice, comfy 2♥ contract to play.

You must recognize that allowing your opponents to play two-level contracts when they have found a fit is losing bridge. Write that down somewhere and repeat it to yourself every day for two weeks. It's extremely important.

With the given auction as a backdrop, suppose you hold the following hand:

♠ Q 8 7 6

♥ K 4

♦ A 8 3 2

♣ J 10 9

Yes, it's a rather dull, 10-point hand. You didn't seriously consider bidding with that hand directly over East's opening bid of 1♥, and you may be reluctant to get involved now. Consider, however, what the auction has told you.

East did not have enough high-card strength to make a move toward game, so probably has a minimum opener. West made a single raise, which could be based on as little as 6 high-card points. In fact, your side might have the balance of power—and you are almost certain to have at least as much as your opponents do or pretty close to it.

So you may be asking why your partner didn't do something. For one thing, he doesn't know how strong East's opening bid is. Taking action could be walking into the lion's den. For all your partner knows, East could be loaded. Remember, an opening one bid could be as strong as 20 high-card points. The other thing is that your partner probably didn't have a suitable hand for entering the auction. He might have been holding the following:

♠ K 10 5 4

♥ A 6 5

♦ K 7 6 5 4

♣ 3

Your partner could hardly double West's 2♥ for takeout: he doesn't have the right shape and is a bit short on high-card points. Overcalling at the three level on that moth-eaten diamond suit would get no consideration either. Your partner's only option was to pass.

Once the auction is about to die out, however, South must start thinking about how to get the opponents out of their comfort level. In the situation described, the best way to do that is to double for takeout. South would not be overjoyed to hear his partner bid 3♣, but at least he has three decent ones. The other thing is that on auctions such as this, the partner will strain to bid a major suit, meaning you can keep the level at two.

If the opponents do not bid on to 3♥, 2♠ might well make. If you are playing duplicate with neither side vulnerable and you make 2♠, your score would be plus 110. If you let your opponents play 2♥, you will probably have minus 110. Which would you prefer? If they bid on and go down, even just one, plus 50 is better than minus 110.

What if the South hand was changed just a bit, perhaps looking like one of these:

Hand 1	Hand 2	Hand 3
♠ Q 5 4 3 2	♠ J 5 4	♠ J 5
♥ 3 2	♥ 3 2	♥ 4 3 2
♦ A Q 4	♦ A Q 4	♦ A Q 4 3
♣ Q 10 9	♣ Q J 8 7 6	♣ K 10 8 7

Instead of balancing with a takeout double, you would prefer to bid 2♠ with hand 1. If you double, your partner might have to bid a weak four-card minor while holding something like ♠ J 10 9, and you would have missed your best spot. With hand 2, you don't have really great support for spades, but you do have an okay, if not robust, club suit. It's best to get that into the picture instead of doubling. Finally, with hand 3, the clear-cut bid is 2NT. Don't panic! You will see that it makes sense.

You want to compete, but if you double and your partner bids spades, it will likely be a poor contract. If you bid one of your minors, you might pick the wrong one and end up worse off than if you doubled. In the context of the bidding, 2NT must be telling your partner to pick a minor. If you doubled and your partner had to bid a minor, it would be at the three level anyway, so just cut out the middleman and tell your partner what you've got. You are a passed hand and the opponents have bid and raised a suit. 2NT cannot be a natural bid.

Ground Rules

Now that you have been introduced to the concept of balancing, here are some key points to remember:

➤ When you are considering a balancing bid, your minimum high-card strength will be in the neighborhood of 8–10 high-card points.

➤ Both partners must remember that when one balances, the balancing player is bidding both hands.

Need to Know

A player who balances is said to be bidding both hands, meaning the player's and his partner's. In general, a player balances when he has passed earlier because he didn't have sufficient values or a suit good enough to introduce directly. When the opponents' bidding threatens to die at a low level, balancing is called for in many cases, but the balancing player still has a hand that has deficiencies. The bidding, however, tells the balancer that his partner has some high cards or the opponents would have at least tried to get higher in the auction. Banking on the partner to have scattered values, the balancer is, in essence, bidding both hands when he takes action.

➤ Bearing in mind that the balancer is bidding both hands, it is incumbent on the balancer's partner not to raise the balancing bid without some unexpected major improvement in his own hand.

➤ A balancing bid of 1NT is possible, as when the bidding goes 1♦—Pass—Pass—? In such a case, 1NT usually shows about 10–14 high-card points and a balanced hand. With a hand good enough to open 1NT in first seat (15–17), the balancer must double first, then bid notrump to describe the strength.

> ➤ Players may decide to employ their normal 1NT system (Stayman and transfers, for example) over the balancing 1NT bid.

> ➤ A balancing jump to 2NT shows 19–21 high-card points, roughly the same strength as an opening 2NT bid. An example auction might be 1♠ – Pass – Pass – 2NT.

> ➤ Balancing is appropriate over a preemptive bid that is followed by two passes, and it is a key element of negative doubles.

Consider this auction:

West	North	East	South
3♦	Pass	Pass	?

Your hand:

♠ K 10 9 5

♥ A J 8 5 3

♦ 6

♣ A Q 7

Holding this hand, you must double. Your partner might be sitting there with something like the following:

♠ 8 4 2

♥ 10 9

♦ K J 9 8 4

♣ K 3 2

As you can imagine, your partner is licking his chops, ready to collect a big number from 3♦ doubled, but your partner can't do it alone. A direct double by your partner would be for takeout, so you must help.

The situation is a bit dicey if your hand is like this one, however:

♠ K 10

♥ A J 10 6 5 3

♦ 6

♣ A Q 7 3

You might still double, but bidding 3♥ will probably work out best in the long run. If your partner does not have a penalty pass of 3♦ doubled and instead is weak, you could be in trouble, as when your partner has this hand:

♠ J 7 6 5

♥ 8 4

♦ 9 7 5 4

♣ K 5 4

Your partner will have to bid 3♠ and you will be in the soup, forced to play 4♥, possibly doubled.

On occasion, you will have a hunch that even with less-than-ideal shape, double is the right balancing action. A hint that it might be right is when your left-hand opponent opens at a high level and the next two players pass. In these days of competitive bidding, most players will give their partners a raise with any excuse so long as they have a bit of trump support. When your right-hand opponent passes his partner's preemptive bid, it might well be because he doesn't have support, increasing the chances that your partner has laid a trap and is waiting for you to spring it.

Just be aware that there are risks. Sometimes the right-hand opponent is the one who has laid the trap as he waits with a strong hand for you to act, but that's part of what makes competitive bidding an exciting element of the game.

CHAPTER 9

Useful Conventions

In This Chapter

➤ Blackwood revisited

➤ Other slam conventions

➤ Negative doubles

➤ Other special doubles

In this chapter, which is oriented somewhat to tournament players, you will find out at lot more about the Blackwood convention. There's a lot more to it than you might have imagined—and there's more than one way to ask for aces.

You will also find out that Blackwood is but one slam convention, and you will learn how to make best use of the others.

Keep reading and you will discover the ins and outs of a convention called the negative double, hailed by one expert as the most important bidding innovation of all time.

By now, you probably won't be surprised to know that the double comes in many different forms. You will find out about them in this chapter.

"Old Black"

Blackwood is arguably the most popular bridge convention in the world. Just about everyone knows that a jump to 4NT asks partner to show how many aces he has. The rudiments are relatively simple.

After one player in a partnership leaps to 4NT, his partner responds as follows:

> ➤ 5 ♣: No aces or 4 aces. The latter is a rare occasion. A player with no aces in his or hand usually will not be strong enough to be interested in slam.

> ➤ 5 ♦: 1 ace.

> ➤ 5 ♥: 2 aces.

> ➤ 5 ♠: 3 aces.

Bridge Basics

Most players consider Blackwood to be an essential tool for getting to slam, and that is a reasonable viewpoint. The fact is, however, that it is more useful in avoiding bad slam —*i.e.*, a commitment to take twelve tricks when the opponents have two cashing aces, or a contract for thirteen tricks when the opponents can cash one ace. It is not unheard of at high levels of bridge play for experts to arrive at grand slams with one of their opponents holding the ace of trumps. In fact, at a recent major championship, it happened at both tables in the same match.

Blackwood, of course, is more than just 4NT. Easley Blackwood thought it might also be useful to find out about kings, so he added another level to his convention.

After hearing the partner's response to 4NT, the Blackwood bidder can continue the interrogation by bidding 5NT, which asks for kings. The responses are similar to the answers to 4NT:

> ➤ 6 ♣: No kings or 4 kings.

> ➤ 6 ♦: 1 king.

> ➤ 6 ♥: 2 kings.

> ➤ 6 ♠: 3 kings.

There are a couple of important points to keep in mind as you add Blackwood to your bidding repertoire:

1. When you bid 4NT and follow with 5NT, you are trying for a grand slam and in so doing are telling your partner that your side has all the aces. It makes sense, doesn't it? If your opponents were holding an ace, you would be rash indeed to make a bid that requires all thirteen tricks.

2. There is a better way to play the responses to 5NT than simply giving numbers of kings. A much better way is to show your kings by bidding them up the line. If you are wondering what up the line means, it is simply the way of saying that you start with the lowest-ranking suit—clubs—and go up the line to the next highest suit until you come to one with a king in it.

Suppose, for example, you and your partner hold these hands:

You (West)	Partner (East)
♠ A J 10 7 6	♠ K Q 8 2
♥ 9 5 3	♥ A
♦ A Q 7	♦ K 9
♣ K 4	♣ A Q J 10 7 6

Here is your bidding:

West	North	East	South
1♠	Pass	2♣	Pass
2♠	Pass	4NT	Pass
5♥	Pass	5NT	Pass
5♦	Pass	?	

East knows that his partner has one king, but which one? It's really important. Bidding a grand slam would be folly if West held this hand instead:

♠ A J 10 7 6

♥ K 5 3

♦ A Q 7

♣ 4 2

In that case, you would be forced to take a finesse in clubs, and if South held the king, you would go down. Disaster!

If, however, your agreement is to bid kings up the line, West would bid 6♣ with the first hand, showing the ♣K, and East could count thirteen tricks. The correct bid with these two hands would be 7NT.

Bridge Basics

When you are bidding anything "up the line" bypassing a suit denies a relevant holding in that suit. No bid, however, denies a holding in a higher-ranking suit that has not been bid to that point. In other words, if 5NT asks for kings up the line and 5 ♦ shows the ♦ K, it denies the ♣ K but does not deny kings in hearts and spades.

With the second hand, West would bid 6♥ over 5NT, showing the ♥K and denying kings of lower-ranking suits. In the up-the-line style, when you pass over something, it means you don't have it. So in passing over clubs and diamonds to bid hearts, West denies having kings in either of those suits.

This is not something that is taught in beginning bridge classes, but it is vastly superior to the system of showing numbers of kings.

Astute readers will be asking at this point, "What if I don't have any kings?" Good question. In that case, you simply go back to your trump suit. It is very likely that your partner has the king of your trump suit or he wouldn't be trying for a grand slam. It's another no-no, of course, to bid a grand slam with the king of trumps missing.

You can read about a new, improved—you might even say high-tech—Blackwood system in Chapter 16.

Taking a Cue

This has been addressed previously, but it's worth a second mention:

Notice that when East bid 4NT over West's 2♠, East did not have two quick losers in any suit. That is a very important principle of using Blackwood. Say you are missing two aces and you have two low cards in one of the side suits. You bid Blackwood and your partner shows one ace. Is it the ace that will cover one of your quick losers in your low doubleton? Maybe, but it's losing bridge to gamble that your opponents won't be able to beat you off the top.

There are better ways to make sure those losers are covered, which will serve as the segue into the next topic—cue-bidding.

With some hands, as soon as you pick them up and hear your partner open the bidding, you are thinking slam. The East hand in the Blackwood 5NT auction is one such hand. With that hand, however, East didn't need to do any cue-bidding. He had at least a second-round contract in every suit. Suppose, however, that the layout was like this:

You (West)		Partner (East)	
♠ A J 10 7 6		♠ K Q 8 2	
♥ A K 7		♥ 10 9 8	
♦ 9 5 3		♦ A K	
♣ K 4		♣ A Q J 9	

West	North	East	South
1♠	Pass	3♠	Pass
?			

Nowadays there are many ways for East to make a game-forcing raise in the partner's spade suit, but for this discussion 3♠ is that raise, old-fashioned though it may be.

What should West do over 3♠? He could sign off in 4♠, but that would be unwarranted given the presence of two aces and two kings.

Bridge Lingo

A bridge hand is said to be "prime" when it is composed mostly of aces and kings rather than queens and jacks. Some experts, in fact, devalue hands with jacks. The reason is that aces and kings can usually take tricks readily, when declarers or defenders want to take them, as opposed to the "slow" process of developing tricks with queens and jacks. It is said that the ace is undervalued at 4 points on the point-count scal —and the jack is overvalued at 1. Always be optimistic with hands that have "prime" values, and go easy with those that don't.

There are different approaches to cue-bidding. The two most prominent will be presented for your consideration.

1. Cue-bids below the level of game can start with second-round control. That means a guarded king, a singleton, or a void.

2. Cue-bids show aces and voids.

In both cases, making cue-bids is like showing kings—you go up the line.

So, taking the two example hands again, what should you (West) do using the first approach?

You (West)	Partner (East)
♠ A J 10 7 6	♠ K Q 8 2
♥ A K 7	♥ 10 9 8
♦ 9 5 3	♦ A K
♣ K 4	♣ A Q J 9

Here's how the bidding should go:

West	North	East	South
1♠	Pass	3♠	Pass
4♣	Pass	4♦	Pass
4♥	Pass	4NT	Pass
5♥	Pass	5NT	Pass
6♣	Pass	6♥	Pass
7♠	Pass	7NT	All Pass

Here are the bids explained:

➤ 1♠: I have an opening hand with five or more spades.

➤ 3♠: I have four trumps and enough to force to game in spades.

➤ 4♣: I have first- or second-round control in clubs and at least mild slam interest.

➤ 4♦: Same here, only in diamonds. Note that East does not bid 5♣ because that skips over 4♦ and denies a control in that suit.

➤ 4♥: I also have at least one control in hearts.

➤ 4NT: Now I am safe to use Blackwood.

➤ 5♥: I have two aces.

➤ 5NT: Any kings?

➤ 6♣: I have the king in this suit, but I don't deny other kings.

➤ 6♥: If you have the ♥K, bid 7♠.

➤ 7♠: You got it.

➤ 7NT: I can count thirteen tricks.

This auction does not go quite as smoothly if East and West have agreed to cue-bid only first-round controls.

Still Searching

There are other ways to find out about aces when your side is in the slam range. One of them is known as Gerber, named for John Gerber, a Texas expert who invented the convention—a 4♣ bid that asks the partner to show aces in the same way that players show aces over a bid of 4NT: first step equals all or none, second step shows one, etc. The convention is most useful when one player has opened 1NT or 2NT, although it is not unheard of for players to agree that whenever either partner bids 4♣, it is Gerber (this is not recommended).

The basics of Gerber are as follows:

4♣ asks the partner to show aces:

> ➤ 4♦: No aces or 4 aces.

> ➤ 4♥: 1 ace.

> ➤ 4♠: 2 aces.

> ➤ 4NT: 3 aces.

To ask for kings, you simply bid 5♣. Responses are the same as over 5NT in Blackwood: first step all or none, second step one, etc.

Gerber is most useful when the opening bid has been 1NT or 2NT. The reason is that 4NT by the opener's partner is usually set aside for a special bid that is known as a quantitative raise.

That means that if you open 1NT to show 15-17 high-card points, a direct bid of 4NT asks you to go on to 6NT if you have a maximum 1NT opener: 17 high-card points or perhaps 16 high-card points with a five-card suit. The 4NT bidder will usually have about 16 high-card points, so if you have 17, you have or are near to the 33 high-card points you need to make a slam in notrump. A bid of 4NT in response to an opening 2NT carries the same message, although the range is narrower. You might accept the invitation with a 20-point hand that has a five-card suit or with lots of 10s and 9s. Judgment is required.

It is also handy to use Gerber after making a Stayman inquiry, as in this auction:

West	North	East	South
1NT	Pass	2♣	Pass
2♠	Pass	4♣	

In this case, East's 4♣ asks West to show his aces. If the partnership is playing Roman Key Card Gerber, which you will learn about in Chapter 16, 4♣ asks West to show key cards (aces and the king of trumps). There is an obvious advantage to using Gerber in this setting: if West's answer to 4♣ tells East that they are missing a couple of aces (or missing the trump queen), the bidding will stop at the four level. That won't be a big deal most of the time, but on occasion you will be glad you could call a halt at the four level.

Now consider this auction:

West	North	East	South
1NT	Pass	2♣	Pass
2♠	Pass	4NT	Pass
?			

Is East asking for aces? No, he would bid 4♣ if he wanted to ask for aces. East has enough to invite 6NT with a quantitative raise, but with a four-card major, he checks to see if there is a fit because playing in a trump suit often produces more tricks than two balanced hands. In some cases, being able to ruff losers can mean the difference between making a slam and going down. In this case, East did not find the fit he was looking for because with two four-card majors, the 1NT opener always bids hearts first. East is disappointed not to find the major suit fit, but he still has slam ambition and wants West to be involved in the decision. Bidding 4NT does that.

Other Slam Conventions

There are many conventions and biddings designed to facilitate slam bidding. The scope of this book does not include a complete discussion of these bidding tools, but two are worth mentioning: splinter bids and the Jacoby 2NT convention.

Splinters

A splinter bid is an unusual jump that indicates excellent trump support and shortness in the suit bid. Here is a classic example:

West	East
♠ A J 10 7	♠ K Q 9 2
♥ A K 9 8 7 3	♥ 10
♦ K Q 4	♦ A J 9 8
♣ 2	♣ 7 6 5 3

West	East
1♥	1♠
4♣	?

West's unusual jump to 4♣ shows a hand good enough to raise East to 4♠ plus a singleton or void in clubs. Using the evaluation tips you learned earlier, the West hand has 17 high-card points plus 3 points for the singleton club. That's 20. East must have 6 high-card points to respond, so the combined hands have 26 points (high-card points and support points).

East looks at his hand for reevaluation and likes what he sees. The opponents have 10 points in the club suit but can take at most one trick, so East feels justified in making a cue-bid of 4♦, indicating at least mild interest in slam. Soon the two will be in the nearly ironclad contract of 6♠.

There are many settings in which splinter bids are appropriate, including after an opening bid, as in this case:

West	East
♠ A Q J 1 0 7	♠ K 9 8 2
♥ 8 7 3	♥ 2
♦ A J 4	♦ K 1 0 9 8
♣ 6 5	♣ A 7 4 3

West opens 1♠ and East bids 4♥ to show four-card trump support (the normal minimum number when using a splinter) and a singleton or void in hearts. West likes his heart holding opposite a singleton or void, but he has opened a minimum and cannot make a cue-bid at the four level, so he signs off in 4♠. East could press on by bidding 4NT, but he also has a minimum for his action, so discretion wins out and the partnership subsides in game. As it is, East-West have reached an excellent game on 22 high-card points.

Splinter bids can be used over minor suit openings as well:

West	East
♠ K J 9 4	♠ 2
♥ Q J 3	♥ A 1 0 4
♦ A K 1 0 4 2	♦ Q J 9 8 7
♣ 6	♣ A Q 1 0 5

West opens 1♦ and East bids 3♠, showing good (usually five-card) trump support and a singleton or void in spades. West is not excited about shortness opposite his second-best suit, but he knows the partnership belongs in game, so he makes the most logical bid: 3NT, indicating good stoppers in the spade suit.

Suppose, however, these were the East-West hands:

West	East
♠ 6 5 3	♠ 2
♥ Q 4 3	♥ A 10 4
♦ A K 10 4 3	♦ Q J 9 8 7
♣ K J	♣ A Q 10 5

Need to Know

Splinter bids might seem confusing at first, particularly when the bidding goes 1♠–Pass–4♥, which sounds like a final contract. What you must ask yourself with any unusual jump is whether it is logical to consider the bid to be natural. Think of it this way: If, after you open 1♠ your partner had a handful of hearts, why would he not just start with 2♥. It's not as though you would pass that bid, after all. In the case where the opener starts at the one level and rebids at the four level (as in 1♥–Pass–1♠–Pass; 4♣), the responder should consider that rebids of 2♣ and 3♣ take care of the natural bids (the latter showing a very strong hand), so 4♣ logically must be a conventional bid.

Now 6♦ is rock solid.

Ozzie's Toy

The great Oswald Jacoby was a genius—a math whiz who could multiply long numbers in his head. During World War II he served as a cryptanalyst, and he wrote books on bridge, backgammon, gin, and poker. His most popular creation is the Jacoby transfer bid, used over 1NT and 2NT openings. Its use is almost universal in the bridge world.

One of his other inventions, nearly as popular as the transfer, is what is known as Jacoby 2NT, which is used by the responder to an opening bid of one of a major.

Assuming the opponents are not bidding, when the opener starts with 1♥ or 1♠, the responder's 2NT is an artificial game force showing at least four-card trump support. The bid also asks a question about the opener's distribution. After opener starts with a major and the responder jumps to 2NT, the opener rebids as follows:

➤ With a singleton or void in a side suit, the opener rebids that suit at the three level.

➤ With no singleton or void and no long side suit, the opener bids four of his major (a signoff) with a minimum opener. With extras (enough to be at least mildly interested in slam) and no shortness, the opener rebids three of his major. A bid of 3NT by the opener shows a balanced hand with extra values.

➤ With a side suit of at least five cards, the opener rebids at the four level. There are different theories about whether the five-card suit should be shown without some minimum high-card strength, perhaps two of the top three honors. Some argue that five to the ace or king is sufficient. In any case, it is a descriptive bid that should allow the opener's partner to assess the slam potential of the two hands.

Need to Know

In theory, a player who bids Jacoby 2NT over his partner's 1♥ or 1♠ opening should have a balanced hand with four or more trumps. There is no hard-and-fast rule about this, however, and players are free to be creative in the use of the convention. For example, a player with a very strong hand, perhaps 18 high-card points, might use Jacoby 2NT with only three trumps just to gain some information about the opener's hand. The extra strength often makes up for the lack of the fourth trump. In bridge, it pays to never say never.

Your partner has opened 1♠. What is your bid with each of the following hands:

Hand 1	Hand 2	Hand 3
♠ A J 10 9	♠ K Q 9	♠ A K J
♥ Q J 10	♥ A Q 10 5 4 3	♥ Q 10 9 6
♦ K Q 5	♦ A 6 3	♦ A Q 8 7
♣ 6 3 2	♣ 4	♣ K 10

➤ Hand 1: You have a textbook Jacoby 2NT bid, a game-forcing raise of spades with a balanced hand. You will like your hand a lot more if your partner shows a singleton club or bids 4♦ to show a second suit of at least five cards.

➤ Hand 2: Bid 2♥, if your partner rebids 2♠, you can raise or even make a splinter bid of 4♣ to show shortness in clubs, three-card spade support (you would have bid a direct 4♣ with four trumps), and slam interest. If your partner raises hearts, you would have several options, including the use of Blackwood.

➤ Hand 3: Try 2NT. You will still be interested in slam even if your partner shows a minimum opener by signing off in 4♠. The information gleaned from his response will help you decide how to proceed.

Negative Is Positive

One of the most important bidding innovations in the history of bridge is the negative double. The origin dates to the early twentieth century, but it was introduced in tournament play in 1957 by Alvin Roth and Tobias Stone. Roth, a giant among bidding theorists, initially called his invention the Sputnik double after the Soviet space satellite that was in the news that year.

The negative double, simple to use and efficient, readily addresses a recurring problem in the bidding.

Suppose this is your hand:

♠ 8 7 6

♥ K J 10 9

♦ A 6 5 4

♣ 6 2

Your partner opens 1♣ and your right-hand opponent overcalls 1♠. You have 8 high-card points, more than enough to respond, but if the negative double is not part of your bidding agreements, you are stuck. You can't bid 1NT because you don't have a spade stopper. You can't bid either of your red suits because doing so shows at least 10 high-card points and guarantees a five-card suit. You don't want to raise your partner's club suit with only a doubleton.

Players who have negative doubles on their list of bidding agreements have an easy time of it. They simply double, which is for takeout, typically showing the two unbid suits, but at the very least showing four hearts. For example, if you switched your minor suit holdings, you would not feel timid about preferring clubs should your partner bid 2♦ in response to your double. Your main aim with the negative double in this case is to avoid losing the heart suit. Your partner might well have four of them, but it will be very difficult to find the fit if you are not using negative doubles.

Negative doubles can be used with much stronger hands as well. Suppose your partner opens 1♣ and you are holding this hand:

♠K J 4

♥K Q 10 8

♦K Q 6 5

♣3

You are planning to bid 1♥, but your right-hand opponent again sticks his nose in with a 1♠ overcall. You know you are going to game, and you want to play in hearts if you have a fit in that suit. The way to find out is to start with a negative double. If the opener's second bid is something other than hearts, perhaps 2♣ or even 2♦, you are prepared to bid 3NT.

Another use for the negative double arises when you hold a hand such as this one:

♠6 5

♥K Q 10 8 7 6

♦Q 9 6 5

♣3

Again, your partner opens 1♣ and your right-hand opponent bids 1♠. You have the length required to bid your heart suit, but your hand is not strong enough. The negative double provides for this. You double, not really expecting your partner to bid hearts, and when he rebids 2♣, you can now introduce your heart suit. Bidding 2♥ says you have a suit long enough to bid but not enough high-card points to do so directly.

Need to Know

When using negative doubles, it's important to establish parameters for the use of the convention. The most important is the strength of the hand making the negative double. The opponents won't always cooperate by overcalling at the one level, and when they jack it up to the two level or three level, you must have more high-card strength when you force your partner to bid higher and higher. When your right-hand opponent overcalls a 1♣ opening with a bid of 3♠, for example, if you make a negative double, your partner will have to bid at the four level. To make a negative double in such a case, you should have an opening hand or very near to it.

You can use this maneuver with any suit, by the way. In the example just provided, your long suit could be diamonds instead of hearts.

The way to look at this situation is that your long suit might not take any tricks if it is not the trump suit. For example, if your partner has a singleton, your opponents will take the ace the first time the heart suit is led, and the dummy will be dead. If your long suit is the trump suit, you will take lots of tricks by using your low hearts for ruffing.

Wielding the Axe

When players new to the negative double hear about it for the first time, the natural question is, "What if I have a penalty double of their overcall? Am I supposed to let them get away with it?"

The answer is no, and the solution is relatively simple. This is your hand and you are West:

♠ A J 6 5

♥ K Q 7 6

♦ K J 1 0 5

♣ 3

This is the auction you hear:

West	North	East	South
1♦	2♣	Pass	Pass
?			

Your partner didn't bid, but that doesn't mean he's broke. He might be, but on this bidding, it is more likely that your partner is sitting over there with a hand like this:

♠ Q 7

♥ J 1 0 5

♦ Q 7 3

♣ A J 9 7 2

If he could have doubled 2♣ for penalty, he would have, but that option is not available for pairs playing negative doubles.

You, as West, must make up for that restriction by picking up the bidding—balancing, in

Bridge Lingo

When you are playing negative doubles and a player overcalls your partner's opening bid in your best suit, you must pass, an action known as a trap pass. The idea is that your pass might sound weak, but you are ready to spring the trap, which is the surprise of passing when the opener reopens the bidding with a double.

other words—with a double. Your partner, of course, will convert your takeout double to penalty when he is sitting there with a handful of the suit his right-hand opponent has bid.

Does that mean the opener will always double when the bidding comes back around to him as in the example auction? No. If the opener has three or four cards in the overcaller's suit, that is strong evidence that your partner's pass is based on weakness, not a desire to penalize the overcaller. When the opener has a distributional two-suited hand that is light on high-card points, it will be preferable in most cases to bid the second suit rather than try to exact a penalty from the overcaller.

When your side is vulnerable and theirs is not, you will consider whether the penalty you might exact from doubling will make up for the game you might bid and make.

You will also carefully consider what might happen if you double back in and your partner bids a suit for which you have inadequate support. The following is an example of this situation:

♠ K 7

♥ A J 4 3

♦ 6 5

♣ K Q 5 3 2

You open 1♣ and your left-hand opponent overcalls a weak 2♠, which is passed back to you. You are short in spades, so your partner could well be sitting over there with a stack. The problem with doubling in hopes that your partner has a bunch of spades is that if your partner is weak or doesn't hold strong spades—perhaps four low ones—he will have to bid at the three level, and if your partner bids diamonds, this deal will quickly turn into a nightmare for you. Where can you go over 3♦ doubled? Yikes!

You must be very careful with these marginal hands when the vulnerability is not in your favor. In general, it pays to be aggressive, but that does not mean rash.

Here's a review of the negative double principles:

> ➤ After a one-level overcall, double shows 6 or more high-card points. When you have enough to force game, you can make that known later, usually via a cue-bid of your opponents' suit.

> ➤ A double of a 1♠ overcall of a minor almost always guarantees four hearts.

> ➤ When the opener starts with a minor and the next player overcalls 1♥, a bid of 1♠ shows five or more spades. Double almost always guarantees four spades.

> ➤ When the overcall is at the two level, double should deliver a hand with at least a good 8 or 9 points (high cards plus length points where appropriate). At the three level, the doubler should be at or very close to an opening bid.

> ➤ Pairs should establish a level beyond which negative doubles no longer apply. Many tournament players say double changes from negative to penalty when the overcall is higher than 3♠. The parlance is that negative doubles are on through 3♠.

Other Un-Doubles

As stated previously, at one time there was only one non-penalty double in the bidding arsenal—the takeout double. Any other time one said double—nowadays, with bidding boxes, you pull out the red double card—it meant the opponents were in trouble. Not so in today's bridge world. There are responsive doubles, game-try doubles, support doubles, lead-directing doubles—even a double with the interesting name of Snapdragon.

Four of the most common will be covered in this chapter. They are:

> ➤ Responsive doubles

> ➤ Support doubles

> ➤ Lead-directing doubles

> ➤ Game-try doubles

Responsive Doubles

It the world of competitive bidding, it's important to be able to get in there and mix it up. You will find that some opponents seem to be bidding on air—or their good looks—so you need ways to communicate with your partner more accurately.

Consider this situation (you are South):

West	North	East	South
1♣	Dbl	2♣	?

This is your hand:

♠ K 9 8 7

♥ Q 6 4 3

♦ J 6 5 2

♣ 5

You have enough to bid, and you would like for your partner to pick a major, but the usual stratagem of cue-bidding is not viable because your hand is not strong enough to go to the three level. If you simply bid one of the suits, you might find that your partner has only three of that suit. He does not, after all, promise four-card support for all unbid suits.

The solution is to roll out the responsive double, which tells your partner you want to compete but are not sure which suit to bid. He also knows from your failure to cue-bid and the bidding by the opponents that your hand is not robust, but you will almost certainly land in the correct spot by using the responsive double.

Here are some important points about responsive doubles:

➤ They apply when your opponents have bid and raised the same suit with some action by your partner in between—a takeout double or an overcall, as with 1♥—Dbl—2♥—? or 1♠—2♣—2♠—?

➤ The higher the opponents' bid, the more strength required to make a responsive double.

➤ In the auction 1♥—Dbl—2♥—Dbl, the double denies four spades. If you had four spades, you would bid the suit, so the responsive double in this context tends to show the minors.

➤ In the auction 1♠—2♣—2♠—Dbl, the double shows the other two suits, diamonds and hearts. With club support, you would simply raise rather than double.

The important point is that when your opponents bid and raise the same suit, it is unlikely you will have a holding in their suit good enough to make you want to double them for penalty. On the rare occasions when you do have strength in their suit, you will have to pass and hope that your partner stirs the pot a bit more. After your initial pass, if you double the opponents' in their suit the next time, your partner should make no mistake about your intentions.

Bridge Facts

The world of competitive bidding has changed significantly in the past three decades to the point that the once-trusty double is almost never for penalty. A famous player and teacher, the late Bernie Chazen once said, "The penalty double has died and gone to heaven." Yes, players make rash bids all the time and should be punished for their sins, but direct penalty doubles are rare indeed. One example is when your partner opens a weak two-bid in first seat and the next player takes a bid. If you double in that setting, you expect your right-hand opponent to go down a lot. Even when your partner opens with a strong 2 ♣ bid, if the next player bids something, a double by you is not for penalty—it tells your partner that you have a very poor hand. He can always convert the double to penalty, but your action is not a so-called business double.

Offering Support

One of the most popular bidding innovations of recent times is the support double, the brainchild of Eric Rodwell, one of the most innovative bidding theorists in recent years.

Here's an auction to show how it works:

West	North	East	South
1♣	Pass	1♥	1♠
Dbl			

In this case, West's second call—a double—shows three-card heart support. If West had bid 2♥ instead of doubling, that would have guaranteed four-card support.

Why, you may ask, is this important?

What if West in the example auction holds the following hand?

♠ 6 3

♥ Q 6 4

♦ K Q J

♣ A J 1 0 9 7

When South bids 1♠, West's best choice is to raise hearts. He can't bid 1NT without a spade stopper, he doesn't want to rebid a five-card club suit, and he doesn't want to pass in case North is getting ready to raise spades, which will blow East and West right out of the water.

It's important for West to let East know that he has some support for East's hearts.

Now consider the auction from East's point of view when he holds the following hand:

♠ Q J 9 8

♥ 10 7 5 3

♦ A 9 6

♣ Q 5

The proper bid for East over an opening of 1♣ is 1♥ despite the disparity in the strength of the two suits. When East learns through the bidding that West has only three hearts, East has an easy decision: he will bid 1NT rather than play a 4-3 heart fit with a such a weak suit. On the other hand, suppose East has been dealt these cards (West raises hearts directly to show four):

♠ A Q

♥ K 6 5 4

♦ A 10 9

♣ 6 5 4 2

East will like his chances in the 4-4 heart fit and will bid game in that suit. Without support doubles, East would have to guess at the best contract. Knowing whether the opener's raise is based on three or four can make a huge difference.

Most pairs cut support doubles off at 2♥ —in other words, if the opponent interferes with a bid of 2♠ or higher, support doubles are off.

An adjunct to the support double is the support redouble, as in this auction:

West	North	East	South
1♣	Pass	1♥	Dbl
Redbl			

South's double shows a decent hand with diamonds and spades. West's redouble shows three-card heart support. A direct raise to 2♥ would show four hearts.

You can use support doubles and redoubles even with very strong hands. The responder will almost never pass your support double, and it might be important for you to get the message of support across before your opponents take away your bidding space.

Show Me the Way

In the world of modern bridge, there are many artificial bids. Two of the most common conventional bids occur over openings of 1NT and 2NT. Over 1NT, for example, a bid of 2♣ does not show clubs—it asks the opener if he has a four-card major. If the responder bids 2♦ or 2♥, neither bid offers to play in the suit named. They are transfer bids: diamonds to hearts, hearts to spades.

You may see where this is going. When you have a good holding in a suit bid artificially, it pays to let your partner in on the secret. After all, when your left-hand opponent opens 1NT and your right-hand opponent bids 2♣, 2♦, or 2♥, your partner is going to be on lead against nearly every final contract. Why not tell him the best lead for your side?

Suppose this is your hand:

♠ A 3

♥ 5 4 2

♦ 6 5

♣ K Q J 9 8 7

As East, you hear this bidding:

West	North	East	South
			1NT
Pass	2♣	?	

North is not proposing to play in clubs. He is bidding Stayman. You must double to get your partner off to the best opening lead. If South denies holding a four-card major, the contract most likely will be 2NT or 3NT. You have a strong suit and an entry (the ♠A), so if your partner leads a club, you will be unlucky not to take six tricks.

Bridge Facts

Every now and then, when you double an artificial bid, especially Stayman, you will hear a dreaded call from an opponent: "Redouble!" That means you're in trouble. There is no rule, for example, that would keep a 1NT opener from holding five clubs to the K-J-10 behind you when the bidding goes 1NT–Pass–2♣–Double (by you). On those rare occasions, you just have to pay off. Whatever you do, don't run from the redouble. Just take your medicine and go on to the next deal.

On occasion, you will double a suit your partner has a lot of and you will be able to buy the contract, either to make or as a profitable save over your opponents' contract.

There is another reason to be an aggressive doubler of artificial bids. On occasion, when your partner is searching for an opening lead, he will be able to rule out a suit you had a chance to double but did not, such as Stayman 2 ♣ or a transfer bid. This is a small thing, but every little bit helps your partner.

There are other artificial bids, such as splinters (discussed earlier in this chapter) and responses to Blackwood 4NT. Such doubles give information to both sides, but you will come out ahead in the long run by helping your partner make the best opening leads.

Space Considerations

One final double worth mentioning is known as the game-try, or maximal double.

In constructive bidding, there are many occasions when one must involve one's partner in the decision about how high to bid. Here's an example:

♠ A Q J 9 8

♥ K J 5

♦ A 6 5 4

♣ 3

You are West in this auction:

West	North	East	South
1♠	Pass	2♠	Pass
?			

You can see there is game potential in your hand, but only if your partner has some complementary cards. For example, you want to be in game if your partner's hand looks like this:

♠ K 1 0 7

♥ A Q 9 8

♦ 8 7

♣ 7 6 5 4

You want to stop short, however, if your partner's hand looks like this:

♠ K 10 7

♥ 6 4 3

♦ J 7

♣ K J 7 6 5

The way to find out if the hands fit together nicely is to make a game try. With the example opening hand, your game try would be 3♥. You want to know if your partner has some honor strength in the heart suit. If so, he will bid 4♠; if not, he will sign off in 3♠.

Sometimes, your opponents' bidding will not give you the chance to make such a game-try. Here's an example auction:

West	North	East	South
1♠	2♥	2♠	3♥
?			

You can't bid a suit to make a game try because anything you bid will be at the four level—you will already be there. You can't pin down the exact suit you want to make a try in, but you can double to tell your partner you want to be in game if he likes his hand. In bidding such as this, you will never have a stack in the opponents' suit, so double might as well be reserved for competing. Of course, your partner can always convert the double to penalty by passing if he has a defensive-oriented hand.

The other benefit of playing maximal doubles is that in the given auction, if West just wants to compete to 3♠, he can make the bid without getting East excited. East will know that West could have doubled if he was interested in game, so he won't put his partner in a shaky or no-play 4♠ contract.

One final note about game-try doubles: When the bidding gives you just a bit of room, you can use the available bid as a general game-try—not tied to the suit bid. Here's an example:

West	North	East	South
1♠	2♦	2♠	3♦
?			

West can bid 3♥ in this situation as a general game-try rather than a game-try in hearts.

PART THREE

Playing Bridge

 Card Play—Taking Your Tricks

> ## In This Chapter
>
> ➤ Your objective as the declarer
> ➤ Slow tricks versus fast winners
> ➤ Counting winners and losers
> ➤ Entries and communication between hands

In this chapter, the discussion turns to what the game of bridge is all about—taking tricks—and what you need to know to get that job done consistently. In some contracts, you count winners. In others, you count losers. You will learn to tell the difference. You will find out that all tricks are not created equal, and how you can use this knowledge to your advantage. Finally, you will find out about communication and why it is critically important for the declarer and defenders.

Your Goal Line

In football, every offensive player seeks to cross the other team's goal line, and every defensive player works at preventing that from happening. When your team is on the opponents' 20-yard line, you know how far you have to go to reach your goal.

In bridge, the contract tells you the "distance" you must travel to succeed. Instead of yards to gain, you have tricks to take.

For example, if you are in a contract of 4♠, you must take ten tricks with spades as trumps. If you are in 6NT, you must take all but one trick, and you don't have a trump suit to lean on.

To review the mechanics of the game, once the bidding is concluded—when a bid, double or redouble is followed by three passes—the auction is over and one of the players becomes the declarer. That is the first person on the side that won the auction to mention the denomination of the final contract. Here's a sample auction:

West	North	East	South
1♣	Pass	1♥	1♠
2♣	4♠	Pass	Pass
Pass			

North bid 4♠, the final contract, but South was the first player to mention spades, so South becomes the declarer.

The rules of the game require that West, the player to the declarer's left, make the opening lead. The rules also state that a player must follow suit if he has a card or cards of the suit led. When everyone follows suit, the highest card played wins the trick.

Each player holds thirteen cards, so there are thirteen tricks to be taken. The player who wins a trick must lead to the next trick, and the cards are played in clockwise rotation. When there is a trump suit, as in the 4♠ contract under discussion, a player who does not have a card in the suit led by an opponent may use a trump to win the trick. Any trump card beats any card in a plain, or non-trump, suit. If two players are out of the suit led and both play trumps on that suit, the player who played the higher trump wins the trick.

Getting It Done

For the purposes of the discussions in this chapter, South is always the declarer, North is always the dummy.

You will recall that when an auction is concluded, the partner of the player who becomes the declarer puts his hand down on the table after the opening lead has been made. The hand is sorted into suits and lined up vertically on the table in descending order, alternating black and red to avoid confusing diamonds and hearts or spades and clubs.

When the declarer is playing a trump contract, the trump suit is always displayed on the table to the far left from the declarer's perspective.

So how do you win tricks in the game of bridge? Consider the following situation (never mind about the contract):

North

♥ A K

South

♥ 2

How many tricks can you take? The answer is two: the ace and king. Try this next combination:

North

♥ A K Q J 10

South

♥ 2

Now your trick total is up to five, but change the layout just a bit:

North

♥ A K Q

South

♥ J 10 9

You have the top six cards in the suit between the two hands, but you are limited to three tricks. Do you see why? When you play a card from North's hand, you must play one from South's. If you play all North's cards, all of South's cards are gone. Did you notice, by the way, that you cannot win a trick in South's hand? So change the cards one last time:

North

♥ A K 10

South

♥ Q J 9

Now you can win two or three tricks in North's hand by simply playing a low heart to the dummy's 10, or you can play the 10 from the dummy and win it with the queen or jack.

What if this were the situation?

North

♥ A K Q J

South

♥ --

If you were not already in the North hand and had no other way to get to that hand, you would not be able to take any tricks in the suit.

Bridge Lingo

When you play good cards in a suit, you are said to cash your winners. If you are within three tricks of your contract and have three winning tricks in your hand, rather than risk disaster by trying for more, you cash out to avoid going down.

Now that you understand how the trick business works, there are some techniques you should know.

One of the most important concepts is the play of a suit that is unevenly divided between the two hands. In such cases, you almost always play high from the short side first. To illustrate:

North

♣K Q 7

South

♣A 3

How many tricks can you see here? That's right—three. If you (South) make the mistake of playing one of North's high cards first, you will discover what it means to block a suit. Just to illustrate, say you play the 3 from your hand to the dummy's king. Now look at the suit:

North

♣Q 7

South

♣A

What happens when you play the suit a second time? That's right—you are back in the South hand with no card left to get to the good queen. If you start with the ace, however, you retain the 3 to play to the good king and queen in the dummy.

Bridge Basics

The process of developing tricks often involves playing on suits with some missing high cards, to knock out the aces and kings so that the lower cards become winners. This process is known as establishment. By using your intermediates to push out the higher cards, you are establishing your lower cards so that they will take tricks. A card that has been established is known as good, which means it's a winner.

The same principle applies when you are working on setting up a suit. Here's a case in point:

North

♦Q J 8

South

♦10 9 7 6

The only high cards you are missing in this suit are the ace and king. When you play this suit, if the defenders want to win a trick, they must use the ace or king to do so. Once the ace and king have been played, you will have established two tricks in the suit.

The proper technique for playing on this suit is to lead low from the South hand and play the queen or jack from the North hand. If a defender wins that with the ace or king, when you get the lead the next time, you can play another diamond to the North hand to knock out the other high honor. Now your 10 and 9 will be good.

Be careful not to lead low from the North hand to the South. It is true that the 10 will knock out the ace or king just the same as the queen or jack, but if the queen and jack are alone in the North hand the second time the suit is played, a defender can win and you will have this situation:

North

♦Q

South

♦9 7

The 9 and 7 are good, but you cannot take them because when you play the suit you will be in the North hand, and if you can't get back to South, a good trick will be lost.

Keeping Track

It is important to watch the cards that your opponents play because it can affect how you go about the business of cashing your tricks. Check out this situation:

North

♠ K Q J 4 3

South

♠ A 5

Start by counting the number of potential tricks you can take. With so many high cards between the two hands, it looks like you can count on five tricks (you will remember, of course, to start with the ♠ A from your hand).

So you play the ♠ A, then follow with the 5 to the king. Did everyone follow suit? Are you aware of how many spades the opponents have between them?

Let's go back and count. You have seven spades between your hand and the dummy, so the opponents have six. What can keep you from taking five tricks in this suit? That's right—if one player has all six spades or even just five. You will play the top four, starting with the ace, but if one player has five or six spades, your last low spade—the 4—will not be good.

But what if the division of the spades is no worse than 4-2 (one player has four, the other two)? In that case, playing the ace, followed by the king, queen, and jack will gather in all the opponents' spades, so your last low one is good. Remember, if you play a card and no one can follow suit or play a trump, that card wins the trick.

Bridge Lingo

The card remaining when all the other cards in a suit have been played is called the thirteener. If the contract is notrump, that card is a winner even if it is the deuce. A player who intentionally wins a trick, especially the contract-fulfilling trick, with a 2 is looking for—and deserves—style points.

Development

So far the discussion has centered on cashing your winning tricks in the correct order so as not the block your suit. In many more cases, it will be necessary for you to develop tricks.

Developing winners usually involves losing some tricks to reach your goal. Consider this suit:

North

♦ Q J 10 9 8

South

♦ 5 4 3

How many tricks can you take in this suit? What do you have to do to get those tricks?

Right—you have to lose a couple first. Here's another:

North

♦ A 7 6 5 4

South

♦ 8 3 2

How many tricks can you take in this suit? How do you go about it? It may help to show the entire suit:

North

♦ A 7 6 5 4

West   East

♦ Q J   ♦ K 10 9

South

♦ 8 3 2

You could play the ♦ A and another diamond, then when you get in again play a third round of the suit. Note that when you play to the ♦ A, West will follow with the jack, East with the 9. Now when you play a second round from the dummy, East will play the 10 and West will win with the queen. At that point, your opponents will have only one diamond left, and when you play the 8 from your hand, the king will win but the 7 and 6 will be high because your opponents will have no diamonds left.

The problem with doing it that way is that you might not be able to get to the North hand by the time you set up those two extra winners. A better plan is to play a low diamond from your hand and a low diamond from the dummy. When you get in again, do the same thing: low from your hand, low from the dummy. Now look at the suit before you play to the third round:

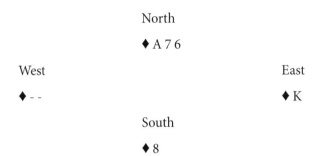

When you play your ♦8, West will have to discard because he doesn't have any diamonds left. You will play the dummy's ace, and that will fetch the king from East. Now your 7 and 6 are good, and you have taken three tricks in the suit without having to worry about how you will get to the dummy.

Sometimes you will have to work on a suit that doesn't seem to hold much promise for developing tricks. Check this out:

North

♣10 9 8 7 6

South

♣5 4 3 2

You are missing all four top honors—the face cards and the ace—so can you take tricks in that suit? Simple—lead it. If you are lucky, this will be the entire suit:

North

♣10 9 8 7 6

West   East

♣A Q   ♦K J

South

♣5 4 3 2

Now look what happens when you play a low club from your hand: West will play the queen, you play a low one from the dummy, and East follows with the jack. The next time you play on clubs, guess what? West has to play the ace and East has to follow with the king. Your poor little suit has just produced three tricks. Suits don't always split so favorably, but when you have only one way to go, you have to hope for the best.

Making It Work

You have learned a bit about managing your suits, now it's time to put it all together in a full deal.

First, one last note: As the declarer, you go about your job of reaching the number of tricks required by your contract differently when you are playing notrump as opposed to a trump contract.

To refresh your memory, a trump contract is one with a suit named—3 ♣, 4 ♠, 6 ♦, etc. In suit, or trump, contracts, you can control your opponents' strong suits by using your trumps when you run out of the suit they are trying to cash against you. Consider the following, where only two suits are shown:

North

♠Q J 10 9

♥5 4

South

♠A K 5 4

♥6 3 2

Say West, to your left, leads the ♥K against your spade contract. The ♥K will win the trick because you don't have a heart that can beat the king. If West continues with the ♥A, that will also win for the same reason. Now suppose West plays a third round of hearts, say, the queen. The heart you have left in your hand is a loser, but you have four trumps in the dummy and you can use one because the dummy is out of hearts. Any hand can play a trump so long as that hand, the dummy included, doesn't have any card in the suit that was led.

If you were playing in notrump, you would have no way of stopping West from winning tricks in hearts as long as he had cards in that suit to play. He might even win a trick with the lowest heart in the deck—the 2.

Bridge Basics

David Burn, a very funny bridge writer who lives in England, facetiously offered what he calls Burn's Law of Total Trumps, which states that when you are the declarer, the total number of trumps held by your side should be greater than the number of trumps held by the opponents. To satisfy this requirement, most bidding systems are geared to find the so-called golden fit of eight trumps, three more than the opponents hold. Occasionally, the best trump fit you can find will be a 4-3, but anything less means you probably had an accident in the bidding.

When a trump suit is present, you do not have to rely so heavily on high-card points. In a notrump contract, if the declarer's hand and the dummy are balanced, you need high-card points.

Finally, via a circuitous route, we get to the difference between playing a trump contract versus a notrump contract.

In a trump contract, you generally count your losers, in no small measure because you usually plan to get rid of at least some of them by using your trumps, as you saw in the example where you ruffed a losing heart in the dummy.

In a notrump contract, you count your winners to see if you have enough to make your contract. If you don't, you will formulate a plan to develop enough winners to get home. Here's an example:

```
                    ♠ A Q 7
                    ♥ K J 9 8
                    ♦ 7 6 5 3
                    ♣ J 4

  ♠ J 9 6 3                        ♠ 1 0 8 2
  ♥ A 4 2                          ♥ 7 6 3
  ♦ Q J 1 0 9                      ♦ 8 4
  ♣ K 1 0                          ♣ Q 9 8 7 3

                    ♠ K 5 4
                    ♥ Q 1 0 5
                    ♦ A K 2
                    ♣ A 6 5 2
```

West	North	East	South
			1NT
Pass	2♣	Pass	2♦
Pass	3NT	All	Pass

A note about the auction: South's 1NT shows 15–17 high-card points. North's 2♣ asks South if he has a four-card major, and the response of 2♦ says no. North has 11 high-card points, so he knows that combined with South's minimum of 15 high-card points, there is enough for game, so North bids it.

If you held the West hand, which suit would you start with considering that your objective is to take five tricks against South's 3NT contract. If your instincts told you to start with the ♦Q, you show promise as a player.

Need to Know

As the declarer, your job is to take at least as many tricks as your contract requires you to. If you are playing a two-level contract, you need eight. If you are in 3NT, you need nine. The defenders, on the other hand, do not need so many tricks to achieve their goal of keeping you from making your contract. Against 3NT, they need only five tricks. In a real sense, especially in notrump contracts, it's a race between the defenders and the declarer to see who gets to their goal first. Although the opening leader can see only his own cards before the opening lead is made, his side does get to strike the first blow, an often crucial advantage.

Back to the example deal. After the opening lead is made, the dummy puts his hand down on the table. A good declarer takes a moment to size up the situation. Here are the two hands the declarer can see after the opening lead is made:

♠ A Q 7

♥ K J 9 8

♦ 7 6 5 3

♣ J 4

♠ K 5 4

♥ Q 1 0 5

♦ A K 2

♣ A 6 5 2

West has started with the ♦Q. How do you like your chances? Well, you can't truly assess your chances until you take stock. Start by counting your sure tricks. You have three spade tricks (ace, king, and queen), two diamond tricks (ace and king) and one in clubs (ace). That's only six tricks and you need nine. How will you find three more tricks? Think about it for a minute and decide on your answer before you read on.

If you are looking closely, you will see your only chance to take nine tricks will be to work on the heart suit. Fortunately, you have really good spot cards in that suit, from the king all the way down to the 8.

Your plan is simple: Win the ♦A (or king if you wish), then play the ♥Q from your hand. You did recall that you play high cards from the short suit first, right?

The player with the ♥A will most likely withhold that card the first time you play the suit, and he might duck again if possible the second time you play it. You have the luxury of being able to overtake the ♥10 with the jack to continue leading the suit until someone gives up and plays the ace—or plays it because he has no other choice.

Now you are good no matter what West does after taking his ace. He will almost surely continue with the ♦J to knock out your other high honor, but no matter. You have your original six tricks, plus three heart tricks for a total of nine.

It's Ruff Out There

You have learned that when you are playing a notrump contract, you count winners to see if you have enough of them to fulfill your contract. Now consider the situation when trumps are involved. In such a case, you count losers to see if there is a way to deal with them. Sometimes you throw losers on winning cards. Sometimes you have to deal with them by using your trumps, as the following deal, a modified version of the previous deal illustrating notrump play:

♠A Q J 7

♥K J 9 8

♦7 6 5

♣4 2

♠9 6 4 2		♠1 0 8 3
♥5 2		♥7 6 3
♦Q J 1 0 9 4		♦8 3
♣K J		♣Q 9 8 7 6

♠K 5

♥A Q 1 0 4

♦A K 2

♣A 1 0 5 3

You have opened the South hand with a bid of 2NT, showing 20–21 high-card points. Your partner bid Stayman, and after finding a fit got a bit overexuberant and put you in 6♥. West starts with the ♦Q.

Taking stock, you see that you have a diamond loser and potentially three club losers. Yikes! Is there anything you can do about it?

Look at your assets in spades. You have three top honors in dummy and four cards in the suit. In the South hand, you have the missing ♠K and only two spades. Here is what the full deal will look like after you pull trumps:

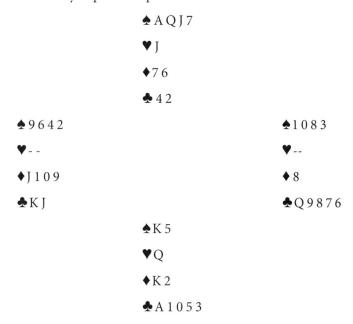

You can now play the ♠K from your hand—start with the short side—then play a spade to the ace. You have the good queen and jack and can use them to discard losers from your hand.

Careful, now: Be sure one of your discards is the low diamond from your hand. If you discard losing clubs instead, you will go down. Do you see how?

You have three losing clubs in your hand, so you cannot discard all of your losers in that suit on the two spades. But look what happens when you throw the losing diamond and one club. Now the full deal will look like this:

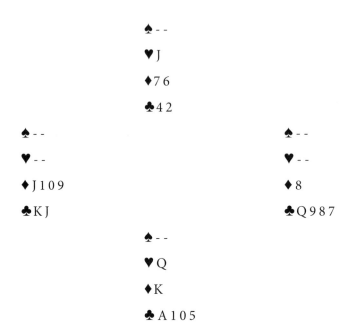

You still have two losing clubs in your hand, but you can play the ace, then a low one from your hand. West will win and continue with a diamond. When you win the king, you will have a losing club and a trump in your hand, plus a trump and a low diamond in the dummy. After you win the ♦K, simply ruff your last club with the dummy's ♥J and play the low diamond to the ♥Q in your hand. Voilà! Twelve tricks.

Congratulations! On this deal, you used two common techniques for getting rid of losers: You discarded two of them on side-suit winners, and you ruffed one of your losers in the dummy. You took two high diamonds, one high club, four spades, three high trumps, plus one ruff in the dummy and one ruff in your hand.

Bridge Lingo

When all the opponents' trumps are drawn and you have trumps in your hand and the dummy, you do not gain tricks by playing more trumps. But you can employ a technique known as separating your good trumps. For example, suppose you (South) are playing a spade contract and these are the remaining cards between your hand and the dummy:

North

♠ K

♥ 2

♦ --

♣ --

South

♠ A

♥ --

♦ 2

♣ --

You can play the ♠ A and win a trick, but you will gobble up the dummy's ♠ K in the process. You gain a trick if you separate your trumps by playing the diamond from your hand and ruffing with the ♠ K, then playing the ♥ 2 from the dummy and ruffing with the ♠ A. Instead of taking one more trick, you take two. This kind of play is known as the crossruff.

Sense of Timing

The play of the hand is often a race between the defenders, who get to take the first shot, and the declarer, who is trying to stay a step ahead. Consider the following deal:

♠ 8 7 6 5

♥ K 5 2

♦ J 3

♣ K Q J 9

♠ Q J 10 9

♥ A 4 3

♦ K Q 10

♣ A 7 6

West	North	East	South
			1NT
Pass	2♣	Pass	2♠
Pass	4♠	All	Pass

You, South, opened 1NT to show 15–17 high-card points, and your partner bid 2♣ (Stayman) to ask about four-card majors. You admitted to owning four spades, so your partner put you in game by bidding 4♠.

West starts with the ♥Q. What is your plan to take ten tricks?

You must start by counting losers—the fast kind and the slow kind. You have three fast losers—the top two spades and the ♦A. Are there any slow losers? Look at the hearts in your hand and the hearts in the dummy. West has already started an assault on your hearts, and if either opponent gets in quickly he will knock out your second high card in that suit, leaving you with low hearts in both hands. The bottom line: you have a slow heart loser, bringing your total of potential losers to four.

That's too many. Can you do anything about it?

Bridge Basics

In most trump contracts, when the declarer gains the lead he immediately considers drawing trumps, and in the majority of cases the declarer continues with that plan. It is silly to fail in a contract because an opponent takes a trick with a low trump, especially if you carelessly neglected to draw that trump. There are reasons, however, for postponing the drawing of trumps. The most notable is when you have reached a contract that is on the thin side in terms of high-card points but on the hefty side in shape. In other words, both hands have shortness, so it behooves you to hold onto your trumps so you can use them to ruff your losers. Remember, every time you play on trumps, two of them go away. If you use them for ruffing in both hands, you get to use them one at a time.

Yes, you can make your contract despite the looming danger in hearts. Do you see how? If you thought about starting on trumps right away, have you reconsidered that plan?

Think about it. If you win the opening heart lead in either hand and start on trumps, you will have to lose the lead twice—the opponents, after all, have the top two trumps.

What do you think is going to happen if you play a trump? Yep—one of your opponents will win and play another heart, knocking out your second stopper in the suit. If you play a second trump, the player who wins will probably have a heart to cash. You have no way to get rid of the diamonds in your hand, so you will lose two spades, a heart, and a diamond for down one in a cold contract, as you can see by examining the full deal:

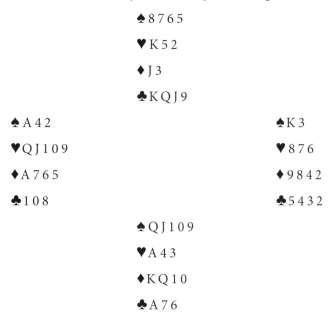

♠ 8 7 6 5
♥ K 5 2
♦ J 3
♣ K Q J 9

♠ A 4 2   ♠ K 3
♥ Q J 10 9   ♥ 8 7 6
♦ A 7 6 5   ♦ 9 8 4 2
♣ 10 8   ♣ 5 4 3 2

♠ Q J 10 9
♥ A 4 3
♦ K Q 10
♣ A 7 6

Do you see now how to take ten tricks in spades? Have you noticed what's going on in diamonds?

Here is your best plan: Win the opening lead in the dummy with the ♥K and play the ♦J at trick two. West can win with the ♦A and play another heart, but you will win with the ♥A in your hand and cash one high diamond then the other, discarding the low heart from the dummy.

Bridge Lingo

Bridge has a jargon all its own, and there are many colorful words players use as substitutes for *ruff*, which means to use a trump to win a trick. *Biff, hit, cut, blow up* are just some of the colorful words players use for using their trumps to win tricks. Defenders are known to try to reduce the declarer's trumps to their advantage by *pumping, punching* or *dinking* him in a plain suit. As noted previously, it's "ruff" out there.

Now when you play a spade, either player can win and play a heart, but you can ruff it in the dummy and continue playing spades. You will knock out the other high spade, and upon regaining the lead, pull the last of your opponents' trumps. You will be down to your good clubs and a good spade. You will have lost two spades and one diamond but no hearts. Your game is made.

Not Fast Enough

Earlier in the chapter, you found out about slow versus fast losers and how to avoid them in many situations. Winners also come in two versions.

Aces are considered fast winners, as are kings when they are in the same suit as the ace. These are also known as quick tricks. A king that has at least one other card with it is usually counted as half a quick trick because the ace will be in the right spot for it to take a trick—to the right—about half the time. Here are some examples:

	(a)			(b)	
	♣6 5			♣6 5	
♣A 10		♣9 8	♣9 8		♣A 10
	♣K 2			♣K 2	

➤ Diagram a: If you lead a low club toward the king and play it, the ace will win and the ♣10 will take the next trick.

➤ Diagram b: You lead low toward the king. If East plays the ace, your king will win the next time the suit is played. If East plays low, you play the king, which will hold the trick.

Playing toward the king hoping the ace is well placed for you is an example of a finesse. There are many variations. Here are some of the most common:

(1)	(2)	(3)	(4)	(5)
♠A Q	♠Q 5 4	♠A K J	♠K J 3	♠A J 10
♠4 3	♠A 3 2	♠9 5 4	♠A 5 4	♠5 4 3

Here's how you play for the maximum number of tricks:

1. Lead the 4 or 3 from your hand, and if your left-hand opponent plays low, insert the queen. It will win a trick whenever the king is to your left.

2. Play the ace and a low spade from your hand, again hoping the king is to your left. If it is, your queen will win now or later.

3. Play low from your hand and insert the jack if your left-hand opponent follows low. You hope he has the queen.

4. Play the ace from your hand, then a low one. If your left-hand opponent plays a low spade, put in the jack. If he has the queen, you win three tricks.

5. Play a low spade and insert the 10 if your left-hand opponent plays low. If that loses to the queen or king, you will try again when next you gain the lead, playing low to the jack. This finesse wins whenever the left-hand opponent has one of the missing high honors.

Back to the concept of fast versus slow tricks. Fast tricks are those you can cash when you want them, as with this holding:

♦ A K Q J 9 8

If you don't have to worry about enemy trumps, you have at least four tricks in the suit even if your partner, the dummy, has none. If the ♦ 10 falls under one of your high diamonds, you will have six tricks.

Note that the queen, not normally considered a quick trick, is a sure thing when accompanied by the ace and king. Honors strung together are much better than honors scattered among different suits. Here are two hands to illustrate this principle:

Hand 1	Hand 2
♠ Q 7 6 5	♠ A K Q J 10
♥ A 4	♥ 6 5 3
♦ J 6 4 3	♦ 8 5
♣ K 7 6	♣ 9 4 2

Hand 1 has an ace, king, queen, and jack, but it does not look like a major source of tricks. It depends, of course, on what the other hand (the partner's) contains, but opposite a very weak hand, Hand 1 is pretty anemic. The ♥ A will certainly take a trick, but the ♠ Q is iffy, the ♦ J is worse, and the ♣ K is no better than 50-50 to take a trick. It's a much different story with Hand 2. In combination, the four high spades plus the 10 are good for five tricks, guaranteed.

So, what bearing does all this have on how you play a contract? Well, you will often have a choice of suits to try to develop. By definition, a suit that needs developing is composed of slow winners. For example, if you have ♦ Q J 9 8 7 opposite ♦ 10 4 3 , you can eventually build three tricks in the suit by leading it enough times to dislodge the ace and king. The question is whether your losing the lead twice will allow your opponents to promote their own tricks.

Here's a simple hand to illustrate the point:

♠ A K

♥ K 2

♦ Q J 8 7 6 4

♣ 8 6 3

♠ Q J 3 2

♥ A 5

♦ 1 0 9 3

♣ A Q J 2

West	North	East	South
	1♦	Pass	1♠
Pass	2♦	Pass	3NT
All Pass			

Bridge Facts

Many newer players become nervous when their partners open 1♣ or 1♦ because of the possibility that the opening bid is based on a three-card suit. In fact, you will have five or more clubs when you open 1♣ more often than you will have just three of them, and there is only one distribution of the cards that would force to you open 1♦ on a three-card suit. That's when you are playing five-card majors and have four cards in each major and two clubs, leaving you with three diamonds. On all other occasions, a 1♦ opener will deliver at least four diamonds.

A note about the bidding. Change one card in the North hand to give him one more spade and one less diamond, and the correct second bid for North would have been 2♠. It is almost never right to rebid a five-card suit, even when the first mention of the suit promised no more than three cards (infrequent when the opening bid is 1♦).

You have an opening hand opposite your partner's opener, so you make the normal bid of 3NT. West starts with the ♥Q. How do you plan to take nine tricks?

First, figure out how many tricks you have on top, that is, tricks you can take without losing the lead. You have four spade tricks, two heart tricks, and one club trick. That's only seven—two short of what you need.

Looking at the diamonds in your hand and the dummy, you can see that there are four tricks available after the ace and king are gone. On this deal, however, you have a serious heart problem. If you play on diamonds right away, an opponent will win and play another heart. You do have the suit double-stopped, but one of your stoppers was taken out on the opening lead, and the other will be dislodged as soon as either opponent gets in. They know they have found your weak spot.

What can you do about it? Well, give the club suit some consideration. In this chapter, you learned about finessing and how that can gain extra tricks. You also learned that any particular missing high card will be where you want it to be about half the time.

One thing is for sure about this deal: if you play on diamonds to develop extra tricks, you will go down. Why not take a 50 percent shot to make it?

Win the opening heart lead in the dummy and play a club right away, inserting the jack if East follows low. On this occasion, you are in luck—the jack holds the trick. Now play a spade to the dummy, cash the other high spade, and lead another low club. Again, East follows low, so you insert the queen this time. Another winner! Now count your tricks. You have four spades, three clubs, and two hearts for nine. You have made your contract, and you are going to make an overtrick if the opponents started with three clubs each.

The full deal:

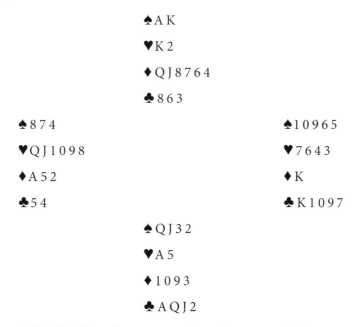

```
                    ♠ A K
                    ♥ K 2
                    ♦ Q J 8 7 6 4
                    ♣ 8 6 3
  ♠ 8 7 4                          ♠ 1 0 9 6 5
  ♥ Q J 1 0 9 8                    ♥ 7 6 4 3
  ♦ A 5 2                          ♦ K
  ♣ 5 4                            ♣ K 1 0 9 7
                    ♠ Q J 3 2
                    ♥ A 5
                    ♦ 1 0 9 3
                    ♣ A Q J 2
```

When you cash the ♣ A, West shows out, so there is no overtrick, but you made your contract by giving it the best shot. Note that even if the club finesse had lost, you still would have had a chance to make your contract if the clubs had been 3-3 between the two opponents' hands. That actually would have given you a bit more than a 50 percent chance, much better than the zero chance you had by playing on diamonds.

Keeping in Touch

A key element of card play is communication between hands. In some areas, transportation is the operative word. What it boils down to is being able to enter one hand or the other when you want to.

Here's a hand to illustrate the importance of managing transportation between your hand and the dummy when you are trying to make a contract:

♠ K 7 6 5 3

♥ A K 7 6

♦ K J 6

♣ 5

♠ Q 4

♥ 5 4 3

♦ A 5

♣ K Q J 1 0 9 7

West	North	East	South
			1 ♣
Pass	1 ♠	Pass	2 ♣
Pass	3 ♥	Pass	3NT
All Pass			

You find yourself in the normal contract of 3NT, against which West leads the ♦ 3. How will you play to make nine tricks?

First, count your winners. You don't have many top tricks—the two top hearts and two top diamonds. That just four tricks, well short of what you need—but your club suit holds real promise because it's so strong. You would be very unlucky not to be able to take five tricks in that suit once you knock out the ace.

Meanwhile, are you tempted by the ♦J in the dummy? You could play the jack, and if it holds because West has the ♦Q, you will probably make at least one overtrick, maybe two.

Bridge Basics

To improve your play and results, avoid playing too quickly at trick one. Any expert will tell you that more solid contracts are sent down the drain at trick one than at any other point in the play. Make it a practice to take your time after the opening lead has been made. Analyze the lead—a low card usually indicates a lead from an honor—and count your tricks and/or losers. If a contract seems too easy to worry about, look again. Consider what might go wrong and what you might do about it. It pays to be pessimistic in many cases.

Yes, there will be occasions when playing the jack will succeed, but if that was your play, take no credit. You badly misplayed the contract, and you will get what you deserve when the full deal is as follows:

	♠K7653	
	♥AK76	
	♦KJ7	
	♣5	
♠AJ109		♠82
♥Q9		♥J1082
♦109432		♦Q86
♣A6		♣8432
	♠Q4	
	♥543	
	♦A5	
	♣KQJ1097	

If you play the jack or the 6 from the dummy, you are doomed. The ♦J will be covered by the queen. Even if you desperately play low, East will simply continue with a diamond—and your transportation back to that nice club suit will have gone up in smoke. When you play a club, West will win the ace, and your hand will be stone dead. All of your clubs will be good, but they will die on the vine. You have no way to get to your hand to cash them.

Do you see how you could have made the contract? Yes, it is counterintuitive, but you must play the ♦K at trick one, preserving your ace as the entry to your hand so that you can enjoy those clubs that will be good for five tricks once the ace is gone. You will make your game by taking two hearts, two diamonds, and five clubs.

The presence of the ♦J was thrown in as a temptation to distract you from the proper play. You must always be on your guard and alert to the need to be in one hand or the other at a crucial time in any deal you play—as the declarer and as a defender.

That's right: Defenders must also work to maintain communication so they can cash their good tricks once they are established. Consider this deal:

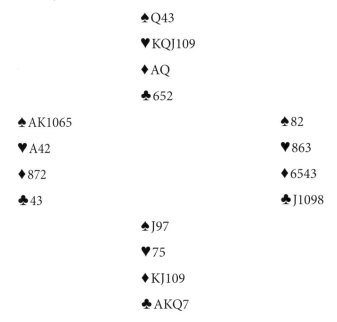

♠Q43
♥KQJ109
♦AQ
♣652

♠AK1065
♥A42
♦872
♣43

♠82
♥863
♦6543
♣J1098

♠J97
♥75
♦KJ109
♣AKQ7

Suppose South is in 3NT, which puts West on lead. West can start off with the ♠A and ♠K, then play a third round. North's queen will win, but West will then have two good spades to cash if and when he gets in. South can win four diamond tricks, but when he plays the club suit, he will see that the suit does not split favorably, so he has no choice but to play a heart, hoping that West does not have the ace. In the given case, West will pounce with the ♥A and cash his two good spades for down one.

Now look what happens if the full deal is changed slightly:

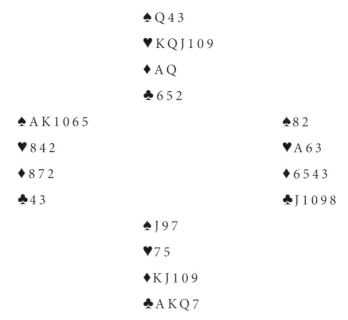

It's the same contract—3NT by South—but now if West starts off with the ♠A and ♠K, the declarer will prevail. West can play a third round of spades to set up two winners in his hand, but how will he get in to cash them? Well, he can't. The declarer will play as before, but when he sees that the club suit won't produce his ninth trick, he will play a heart. East can win and cash a good club, but that will be the end for the defenders. They will get two spades, one club, and one heart—not enough to defeat 3NT.

Do you see how the defenders can prevail anyway?

The key is to maintain communication between the East and West hands, and the way to do that is for West to lead a low spade against 3NT instead of one of his high ones. It is standard among experienced players to lead fourth-best from their best suit (providing it has not been bid strongly by the declaring side), so West would start with the ♠6 on this occasion. The declarer will play low from the dummy and win in his hand, but when he plays a heart after testing clubs, East will win and fire back his remaining spade.

West's ♠A and ♠K will win the next two tricks, and North and South will have no more of the suit, meaning West's two remaining spades will be winners. By starting with a low spade instead of a high one, East and West maintained communication between their two hands. Note that playing even one high spade at the start would have fouled up the communication.

Finally, here is a classic deal for teaching how to maintain communication between two hands.

♠1087

♥QJ6

♦KQJ106

♣65

♠AKJ

♥A43

♦92

♣A10982

West	North	East	South
			1NT
Pass	2NT	Pass	3NT
All Pass			

North's 2NT was invitational, and South liked his good club intermediates, so he bid the game. West leads the ♥2. What is your plan for taking nine tricks?

It looks as though you have what is known as a free finesse. You can play the queen, and if it holds, you have two tricks. If East covers, you take the ace and the dummy's ♥J will be good. In this case, the finesse is anything but free. In fact, it would cost you your contract.

$$\begin{array}{ccc} & \spadesuit 1087 & \\ & \heartsuit QJ6 & \\ & \diamondsuit KQJ106 & \\ & \clubsuit 65 & \end{array}$$

♠1087

♥QJ6

♦KQJ106

♣65

♠Q92   ♠6543

♥K1082   ♥975

♦54   ♦A873

♣KQ43   ♣J7

♠AKJ

♥A43

♦92

♣A10982

Consider what happens if you play the ♥Q. You don't have enough tricks to make your contract without developing tricks in diamonds, and when you play the suit, your opponents are not going to be so obliging as to win the first round of the suit. When East wins the second round (you will find out later in this book how he knows just when to win his ace), he will return a heart, the suit his partner led. Now what?

If you play low, West will win the ♥K and return the suit. You will have nothing left but the ace, so you will have to win. You will be in your hand with no way to get to the three good diamonds in the dummy. If you go up with the ace and play another heart, West will take the king, and once again the winning diamonds will be stranded in the dummy.

But what if East has the ♥K and plays it at trick one? Then you will have the jack to get to the dummy once diamonds are established. Unless East is fast asleep, he will never cover the ♥Q and give you that entry to the diamond suit. He knows he can cut you off from the dummy by taking his ♦A at just the right time. East would never give you an easy entry to the dummy.

So what is the answer? How can you make 3NT? Easy, just play the ♥6 from the dummy and win the ace in your hand. You will then have two low hearts in your hand and the QJ in the dummy with only the king missing. You can knock out the ♦A, win the return (East probably won't play a heart), and play a low heart from your hand. No matter what West does, you cannot be prevented from getting to the dummy to cash your good diamonds and make your contract.

CHAPTER 11

The Power of Trumps

In This Chapter

➤ Getting rid of losers by ruffing

➤ Drawing trumps—when to do it and when not to

➤ Managing a shaky trump suit

➤ The crossruff

In this chapter, you will learn more about how too many losers can turn into a making contract. You will learn everything you always wanted to know about drawing trumps—and when to postpone it. The 4-3 trump fit is a necessity on occasion, and you will find out how to manage that situation to the fulfillment of your contract. You will also learn about the magic of the crossruff—and the most important part of preparing for it.

Small Cards, Big Results

Strictly speaking, all cards are the same size, so it's technically not correct to refer to the lower spot cards such as 2s and 3s as small. That is the vernacular, however, and everyone knows what it means to play a small heart.

The point is that any trump card, even the 2, can win a trick over any plain suit, even the ace, so long as the hand playing the trump is out of the suit led. Therein lies the magic of the trump suit.

Good things can happen for a declarer who has lots of trumps between his hand and the dummy, as documented in one of the most famous and influential books of recent times. The book *To Bid or Not to Bid: The Law of Total Tricks* was written by many-time North American champion Larry Cohen, who now lives and works in Florida.

In the book, Cohen explained that having extra trumps can mean extra tricks. It's an oversimplification to be sure, but in general the law as Cohen laid it out says that you and your partner can safely bid to a contract at the same level as the number of trumps you hold between your two hands.

That means, for example, that when you have ten trumps, it is usually safe to bid up to the four level, which means you have to take ten tricks. *Safe*, of course, is used in a bridge sense, and can mean that you will make your contract—or that even if you go down, you will have prevented your opponents from scoring their contract for a greater reward.

Add Them Up

The "total tricks" part comes from the theory, first put forth by Frenchman Jean-Rene Vernes in the fifties, that the number of tricks available on any deal is equal to the number of trumps held by the two opposing sides in their best fits. In other words, if each side's best fit is eight cards, there should be sixteen tricks available on the deal.

The theory is best put to practice in competitive bidding situations, where the high-card points are more or less equally distributed between the two sides.

Here's an example

♠ K 10 9 8 4
♥ 5 3
♦ 8 7 6 4
♣ Q 3

♠ J   ♠ 3 2
♥ A K J 2   ♥ Q 10 8 7 6
♦ Q 10 9 2   ♦ K J 5 3
♣ A J 9 7   ♣ 8 4

♠ A Q 7 6 5
♥ 9 4
♦ A
♣ K 10 6 5 2

West	North	East	South
			1♠
Dbl	4♠	All Pass	

This is a typical competitive auction. South has a normal 1♠ opener, West has a classic takeout double, and North has just the right hand for a preemptive raise to the four level based on his knowledge that he and South have at least ten trumps between the two hands.

Having so many extra trumps makes playing the contract very easy. West will probably start with a high heart and continue the suit when East encourages by signaling with a high heart. There will be more on that topic in the sections on defense.

After cashing a couple of hearts, West might switch to a trump. The declarer can win, play another round, ending in his hand, then play a club toward the dummy's queen. West can duck and win the next round of clubs, but the declarer will be in control. He will have three trumps left in the dummy to ruff clubs (the king actually becomes good after two ruffs) and three trumps in his hand to ruff losing diamonds.

Easy as pie, right? Try it without all those extra trumps. The fact that the contract was made is a bonus. North's hand was weak in high-card points, so it would not have been surprising for South to go down in 4♠. As it is, East-West can make 4♥ with relative ease, so even down one is a good result for North-South.

Bridge Basics

In the early days of bridge, players led the king from two different holdings: the AK and the KQ. Unless the partner of the opening leader was looking at the ace of the suit led, he didn't know which holding the lead was from, and it can make a difference at times. For example, if the dummy has three low cards in the suit and the third hand has, say, three to the jack, the partner of the opening leader will not want to encourage the opening leader to continue the suit in case the declarer has three to the queen and the leader has started with the AK. If, however, the lead is from the KQ, the third hand should encourage holding the jack because continuing the suit will knock out the declarer's ace and promote winners in the suit.

To help with this and other situations, most modern players now have the agreement that the ace is led from the AK and the king from KQ to make a clear distinction between the two holdings.

On this deal, North-South had the advantage of possessing the boss suit—spades. In the given auction, if East-West want to compete, they have to bid at the five level, and that's one level too high. If East bids 5♥, he will lose a spade, a diamond, and a club and go down one. Looking at all the cards, North-South can actually defeat 5♥ two tricks. Do you see how?

It's unlikely that anyone would try it, but if East bids 5♥, South can start with the ♦A and continue with a low spade. North wins the ♠K and returns a diamond for South to ruff. That's three tricks in already for down one, and East will not be able to avoid losing a club for two down. This defense is not as far-fetched as it might seem, but it is risky. North would bid 4♠ with five trumps to the ten just the same as he did with five to the king.

One further point: when the bidding escalates so steeply in one fell swoop, it's often difficult to tell which side is bidding to make and which side is just trying to get in the way, not caring if they go down. With the deal under discussion, it would actually pay East-West, who have 22 high-card points to their opponents' 18, to continue bidding as a sacrifice. Down one in 5♥ is better than defending the unbeatable 4♠.

It is also worth noting that on the deal under so much discussion, even if West had passed, North would still have bid 4♠ with the same hand. A jump to game in that fashion does not promise strength, only lots of trumps. Unless South has an exceptional hand, he is not invited to bid on in such an auction.

Shape, Beautiful Shape

It has been pointed out elsewhere in this book that shapely hands—two five-card suits, for example—can produce lots of tricks. That assumes, of course, that the partner of the shapely hand holder has good trump support. If you don't have enough trumps, the opponents will run you out of them, and all those tricks you hope to take by ruffing will never materialize.

Here's an example, with neither side vulnerable:

♠92
♥7
♦QJ987
♣A8654

♠KQJ104		♠85
♥AJ32		♥Q1098
♦A104		♦K3
♣10		♣KQJ97

♠A763
♥K654
♦652
♣32

West	North	East	South
1♠	2NT	Dbl	3♦
Dbl	All Pass		

A note on the bidding: North's bid is the Unusual 2NT, showing at least five cards in each minor. Bidding with that hand is not recommended, but players often enter the auction with even worse collections, so you must be prepared to exact the optimum penalty when they do. East's first double delivers this message: "It's our hand, partner, and I can double one or both of North's long suits." East has 11 high-card points, so he isn't sure that game will make for his side. He is sure that he and his partner have most of the high-card strength, so he tells West that he prefers to try for a penalty.

With two clubs and three diamonds, South has a definite preference. With some of his strength in diamonds, West lets East in on the good news with a double when South chooses between North's two suits.

North-South are unlucky that South's hand is somewhat weak and that South did not have better trumps, but more judicious bidding by North would have produced a luckier outcome on the deal.

When one opponent shows a two-suited hand and forces his partner to pick one of them, the best strategy for the defenders is usually to lead a trump. There is a good chance that the declarer, South, will try to ruff losing clubs in his hand—the hand with the shorter trumps. It is best for the defenders if they can start pulling trumps—usually the declarer's job—to prevent all that ruffing.

Accordingly, West leads a low diamond to East's king. A second diamond comes back to West's ace, and a third round takes South's last trump. It's a grim situation for poor South, who is somewhat of an innocent bystander—the victim of his partner's poor judgment. It's too bad that South couldn't somehow make North play it. Even if West starts with the ♦ A in order to make sure two rounds are played, East can win the ♦ K and return a spade. When the declarer desperately plays North's ♣ A and another club, East will win and put his partner in with a spade to play a third round of trumps.

When the smoke clears, South will have three diamond tricks in the North hand and two tricks with the black aces—and that's it. Down four and minus 800.

Even without any extra high-card points, it's a much different story if North-South had uncovered a nine-card trump fit, perhaps with this as a full deal:

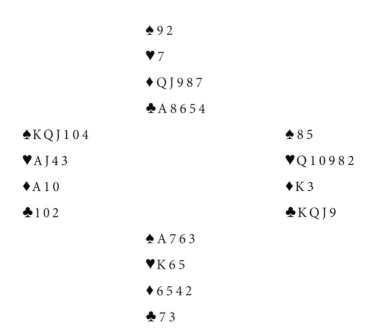

♠ 9 2
♥ 7
♦ Q J 9 8 7
♣ A 8 6 5 4

♠ K Q J 10 4
♥ A J 4 3
♦ A 10
♣ 10 2

♠ 8 5
♥ Q 10 9 8 2
♦ K 3
♣ K Q J 9

♠ A 7 6 3
♥ K 6 5
♦ 6 5 4 2
♣ 7 3

Consider how well South would do playing 3♦ with that extra trump. The opponents can play two rounds of diamonds, but the declarer can take the two black aces, three trump tricks in the North hand, and two club ruffs in the South hand. That's seven tricks, a huge improvement over the result with the eight-card diamond fit.

Given this new layout, an experienced East-West pair would not double South in 3♦, preferring instead to bid their cold game in hearts. With East and West both holding doubletons in the diamonds, they know it's better to go on the offensive rather than doubling for penalty. There's an adage in bridge that is worth remembering for situations like this: Points don't take tricks. Trumps take tricks.

Mind Your Trumps

The previous section was meant to reinforce how important trumps and their management are to your success. In general, the more trumps you have, the more options you have as the declarer.

Here's a case in point:

♠ A K 8
♥ A Q 10 9
♦ K J 10 2
♣ 3 2

♠ Q 4 3

♥ K J 8 4 3

♦ A 6 5

♣ A 7

You are in 6♥. West leads the ♣5 to East's jack and your ace. How will you play this contract?

First, take stock. How do you assess this contract? Hint: Unless one opponent has all four outstanding trumps, the contract is ice cold.

What is the key to making twelve tricks? That's right: Avoiding a diamond loser. You could pull trumps and play the ♦A and a low diamond to the 10 in the dummy. If it wins, you could return to hand and take another diamond finesse. On the fourth diamond, you could discard your losing club. Easy game, eh?

Not so fast. If the diamond finesse loses, you are down because your opponents can then cash a club. Why not guarantee the contract? Here's how you do it: After winning the ♣A, pull trumps in two or three rounds, then play your spades, leaving this position:

♠ - -

♥ Q

♦ K J 1 0 2

♣ 3

♠ - -

♥ J 8

♦ A 6 5

♣ 7

Now all you need to do is play the ♣7 from your hand. You don't care which opponent wins it because either one will have to hand you the contract when he gets in. Whoever wins will have to play a diamond, which solves your problem about the location of the queen, or he will have to play a spade or another club. If a non-diamond is played by East, you discard a low diamond from hand and ruff in the dummy. If it comes from West, take your diamond discard after ruffing in the dummy. Either way, you can claim at that point.

It's an entirely different story if you have only eight trumps between your hand and the dummy, perhaps in this layout:

♠ K Q 5

♥ Q J 3

♦ A J 10 8 2

♣ 6 5

♠ A J 7

♥ A K 10 8 4

♦ K 6 5

♣ A 7

You are playing 6 ♥ again, and this time West leads the ♣ Q. You win with the ace and pull trumps, but when you exit with your low club after cashing the spades, either opponent can win and simply play a black card. You have to ruff in hand—and you still have to find the ♦ Q on your own.

Do you see how useful that extra trump can be? Modern bidding systems are geared to uncovering those nine-card (or better) fits because your options are increased considerably when you can pull trumps and still have at least one left in each hand.

Here's another example of how an abundance of trumps can make your life easy:

♠ A K 4

♥ 6 5 4

♦ A Q 8 7 6

♣ J 4

♠ Q J 6

♥ A Q

♦ K J 10 4 3 2

♣ A 3

You are South, playing in 6 ♦. West leads the ♣ K and you win with the ace (good play). If the dummy had just one more spade, you could discard your losing club and take the heart finesse for an overtrick. That's not possible, so you must consider another plan to bring home the slam. Any ideas?

First, consider the opening lead. You can bank on West to have the ♣Q to go with his king. A plan is starting to take shape. What if you pull trumps (the opponents have only two) and cash your spade winners, eliminating that suit, then play the ♣J from the dummy?

West will have to win, and then what? If he plays a heart, it's right into your AQ. If he plays another club, you ruff in dummy and pitch the ♥Q from your hand. The only cards you will have left in your hand will be the ♥A and your winning diamonds. Slam made! Congratulations!

If someone had described this play to you, calling it a strip and end play, you might have thought, "That's for experts. I can't do that." Look it over again. It was really pretty simple, wasn't it? All those extra trumps made this slam easy to play.

Bridge Lingo

When a contract is so easy that it almost plays itself, it's often called a pianola, after the player pianos of yesteryear that did, in fact, play by themselves. They were sometimes also called auto-pianos, but that doesn't have the cachet of pianola. Another way of saying that a contract is super easy is to say, "You could have thrown it against the wall and it would have made." A caution is in order regarding these seemingly easy contracts: if it appears to be a pianola, look again. There might be a problem lurking that can spoil your fun.

Kiddies Off the Streets

One of the first things most players are taught about trump contracts is to pull trumps—get the kiddies off the street, in the vernacular. That is most often a good idea, but there will be occasions when it's the wrong strategy.

First, an example of a situation that requires prompt action with the trump suit:

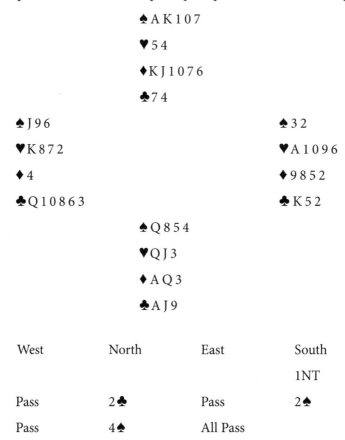

♠ A K 10 7

♥ 5 4

♦ K J 10 7 6

♣ 7 4

♠ J 9 6

♥ K 8 7 2

♦ 4

♣ Q 10 8 6 3

♠ 3 2

♥ A 10 9 6

♦ 9 8 5 2

♣ K 5 2

♠ Q 8 5 4

♥ Q J 3

♦ A Q 3

♣ A J 9

West	North	East	South
			1NT
Pass	2♣	Pass	2♠
Pass	4♠	All Pass	

The auction is normal: South's 1NT shows 15–17 high-card points. North's 2♣ asks South if he has a four-card major, and when South admits to four spades, North places the contract.

West starts with his singleton diamond, also normal. As it turns out, East does have an ace, and if it were the ♦A, the defenders could start off with the first two tricks: diamond to the ace, diamond back, ruffed by West. If East had another fast entry—say, the ♣A instead of the ♣K—the contract would be defeated with a second diamond ruff.

The singleton lead does not prove fruitful, but South must be careful in assessing the situation. So long as East does not have four spades to the J-9, South can see four spade tricks. The diamond suit will always produce five tricks, and there is the ♣A. That's ten tricks.

Don't mess around. Just pull trumps, ending in dummy, and if you want to try for an overtrick, play a heart toward your Q-J. If the queen loses to the king on your left and a club comes back, win the ace, cash your diamonds, pitching the ♣J and the ♣9, then play another heart from the dummy. If the two top honors were split—that is, East had one, West had the other—East will have to win, setting up your jack. You can ruff the club return and play the ♥J for trick number eleven.

It would be a different story if trumps did not divide 3-2.

Bridge Basics

There are some suit combinations that allow for managing bad trump splits, and you must be aware of the correct way to manage those combinations. Here is an example of a suit in isolation: A K 10 7 in the North hand facing Q 8 5 4 in the South hand. You cannot guard against your right-hand opponent's holding J 9 6 2. He will always come to a trump trick because when you play toward the queen in the South hand, East will insert the 9, forcing the queen, and assuring a trick for his side. If however, West has four to the jack, you can play to the ace first, then low to the queen. When your right-hand opponent shows out, you win the queen and have the K10 poised over the J9 for four tricks.

If the spade suit breaks badly for you but you find that you can escape with no spade loser—as when West, not East, has four spades including the jack—you must simply cash your winners. If you pull trumps and attempt to develop a trick in hearts, your opponents will win and knock out your ♣A. When you play the second heart, they will win and cash enough clubs to defeat your contract, and you will be helpless to prevent it because in the course of pulling trumps, you used all of yours.

Master Concession

When you are playing on trumps and you find that one of your opponents has the master trump—the highest trump remaining after you have played your high ones—it is usually not correct to continue playing on trumps. Remember, leading a trump from the dummy or your hand often uses up two trumps, and you can't always afford that. Here is an example:

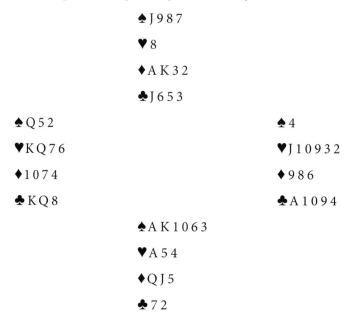

♠ J 9 8 7
♥ 8
♦ A K 3 2
♣ J 6 5 3

♠ Q 5 2   ♠ 4
♥ K Q 7 6   ♥ J 10 9 3 2
♦ 1 0 7 4   ♦ 9 8 6
♣ K Q 8   ♣ A 1 0 9 4

♠ A K 1 0 6 3
♥ A 5 4
♦ Q J 5
♣ 7 2

South plays in 4♠ on the lead of the ♣K by West. South ruffs the third round of clubs, and plays the ♠A and ♠K. It would be folly for South to play another round of trumps, conceding the ♠Q to West. Doing so would remove a trump from the dummy, so only one heart ruff would be possible. The contract would fail as a result.

In the given case, South should cash the ♥A, ruff a heart, return to hand with the ♦Q, and ruff his last heart with the dummy's last trump. Now South plays winning diamonds and West can take his ♠Q whenever he wants to, but that's the third and final trick for the defense.

Change a few cards in each hand and it's a different story.

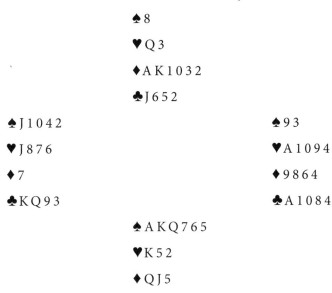

```
                          ♠ 8
                          ♥ Q 3
                          ♦ A K 1 0 3 2
                          ♣ J 6 5 2
        ♠ J 1 0 4 2                        ♠ 9 3
        ♥ J 8 7 6                          ♥ A 1 0 9 4
        ♦ 7                                ♦ 9 8 6 4
        ♣ K Q 9 3                          ♣ A 1 0 8 4
                          ♠ A K Q 7 6 5
                          ♥ K 5 2
                          ♦ Q J 5
                          ♣ 7
```

Again, South plays 4♠ and West again starts with the ♣K, continuing with the queen, which South ruffs. South cashes the top three spades. When the suit proves to be 4-2 (the normal expectation), South must concede the trick to the jack immediately. Do you see why?

South has already lost a club trick and he has a sure loser in spades. If he can't get at least one heart discard on diamonds, he will lose two heart tricks. South must be able to cash at least four diamonds to be able to take ten tricks.

The problem is that if South leaves the ♠J outstanding, he will collect only two diamond tricks. West will not ruff the first or second round of diamonds, but he will ruff the third round and South will be cut off from the diamond suit. He will end up losing two heart tricks, a spade, and a club.

If South continues with a fourth round of spades, West can win and continue with a club, but the declarer can then ruff and cash all his diamonds, discarding two hearts from hand, and conceding a trick to the ♥A at the end. That's ten tricks and game made.

Let Them Stay Out

There will be times when it will be fatal to draw even one round of trumps, and that's usually when you need to take some ruffs in the dummy. Look at this deal:

♠ 6 4 3 2
♥ 7 2
♦ J 1 0 7
♣ A 8 4 2

♠ A K Q 1 0 9 5   ♠ J 8 7
♥ Q J 8   ♥ K 1 0 9 4
♦ 6 5   ♦ 3 2
♣ 7 5   ♣ Q J 1 0 9

♠ - -
♥ A 6 5 3
♦ A K Q 9 8 4
♣ K 6 3

You are South in an ambitious contract of 5♦. West could make your life very difficult if he started with a trump, but most players holding his hand would start with a high spade.

You ruff and consider your prospects. Your trumps are strong, so you can pull trumps with ease if you choose to. The problem is that pulling trumps will leave you at least one trick short, and that's if the clubs prove to be 3-3, providing you with three tricks from that suit.

Bridge Facts

There's an interesting and useful fact when it comes to considering how a particular suit will break for you when you are the declarer: When the number of cards out against you is an odd number, the suit tends to break as evenly as possible. That is, seven cards will break 4-3 more often than 5-2; five missing cards will break 3-2 about three times as often as 4-1. When it's an even number, the suit is less likely to break evenly (2-2 or 3-3, for example) than unevenly. When there are six cards missing, expect a 4-2 split 48.45 percent of the time versus 35.53 percent for 3-3. With seven cards missing, expect a 4-3 split 62.17 percent of the time versus 30.52 percent for a 5-2 break.

Even if you get lucky in clubs (a 3-3 split), you still have only ten tricks: six diamonds, three clubs, and the ♥A. The odds say you will need two heart ruffs in the dummy.

Consider what will happen if you play even one round of trumps before starting to work on hearts. Say you play a low heart from your hand after cashing one high diamond. West will win and won't make the same mistake twice. A trump will hit the table as soon as West can get one out of his hand. That will leave you with one trump to deal with two heart losers.

If you start on hearts at trick two without touching trumps, you are in a much better position. Say you play a low heart from your hand at trick two. West wins and plays a trump, which you win in hand. Now play the ♥A and ruff a heart. You can return to hand with the ♣K and ruff your last losing heart. Now a spade ruff allows you to remove all the opponents' trumps and play a club to the ace, your eleventh trick. You took six trumps in your hand, two in dummy, the ♥A, and the two high clubs. Well done!

Moving About

Another reason to postpone drawing trumps is to maintain communication between your hand and the dummy, usually for a specific reason.

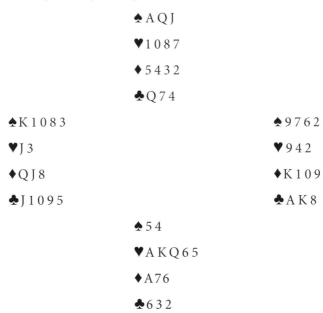

```
                    ♠ A Q J
                    ♥ 1 0 8 7
                    ♦ 5 4 3 2
                    ♣ Q 7 4
   ♠ K 1 0 8 3                      ♠ 9 7 6 2
   ♥ J 3                            ♥ 9 4 2
   ♦ Q J 8                          ♦ K 1 0 9
   ♣ J 1 0 9 5                      ♣ A K 8
                    ♠ 5 4
                    ♥ A K Q 6 5
                    ♦ A 7 6
                    ♣ 6 3 2
```

West	North	East	South
			1♥
Pass	2♥	Pass	Pass
Dbl	Pass	2♠	3♥
All Pass			

Those annoying opponents have pushed you to the three level, thanks to West's balancing double. You can beat their contract, but it's hard to tell sometimes, and you do have a nice heart suit.

No matter what might have been, you must concentrate on the task at hand—making nine tricks. West starts with the ♣J, which you duck. East has to overtake when West continues with a club. After winning with the ♣K and cashing the ace, East defends accurately by switching to a diamond, playing the 10. There's little point in ducking, although in this case it wouldn't hurt, so you win the ♦A and consider your game plan.

If you are to make this contract, the spade finesse must be right—that is, West must have the king. You can lead to the ♠J and then the queen and discard one of your losing diamonds on the ♠A.

You must take care, however. If you pull your opponents' trumps, it will take three rounds. If you turn your attention to spades then, your hand and the dummy will look like this:

♠ A Q J

♥ - -

♦ 5 4 3

♣ - -

♠ 5 4

♥ 6 5

♦ 7 6

♣ - -

You can play a spade to the jack, which holds, but now what? If you play a diamond from the dummy, your opponents will take two tricks in that suit. They already have three club tricks, so you will be down. It doesn't help to cash the ♠A. You don't gain a trick that way.

Here's a better plan: After taking the ♦A, cash two high hearts, then play a spade to the jack. You can use the dummy's last heart to get to your hand to play a second round of spades.

You insert the queen, and when it holds you can cash the ace to get rid of one of those losing diamonds in your hand. You are home with five hearts, three spades, and the ♦ A. You were thinking ahead, and it paid off.

Extra Care Needed

There will be times when you won't be able to rest in a traditional eight-card fit, and that applies whether you are playing a part score, game, or even slam.

When there is no so-called golden fit—at least eight cards in the same suit between the partners' hands—a partnership typically plays in notrump. On occasion, however, the bidding makes it apparent that a notrump contract is not going to be success, and that usually means that neither partner can stop a long suit announced by one of the opponents.

A fallback position in many of those cases is a 4-3 fit, which can be tenuous and often requires extra care.

Bridge Lingo

In bridge's colorful vernacular, there is a name for the 4-3 trump fit. It's called a Moysian. That's because Alphonse "Sonny" Moyse, publisher and editor of *The Bridge World* in the Fifties and Sixties, was an adherent of four-card major suit openings and raising with three-card support. That landed him in many 4-3 fits, and he often wrote in favor of the practice.

	♠ 4 3	
	♥ J 9 8	
	♦ K Q 10 6 5	
	♣ A Q J	
♠ A K Q J 8		♠ 10 9 2
♥ 10 7 5 2		♥ 4 3
♦ J 8		♦ 9 7 3 2
♣ 5 2		♣ K 6 4 3
	♠ 7 6 5	
	♥ A K Q 6	
	♦ A 4	
	♣ 10 9 8 7	

West	North	East	South
			1 ♣
1 ♠	2 ♦	Pass	2 ♠
Pass	3 ♣	Pass	3 ♥
Pass	4 ♥	All Pass	

A note about the auction: South's 1 ♣ is normal, as is the 1 ♠ overcall by West. North has enough high-card strength to bid 2 ♦ freely. South has a problem: If he bids 2 ♥, that shows about a king more in high-card strength than he actually has. He has no semblance of a spade stopper, so he can't bid notrump, and he doesn't want to bid 3 ♦ with only two of them.

So South marks time with a cue-bid of 2 ♠, which asks if North can stop spades. If so, North should bid 3NT. He does, after all, have an opening hand.

North has no spade stopper and only five diamonds, so he does not want to rebid that suit. He settles for a preference to South's first-bid suit. North would prefer to have at least one more club, but at least he has three honors.

South is not happy about playing in clubs at a high level with a suit headed by the 10, so he makes a stab at an alternate contract with a bid of 3 ♥. He knows North does not have four hearts because North did not make a negative double over the 1 ♠ overcall. North also knows that South is aware of the situation in hearts, but game in a major requires only ten tricks compared to the eleven needed to make five of a minor. North, therefore, opts for game in hearts.

With North's running diamond suit and the ♥ J, 4 ♥ is a good contract. Note that 5 ♦ has no chance. West will cash two spades and East will eventually win the ♣ K. Because North and South have the top four hearts, only a 5-1 trump split would put 4 ♥ in jeopardy. It does not help the defense for West to play a third round of spades. The declarer simply ruffs in dummy and goes about his business.

Much more care is needed when the layout is as follows:

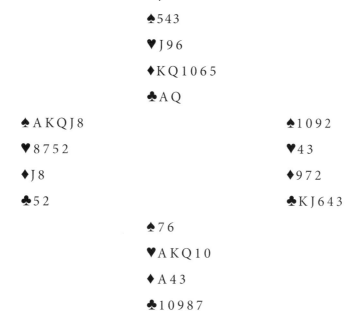

♠543
♥J96
♦KQ1065
♣AQ

♠AKQJ8
♥8752
♦J8
♣52

♠1092
♥43
♦972
♣KJ643

♠76
♥AKQ10
♦A43
♣10987

A contract of 4♥ is still a good bet, but when West plays three high spades to start the defense, the declarer must decline to ruff, instead discarding a club or a diamond from hand. Can you see what happens to the contract if the declarer ruffs the third round of spades? All of a sudden, West has more trumps than South, and if the declarer plays three rounds of trumps and starts on diamonds, West will ruff the third round and cash two more spades.

As noted previously, when your opponents have six of a suit out against you, they will divide 4-2 more often than 3-3, so South is betting against the odds if he ruffs the third spade. If South pitches from his hand instead, it does not help West to continue with a fourth round of spades. The declarer can simply ruff with the ♥9 or ♥J and take five diamonds, four hearts, and the ♣A for ten tricks.

Sometimes, even when you have control of a suit, some foresight can pay big dividends.

♠K Q 3

♥5

♦A Q 6 5

♣K J 9 3 2

♠A J 7 6

♥A 6 4

♦7 3 2

♣Q 1 0 4

South plays in 4♠ after East has overcalled in hearts. West leads a low heart, and East plays the queen. How will you come to ten tricks?

It may be counterintuitive to play a low heart when you have the ace in your hand and a singleton in the dummy, but it's the only play to make the contract when the layout is as follows:

♠K Q 3

♥5

♦A Q 6 5

♣K J 9 3 2

♠10 9 5 4		♠8 2
♥J 9 3 2		♥K Q 1 0 8 7
♦J 9 4		♦K 1 0 8
♣8 7		♣A 6 5

♠A J 7 6

♥A 6 4

♦7 3 2

♣Q 1 0 4

By playing low on the first round of hearts, you can ruff the second round with the dummy's low spade, cash the dummy's high trumps, and play a low club. If East goes up with the ace and plays a heart, you win the ace, pull the remaining trumps with the ace and jack, then take your club winners, actually ending with an overtrick. You take four clubs, four spades, one heart ruff in the dummy, plus the ♥A and the ♦A for eleven tricks. You play so well!

Fun With Trumps

You have already read about how advantageous it can be to separate your trumps—that is to use them one at a time from each hand instead of crashing two of them together each time you pull a round. Here's an extreme example of a maneuver known as a crossruff, so called because you ruff back and forth between two hands, making all or nearly all of your trumps one at a time:

♠ A K Q 1 0 9

♥ 6

♦ A 8 7 6 5

♣ 1 0 9

♠ J 8 7 6 5

♥ A 7 5 4 3 2

♦ 2

♣ A

In a spade contract, the only way to hold North-South to twelve tricks is to lead a trump. On any other lead, the declarer will be able to win, cash the red aces, and ruff five times in each hand. Taken together with the ♣A, that's thirteen tricks. Even on a trump lead, the declarer will win three aces, eight separate trump tricks, and one other trump for twelve tricks.

Most of the deals in which you use a crossruff will not be as extreme, and there is one element to the crossruff that is key to its success. See if you can identify the key play or plays in this example:

♠ 2

♥ A J 2

♦ A J 10 9

♣ A 9 6 5 3

♠ A 6 5 4 3

♥ K Q 8

♦ K Q 8 3

♣ 2

You, South, land in 6♦ after East opens the bidding with 3♣. West annoys you by leading a trump, and the dummy's 9 wins. How do you proceed? First, count your tricks.

Outside of diamonds, you have only five top tricks, so you must make the rest of your trumps separately. Fortunately, your remaining trumps are all high, so there's no problem there. You have to hope that the ♣A will live—that this is one of those aggressive preemptive bids made on a six-card suit. You can't afford for West to ruff and play another trump.

There is an even bigger issue, however. Have you identified it yet?

If you cash the ♣A and ♠A right away and start ruffing back and forth between your hand and the dummy, what do you think your opponents will be doing while you have all that fun? That's right, they are going to start getting rid of hearts. Inasmuch as you are going to use all your high trumps for ruffing, your opponents are going to have low trumps left at the end, when you are down to no trumps. Do you think they might use them on your hearts? Right you are.

With that in mind, your only chance is to cash your heart tricks before you start ruffing. You hope this is the full layout:

♠ 2

♥ A J 2

♦ A J 10 9

♣ A 9 6 5 3

Bridge Basics

An examination of the crossruff and its elements can give you a valuable insight into what is often the best defense against a so-called sacrifice bid by your opponents. Such a bid is usually made because your opponents believe you will make your contract, and they are hoping that their contract, even doubled, will result in a smaller minus than allowing you to play your contract. In many such cases, your opponents will be hoping to make up for their lack of high-card points with shape, allowing them to make enough trump tricks between the two hands to make up for your greater strength. You can often spoil this strategy by leading trumps at every opportunity, forcing them to use their trumps two at a time instead of separately.

♠ K Q 10 9 7	♠ J 8
♥ 9 7 5 3	♥ 1 0 6 4
♦ 6 5 4	♦ 7 2
♣ 4	♣ K Q J 10 8 7

♠ A 6 5 4 3
♥ K Q 8
♦ K Q 8 3
♣ 2

If all three hearts stand up, now you can cash your black aces and merrily ruff three times in each hand. That gives you the trump trick you took at the first trick, three hearts, two black aces, and three ruffs in each hand for a total of twelve. You will have the fun of seeing your opponents underruffing at the end.

If West can ruff the ♣ A or if East ruffs the third round of hearts, at least you can console yourself with the knowledge that you played the contract correctly.

Here's another trump suit trick—pun intended—that can come in handy on occasion:

♠ A J 6

♥ Q 8 4

♦ 5 2

♣ 9 6 5 4

♠ K 5

♥ A K J 9 6

♦ A K 4 3

♣ A K

West	North	East	South
			2 ♣
Pass	2 ♦	Pass	2 ♥
Pass	3 ♥	Pass	4NT
Pass	5 ♦	Pass	6 ♥
All Pass			

The auction is straightforward with one noteworthy aspect. South's 2♣ describes a very strong hand. North's 2♦ is known as a waiting bid—possibly weak but also possibly unable to make a descriptive positive bid. South shows his suit and North's 3♥—the noteworthy bid—shows a raise in hearts with some additional feature. A jump to 4♥ would say, "I have heart support, Partner, but I have no aces, kings, or singletons for you."

West starts with a trump to the 4, 7, and your 9. You have eleven tricks and the need to do something about the two low diamonds in your hand. If you can ruff them both, you can make an overtrick. If that thought entered your mind, beware. The full deal might be as follows:

♠ A J 6

♥ Q 8 4

♦ 5 2

♣ 9 6 5 4 3

CHAPTER 12

Goodbye, trumps

The Declarer Play at Notrump

In This Chapter

➤ The tempo principle and counting tricks

➤ Developing long suits

➤ You duck, you win

➤ Avoidance

In this chapter, you will learn about tempo and why the defending side often has an advantage in this area. You will also read about some tricks for developing your long suits and, while you are doing so, how to keep the danger hand off lead.

The holdup, or duck, will become an important part of your repertoire, and you will read about when to do it and when to lay off. You will also learn how to identify the danger opponent and ways to keep that opponent from gaining the lead.

A Step Ahead

Once a contract has been determined—a bid, double, or redouble is followed by three passes—the player to the left of the declarer gets to fire the opening shot. In some settings, the player must lead more or less blindly. Usually that's because the bidding has provided virtually no clues to the best opening lead. An example:

West	North	East	South
			1NT
Pass	3NT	All Pass	

West holds

♠ Q 7 6 5

♥ Q 4 3

♦ A 8 6 4

♣ 1 0 9

What should West lead? It's a tough call because the auction has been so uninformative. Contrast the auction above to this one:

West	North	East	South
			1NT
Pass	2♣	Pass	2♠
Pass	3NT	All Pass	

What have you learned from this auction? It has been much more helpful to you than the first.

Can you tell what happening with the majors? You should be able to. North must have four

Bridge Basics

When you open 1NT and your partner bids 2 ♣ to ask you to tell about your major suits, if you have two four-card majors, you should bid hearts first. Why? Because every now and then you will get to play at the two level, providing just a bit of safety when game is not in the picture. It works this way: a 2 ♥ response to 2 ♣ does not deny having four spades, so the Stayman bidder can continue with 2 ♠ to show a hand with invitational values and four spades. When the opener has a minimum and four spades, he can pass. It follows, then, that a response of 2 ♠ to Stayman denies four hearts.

hearts because he bid Stayman (2♣, asking South about majors).

By responding to 2♣ with 2♠, South denied having four hearts. North would not have used Stayman unless he had at least one four-card major, and he did not raise spades, so he must have hearts.

So here's what you know so far: South has four spades, North has four hearts and fewer than four spades. Leading a spade does not seem very attractive knowing that South has four of them. Knowing that North has four hearts should make you leery of leading that suit. You might well locate the queen for the declarer when a non-heart lead would leave him with a guess.

What else do you know?

What about your partner's two passes? Could he have a robust holding in clubs? Not likely. If he did, he would have doubled the Stayman bid to say so.

By process of elimination, you select a low diamond for your opening lead. You hope your partner can provide a bit of help, perhaps the king. On a good day, your partner will have the king and the queen.

This discussion is meant to introduce you to the concept of tempo, which is the element of timing in the play that often decides the outcome.

Consider this full deal:

```
                    ♠ A 6 5
                    ♥ K Q J 8
                    ♦ J 5 4 3
                    ♣ 6 2
     ♠ K Q J 10 3                    ♠ 9 4
     ♥ A 4 3                         ♥ 7 5 2
     ♦ 9 6                           ♦ Q 7 2
     ♣ 7 4 3                         ♣ Q 10 9 8 5
                    ♠ 8 7 2
                    ♥ 10 9 6
                    ♦ A K 10 8
                    ♣ A K J
```

West	North	East	South
			1NT
Pass	2♣	Pass	2♦
Pass	3NT	All Pass	

West has an easy lead against 3NT, and by starting with the ♠K, West has assured that the tempo favors the defense. In fact, on the given layout, the declarer has no chance to make his contract. South can see that even if both minor suit finesses work, that's only eight tricks (four diamonds, three clubs, and the ♠A). That means the declarer must play on hearts. When he does, West will pounce with the ♥A and cash his spade winners.

As a point of technique, the declarer will duck one round of spades in the hope that East has the ♥A and two or three spades. The declarer doesn't mind if East has three spades, because that would mean West has only four, so the defenders can take only three spade tricks and the heart ace. If the diamond finesse fails, the contract was never going to make anyway, so the declarer must assume it works.

The point of this lengthy discourse is to show how tempo works. Look what happens when you switch the East and West hands to make this the full deal:

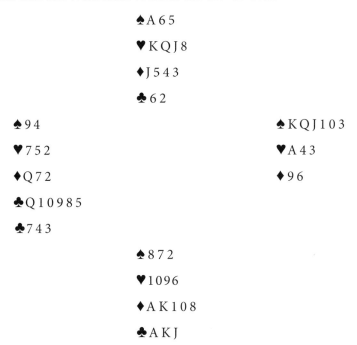

On the same bidding, West might well lead a club, hoping his partner could contribute an honor—preferably the ace or king. On a club lead, the declarer has the tempo advantage. The defenders have not found his weak spot as before, so he can get to work on hearts right away. East may duck a round of hearts—leaving the declarer in dummy to take a diamond finesse, but he will eventually have to win, and even if he switches to the ♠K, the declarer has eleven tricks in the form of three clubs, three hearts, four diamonds, and a spade.

You see, timing is everything. On the bidding, it would be virtually impossible for West to find the killing spade lead. After all, North bid Stayman; he could have both four-card majors.

Tempo With Trumps

This chapter is about notrump play, but the issue of tempo can apply to suit contracts as well. Consider this deal and how tempo can play a role.

♠ 6 5 4 3

♥ 7 3

♦ A 1 0 8 6

♣ K Q 8

♠ 7

♥ A K J 1 0 9

♦ K 4

♣ A J 5 4 3

South lands in 4 ♥, against which West leads the ♠A. When East plays the ♠J, showing the 10 and possibly the 9, West continues with the ♠Q. South ruffs and pauses to take stock. If you are South, how should you continue?

You could go over to the dummy in one of the minors and take a heart finesse, but if it loses, West will play another spade—and your contract will sink like the Titanic when the full deal is as follows:

♠ 6 5 4 3

♥ 7 3

♦ A 1 0 8 6

♣ K Q 8

♠ A K Q 8   ♠ J 1 0 9 2

♥ Q 6 4 2   ♥ 8 5

♦ Q J 5   ♦ 9 7 3 2

♣ 1 0 7   ♣ 9 6 2

♠ 7

♥ A K J 1 0 9

♦ K 4

♣ A J 5 4 3

When West wins the ♥Q and punches you with a third spade, you will be down to two trumps, one fewer than West. To keep the tempo in your favor, you must forget about the finesse and consider that a 4-2 trump split is more likely than a 3-3 break. In that case, your best plan is to cash the ♥A and ♥K and start in on clubs. West will make his low trump, but even if he also cashes the ♥Q, you will still have a trump left to ruff a third round of spades. Your minor suit winners will then see you home.

Here's another illustration of how your opponents can gain a tempo with their opening shot:

♠ A K J 4

♥ Q 5 4 2

♦ 1 0 9 4

♣ 3 2

♠ 3 2

♥ - -

♦ A K Q J 3 2

♣ A 8 7 6 5

West	North	East	South
			1 ♦
1 ♥	Dbl	2 ♥	3 ♣
Pass	3 ♦	Pass	4 ♦
Pass	5 ♦	All Pass	

West—the rat!—was listening to the auction and starts with the ♦8. Without that lead, you would be able to ruff two clubs in the dummy, but the defense is a tempo ahead. When you duck a club or play the ♣A and another club, you can expect a second trump to be played, leaving you only one trump to ruff clubs with. If the suit splits 3-3, you will be okay, but you're not really expecting a 3-3 break in this exercise, are you?

Do you have another string to your bow? Yes: the spade finesse. You could play the top two spades and hope the queen drops when you ruff the third round, but a better play is to finesse against the ♠Q in the West hand—a 50 percent chance. You hope this is the full deal:

♠A K J 4

♥Q 5 4 2

♦1094

♣3 2

♠Q 6 5   ♠10987

♥A J 9 8 3   ♥K1076

♦875   ♦6

♣K 1 0   ♣Q J 9 4

♠3 2

♥- -

♦A K Q J 3 2

♣A 8 7 6 5

Without the trump lead, you would have had an easy time, ducking a club and ruffing two of them in the dummy even if they switched belatedly to a trump. The trump lead gave your opponents a tempo advantage, but you overcame it by considering different lines of play and selecting the one that gave you the best mathematical chance to succeed.

Let's get back to the notrump discussion and the subject of tempo.

Good players rarely look to the finesse as the first option when looking over the dummy as they decide how to play. Sometimes, however, there is no other option. Consider the following deal:

♠8

♥7 2

♦A Q J 9 3

♣K Q 1 0 9 4

♠A K Q 3 2

♥K Q

♦1 0 5 4

♣J 8 7

Bridge Lingo

It is not unusual for the opponents of a declarer who played a contract extremely well to say, "He played it double dummy!" That means he played as though he could see all the cards. Most play problems are presented as single dummies: the dummy in the North position, the declarer as South, with East and West not shown. *Double dummy* means all four hands are shown. In the early days of bridge, clever writers devised double dummy play problems that were tough even looking at all four hands.

South lands in 3NT, and West leads the ♥J. Looking at the dummy, it appears that 5♦ is a much better contract, but it would be a major mistake for South to dwell on that fact. South must concern himself with the best way to make the contract he is in.

East wins the ♥A and fires back the ♥3. South wins the king and stops to assess the situation. Without the heart lead, the declarer might go to work on the club suit. The spot cards in clubs are so good that four tricks are guaranteed. All you have to do is knock out the ♣A. Four clubs, three spades, one heart, and the ♦A make nine tricks.

There's only one problem with that plan: You can't get four club tricks without letting the defenders in with the ♣A, at which point you will have to start making decisions about what to discard while your opponents cash their heart tricks.

You're only real chance is to take the diamond finesse. You hope the full deal looks something like this:

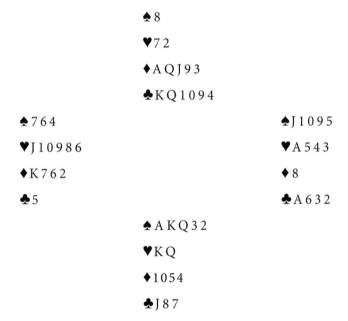

```
                  ♠8
                  ♥72
                  ♦AQJ93
                  ♣KQ10 9 4
  ♠764                            ♠J1095
  ♥J10986                        ♥A543
  ♦K762                          ♦8
  ♣5                             ♣A632
                  ♠AKQ32
                  ♥KQ
                  ♦1054
                  ♣J87
```

After winning the ♥K, you play the ♦10 from your hand, letting it run. You breathe a sigh of relief when it holds, and you follow with a second diamond, putting in the 9 as East shows out. All you have to do now is play a spade to your hand so you can take another diamond finesse.

Careful, now. Be sure you cash your other two high spades. If you don't, you'll be stuck in the dummy after the ♦Q holds, and, although you can cash the ♦A and ♦J, you will have to play a club next, and your opponents will be in to cash the setting trick in hearts.

Your opponents got in the first blow and it put you in a bad spot, but you overcame it by taking your only chance. On a different day, the diamond finesse would have been unsuccessful and you would have gone down two tricks, but it pays to take your best shot anyway. Bold players are often luckier players.

Building Blocks

Nothing helps your cause in notrump play as much as a long suit. If it's also strong, that's even better. You won't always be blessed with such an asset, but when you do have the pleasure, you must know a few tricks to keep from wasting it. Try this on for size:

♠A Q

♥6 5

♦Q J 10 9 8 7 6

♣7 6

♠K 9

♥A K 7 4

♦A 5

♣K Q 5 4 3

West	North	East	South
	3♦	Pass	3NT
All Pass			

Your side is vulnerable, so your partner is not being frisky. It would not be unreasonable of you to expect seven diamonds to the KQ on this bidding.

West leads a spade, and although North does not deliver exactly what you wanted in the diamond suit, his bidding is not off the wall.

You let the ♠Q hold at trick one. What is your plan?

You have the queen down to the 6 in diamonds, and if you can trap the king in the East hand, you will take a lot of tricks: seven diamonds, two spades, two hearts, and a club. You might have to consider such a maneuver if your contract was 6NT, but it's not. You are in 3NT.

If you run the ♦Q at trick two and it loses, it will be a disaster. After winning the ♦K, West will return a spade, and the dummy will be stone dead. All those remaining diamonds will be good, but the suit will be blocked because the only diamond left in your hand will be the bare ace. Argh! You will end up with one diamond, two spades, two hearts, and probably just one club. Down three!

How should you have played? You cannot go wrong if you play a diamond to the ace, followed by a low diamond from your hand. Your opponents can take the king, but they cannot prevent you from taking six diamonds, two spades, and two hearts. Every now and then, when you play the ♦A instead of finessing, one of your opponents will have a singleton king and you will make twelve tricks after all.

Connections

There will be occasions when you will deliberately lose a trick or two in order to be sure of a certain number of winners. You might remember a suit like this from an earlier chapter:

♣A 8 7 4 3

♣6 5 2

You could play a club to the ace and a second club, and that would be okay if the dummy with the long clubs had plenty of entries. Suppose the dummy has no entry other than the ♣A. In that case, you must be clever.

Your first play in clubs should be the 2. Whatever your left-hand opponent plays, the dummy contributes the 3. You can win the return and play a second club from hand. Again, no matter what your left-hand opponent plays, you play the ♣4.

If everyone has followed suit to both leads in clubs, your strategy has been successful: two clubs from you, two clubs from your left-hand opponent, two clubs from the dummy, and two clubs from your right-hand opponent equals eight clubs. The dummy has three clubs to the ace left, so that's eleven clubs accounted for, and you have one for a total of twelve. That means one of your opponents has the only outstanding club, and you have the ace in the dummy to capture it.

Voilà! You have just come up with three tricks, whereas, if the dummy had no entry outside the ♣A, you would have taken only one trick had you started with the ♣A.

Take Care

The suit you want to develop won't always be so anemic, but you must take care even with a seemingly powerful collection. Take a look:

♠ 8 3 2

♥ 5 4 3

♦ A K Q 7 6

♣ 9 6

♠ A K 1 0 9

♥ A J 1 0

♦ 5 4

♣ A 7 5 4

West	North	East	South
			1NT
Pass	3NT	All Pass	

This is a normal auction. North's diamond suit often produces five tricks, and there are chances even if, as in this case, South has a low doubleton. North has only 9 high-card points, but they are good ones.

West leads the ♥7, you play low from the dummy and East contributes the queen. Your good holding in hearts guarantees two tricks in that suit. Following the guideline about the difference between notrump and suit contracts, you count winners. Top winners are two in spades, two in hearts, three in diamonds, and one in club. That's eight. Where will that ninth trick come from?

The diamond suit is powerful and could produce five tricks if each opponent has three diamonds. There are a couple of considerations, however, in deciding what to do next. One is that you don't need five diamond tricks to make your contract—four will do just fine. The other consideration, which has been pointed out previously, is that when there are six cards missing in a suit, they will divide 4-2 more often than 3-3. If you cash the top three diamonds in the hope of taking five tricks, you will end up with only three and you will go down.

So what is the answer? Look at the full deal before deciding on your move at trick two:

                    ♠ 8 3 2
                    ♥ 5 4 3
                    ♦ A K Q 7 6
                    ♣ 9 6

    ♠ Q 6 5 4   ♠ J 7
    ♥ K 9 8 7   ♥ Q 6 2
    ♦ 3 2   ♦ J 1 0 9 8
    ♣ Q 3 2   ♣ K J 1 0 8

                    ♠ A K 1 0 9
                    ♥ A J 1 0
                    ♦ 5 4
                    ♣ A 7 5 4

You have won the first trick with the ♥ A. Look what happens if you play a low diamond from your hand and play low in the dummy. East will win and probably fire back a heart (for all he knows, his partner started with four hearts to the K10). West will take your jack with the king and return the suit, but you are in control.

Bridge Basics

When you have two cards that are equals, such as the jack and 10, it can matter which card you play from your hand when you are the declarer. In a situation where a low card has been led and a low card has been played from the dummy, if East plays the queen and South wins the ace, West knows that the declarer (South) has the jack. How does he know? With the queen and jack, East would play the jack, the lower of the equals (more on that in Chapter 14). When East gets in and plays back a heart, the declarer should play the card he is known to hold.

You win the ♥ 10 and play another diamond, this time playing the ace from the dummy. When both opponents follow, you know that you can run the suit. There are only two more diamonds out against you, and the ♦K and ♦Q will pick them up. You will take at least four diamonds, two hearts, two spades, and a club. If West has difficulty finding three discards as you run your diamonds, you might even end up with an overtrick.

Different Looks

There are other situations in which it's a good idea to duck, and they may not all be obvious. Try this one:

♣A Q 6 5 4 2

♣7 3

If you need this suit to produce five tricks for you, and the dummy is short of entries, you must count on the king to be on your left. But that won't be good enough given the weak spots in this suit.

The way to play this suit is to play low from your hand and also low from the dummy no matter what card West plays. Suppose you lead low from your hand and put in the queen, which holds. Now what? If you play the ace, it will win, but it will also be your last trick, even if the king falls under the ace. Consider that the opponents have the KJ1098 out against you. If West has the K10, that means his partner has the J98. So when you play the ace, the king will fall but the jack will be a winner.

Bridge Basics

A lot of successful play at bridge is detective work, and the first place to look for clues to trick taking is in the bidding. For example, if your hand and the dummy have a total of 27 high-card points and one of your opponents opened the bidding, you can be virtually certain of the location of all the outstanding high-card points. They are in the opener's hand. That can help you immeasurably in the play. If one of your opponents has passed his partner's opening bid and later turns up with an ace, he should not have more than a jack in his hand. With 6 high-card points, your opponent would have responded. Stay on the alert for clues. They are everywhere.

Another combination that will see you home is a doubleton king in the East hand, but you have to guess well in that case. On occasion, you will have evidence that helps you in that situation.

Perhaps West passed as the dealer and has shown up with 10 high-card points in the course of the play. He can't have the king would have opened the bidding, right? In that case, your only hope is to find a doubleton king on your right. A singleton won't do because that would give West four cards, so you would never be able to establish the suit.

You would not want to find yourself in such situations on a regular basis, but it will pay you to know how to give yourself the best chance when it's your only chance.

Here's another occasion when playing low is called for. Again, it's not obvious unless you have seen it before.

♣A Q J 5 4 2

♣7 3

Again, you are in a situation where this suit must produce a lot of tricks for you—and you don't have entries to the dummy outside of that suit.

This is a stronger holding than the one previously shown, but be careful. If you play low from your hand and West plays the king, it will be natural for you to reach for the ace. After all, you have the ace, queen, and jack. But what if the layout is as follow?

♣A Q J 5 4 2

♣K   ♣1 0 9 8 6

♣7 3

If you call for the ace from the dummy, you will be limited to three tricks in the suit. Your ace, queen, and jack will win, but East's 10 will be a winner. No more diamond tricks for you.

Now if you play low, those three high cards in the dummy will pick up all of East's cards, turning the 5 and 4 into winners. Now you take five tricks instead of three.

It is worth noting that it would be a good play by West to put up the king from a doubleton, counting on you to make the safe play of ducking to make sure you take at least five tricks.

Holding a doubleton king in front of the AQJ, West knows that if you have at least two clubs, you can take all six tricks by playing the jack or queen if he plays low. In that sense, he has nothing to lose by playing the king. Watch out for those sneaky defenders—and for the opportunity to return the favor.

High, not Low

There are certain situations where you want to play high, not low. One of them is a familiar maneuver known as a safety play.

Suppose you find yourself in 6NT on this deal:

♠ A K J

♥ Q 10 7

♦ 9 4 3 2

♣ K 5 4

♠ Q 6

♥ A K 4

♦ A Q 10 8 5

♣ A 3 2

Bridge Basics

As you read about bridge and play more, you will encounter the term *safety play*. You make such a play as insurance against bad breaks or to keep a particular opponent out of the lead. Safety plays often involve giving up a trick, as was demonstrated with the suit of AKQ76 opposite the 54. The safety play to assure four tricks whenever possible is to play low from both hands. The play gives up a trick when the suit is split 3-3, but it guarantees four tricks so long as the suit splits no worse than 4-2.

West leads the ♠10 and you check out the dummy. You have three spades, three hearts and two clubs outside of diamonds. That's eight tricks. Clearly you will have to develop diamonds for four tricks.

How should you play the diamond suit?

If you win the opening spade lead in the dummy and play low to the ♦Q, losing to the king, what will you do after regaining the lead? There are two diamonds out against you—the jack and the 7. You could cash the ♦A, hoping the suit originally divided 2-2, in which case the jack would fall.

What if East started with three diamonds to the jack? Now if you cash the ace, East will have the setting trick in the form of the ♦J.

So that means you should go to the dummy and play a low diamond, putting in the 10 if East follows with the 7. But that loses if West started with the KJ.

So what is the answer? The best play, assuming your goal is to make your contract, is to win the opening lead and play the ♦A. This will assure that you make your contract whenever it can be made.

Consider how the diamonds may be divided

West	East
KJ 7 6	--
KJ 7	6
KJ	7 6
K	J 7 6
--	KJ 7 6
6	KJ 7
7 6	KJ
J 7 6	K

Bridge Lingo

Bridge players have assigned a number of unusual ways to describe a finesse. The most popular is *hook*, as in, "I had to take the spade hook," meaning the player felt his contract depended on a successful finesse in spades. The act of playing a card and running it through another player can be described as floating or swinging the card through to try to gain a trick. A card that is favorably placed for the declarer to take a finesse is said to be in the slot.

When West has KJ76 or KJ7, you cannot make the contract, so playing the ace doesn't affect the outcome at all. But when West has KJ doubleton, playing the ace catches the jack, so you can simply drive out the king by playing the queen. When West has the singleton king, you will take thirteen tricks because you can finesse against the ♦J in the East hand.

When West shows out, you simply enter the dummy twice and lead toward your diamond honors two times. If West plays a low diamond under your ace, you go to the dummy and play a diamond toward your Q1085. If East plays the king and West discards, your queen will pick up the jack next time the suit is played. If East plays the jack, you put in the queen. If it loses to the king, all the rest of your diamonds are good.

When you are playing a form of scoring where making overtricks is important, you might play this suit differently. When your objective is to make your contract whenever it is possible to do so, you will make the safety play of the ace.

You want to guard against having to guess what to do when this is the full deal:

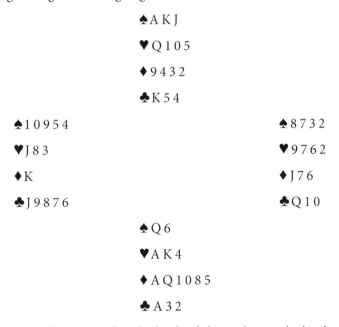

                    ♠A K J
                    ♥Q 1 0 5
                    ♦9 4 3 2
                    ♣K 5 4

♠1 0 9 5 4   ♠8 7 3 2
♥J 8 3   ♥9 7 6 2
♦K   ♦J 7 6
♣J 9 8 7 6   ♣Q 1 0

                    ♠Q 6
                    ♥A K 4
                    ♦A Q 1 0 8 5
                    ♣A 3 2

There are other combinations of cards that lend themselves to the kinds of safety plays that guarantee contracts. Here's one:

    ♣K J 4 3
    ♣A 9 5 2

If you need four tricks from this suit, you should play the ace and then low to the jack if West follows low twice.

If you need just three tricks, the proper play is low to the king and low from the dummy. If East follows low twice, insert the 9 from your hand. If it loses to the 10, there is only one other left for the opponents, and the ace will pick it up. If East follows low then plays the 10, win the ace and play the 9, which will knock out the queen and make your jack good. If East follows low once then discards, just win the ace and lead toward the jack.

So long as both opponents follow once, you can always guarantee three tricks in this suit by playing in this fashion.

Finally, a safety play that is kind of a hybrid between playing wide open, which you might do in a tournament, and playing safe to assure your contract whenever possible.

Suppose you find yourself in the normal contract of 3NT with these two hands:

    ♠ Q 4

    ♥ 6 5

    ♦ 5 4

    ♣ A K J 7 6 4 3

    ♠ J 8 7 6

    ♥ A J 1 0

    ♦ A K Q 6

    ♣ 5 2

When you have a long suit such as the one held by North, if you play a game contract it will almost always be 3NT. On this layout, 5♣ would be a poor spot, and even if it made, 3NT would score better.

West leads a low heart to East's king and your ace. When you play the ♣2 from your hand, West contributes the 8. If you are concerned only with making your contract, what should you play?

You have nine clubs between the two hands, so there are only four out against you. That means you could easily take seven club tricks by cashing the ace and king if the queen is a singleton or doubleton in either hand. In fact, playing the top two clubs is the percentage play. It will be successful 53 percent of the time.

Before you decide on your play, consider the clubs that the opponents hold. Between them, they have the Q1098. If West's ♠ 8 is a singleton, you should play low from the dummy. East will have to win and you will later play the ace and king to pick up his queen and 10, and you will end up with six tricks. If West has played the 8 from Q1098, the 8 will win, but East will show out, so you will have a marked finesse against the queen the next time you play diamonds.

You can compromise in this case by playing the jack. Even if it loses, you will have seen two of your opponents' four diamonds, so you will be assured of taking the rest no matter how the cards were distributed—and you will win all seven tricks whenever West is dealt the queen so long as he does not have all four clubs. A 4-0 split occurs only 9.57 percent of the time.

To Be Avoided

In notrump play, there will be times when you want to keep one of your opponents from gaining the lead. Usually, it is because you don't want to allow him to lead through some vulnerable holding in your hand or dummy. Consider this deal:

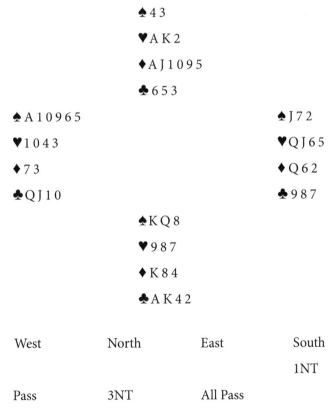

	♠ 4 3	
	♥ A K 2	
	♦ A J 1 0 9 5	
	♣ 6 5 3	
♠ A 1 0 9 6 5		♠ J 7 2
♥ 1 0 4 3		♥ Q J 6 5
♦ 7 3		♦ Q 6 2
♣ Q J 1 0		♣ 9 8 7
	♠ K Q 8	
	♥ 9 8 7	
	♦ K 8 4	
	♣ A K 4 2	

West	North	East	South
			1NT
Pass	3NT	All Pass	

West starts with the ♠6, fourth from his best suit. East plays the jack, and the declarer takes the trick with the king. Winning with the king is a standard play because it creates doubt as to the location of the queen. East should and would play the jack from the QJ, but he would not play the jack from KJ. For all he knows, South started with three spades to the queen, so playing the jack in that case would give the declarer a trick he could never get on his own. So if South wins with the queen instead of the king, West will know he started with the king and queen.

At any rate, South likes his chances, but he must be careful. The one thing he does not want to do is let East in. Do you see why?

If East gains the lead, he will fire back a spade, and South's remaining Q8 will be gobbled up by West, still holding the A 1 0 9 5 .

It's obvious that you must develop the diamond suit if you are going to take nine tricks, and looking at South's hand and the dummy in isolation, the proper play is to cash the ♦ K and play low to the jack, 10, or 9. The problem with that plan is that if East has the queen, the spade through will defeat you.

On this deal, you must practice a maneuver known as avoidance. That means, you want to avoid letting the danger hand gain the lead. In this case, the danger hand is East. So what can you do about it?

You are lucky that your diamond suit has sufficient strength that you can make sure East never gains the lead. Simply go to the dummy with a heart to the ace and play the ♦ J. If East follows low, let the jack run. You don't care if it loses to West, even to a singleton queen, because West can't hurt you. He can cash the ♠ A if he wants, but then your queen will be good.

The reason you want to run the jack without playing the ace first is that it protects you in case East has four diamonds. If you cash the ace first, you can play the 10 next, and it will win, but East will not be so accommodating as to cover, so when you play your next diamond, the king will take a low card from East, and suddenly his queen will be good even though you successfully finessed against it.

When you play the jack first and East has the queen, your jack wins, as does the 10, and after you play to the king, you can go back to the dummy with a heart and cash the ♦ A. At last, the ♦ Q falls. Whew! That was a hard-earned five tricks in diamonds, but it was worth the effort.

Even if West wins the ♦ Q, you still have four diamond tricks to go with one spade, two clubs, and two hearts for nine tricks.

Take Your Best Shot

Sometimes you will make an unusual play with the familiar goal of avoidance. Check this out:

♠ K 5 4

♥ 3

♦ A Q J 9 8 3

♣ Q J 5

♠ A 3 2

♥ K J 4

♦ 7 5 4

♣ A 9 8 4

West	North	East	South
1♥	2♦	Pass	2NT
Pass	3NT	All Pass	

West leads the ♥8 and East plays the 10. You win the ♥J and take stock of your situation.

You will rely on the diamond suit for the tricks you need to make your game, and the usual way to play the suit is to play low from your hand, inserting the queen if West plays low. West, after all, did open the bidding, and the chances are good that he has the ♦K.

If you think about it, you will realize that if West has the ♦K, there is no need to take the finesse. If West's hand looks like this

♠ Q J 10

♥ A Q 9 8 7

♦ K 6 2

♣ 7 2

You can play low to the ace and if the king doesn't fall, return to your hand with a spade and play another diamond. West will be without recourse. If he plays a low diamond, the dummy's queen will win and East will show out. Now you just play a third round of diamonds and West is in. Your ♥K remains protected.

The full deal you are guarding against looks like this:

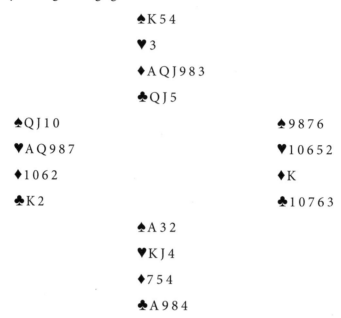

♠K 5 4

♥3

♦A Q J 9 8 3

♣Q J 5

♠Q J 10   ♠9 8 7 6

♥A Q 9 8 7   ♥10 6 5 2

♦1 0 6 2   ♦K

♣K 2   ♣10 7 6 3

♠A 3 2

♥K J 4

♦7 5 4

♣A 9 8 4

If this is the layout, finessing the ♦Q at trick two would have been a disaster. East would have scooped up his king and fired back a heart, giving his side four hearts plus the ♦K for down one.

There are other ways of keeping a particular hand off lead, and it helps to see the situation in print so you can recognize it at the table.

Suppose you need three tricks from this suit and you want to keep your left-hand opponent from gaining the lead:

♦6 5 4

♦A K 7 3

You have to hope that your right-hand opponent has three diamonds to the queen. With ample entries back and forth between your hand and the dummy, you play the 4, going up with the ace if East follows low. Return to the dummy and play another low diamond, again going up with an honor if East plays low. Now you play a low diamond from your hand and hope this was the full layout of the diamond suit:

♦6 5 4

♦J 1 0 9   ♦Q 8 2

♦A K 7 3

If East is on the ball, he may try the plot of playing the queen the first or second time you lead from the dummy. To counter that, all you have to do is play low. Now the 3-3 split will see you home, and you will get your three tricks.

Be careful, however, about cashing tricks in other suits. A really wide-awake East might make the sensational play of discarding the queen!

Quack! It's Another Duck

It's been said before, but it bears repeating: Take your time at trick one. Don't play before considering your options.

Check out this deal with your thinking cap on.

♠ 10 9 6 2

♥ 3 2

♦ A 4

♣ A K J 9 8

♠ A Q J 7

♥ K 5 4

♦ 6 5 3 2

♣ Q 4

West	North	East	South
1 ♥	Dbl	Pass	4 ♠

All Pass

Your partner's takeout double was a bit eccentric, and your jump to 4 ♠ was pretty optimistic considering that your ♥K is more or less worthless, but here you are in game. It's nowhere near the worst contract you will ever play.

West starts with the ♦K. How are you going to take ten tricks on this layout? Consider how you will play this contract before you decide on your play at trick one—and be specific.

If you play the ♦A at trick one, you will go down. East will follow with the jack, showing the 10 and probably the 9 as well. If the spade finesse loses, West will not be so friendly as to play the ♦Q or the ♥A. He will put his partner in with a diamond to play a heart through your king. If the full deal is as follows, down you go.

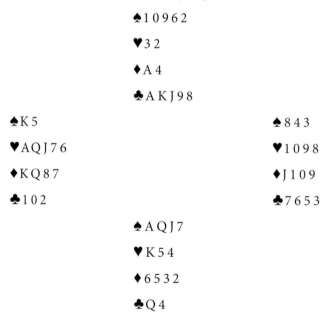

The defenders will win a diamond, two hearts, and a spade for four tricks.

Your key to making this contract is an avoidance play—to keep East off lead at all costs. You must play low on the diamond lead. If you don't make that play, the defenders will defeat you.

West might threaten the communication between your two hands by playing a club, but you can win in the dummy and take the spade finesse. West can win the ♠K, but he can do no better than play another trump. You can win, pull the other trump, cash your ♣Q and enter the dummy with a diamond to the ace to play three more rounds of clubs, discarding your hearts. Now you can ruff a heart and then ruff a diamond, giving up a heart at the end

CHAPTER 13

More Card Play Technique

In This Chapter

➤ Clues from the bidding

➤ What the opening lead tells you

➤ Assumptions in declarer play

➤ Counting: the most valuable skill

In this chapter, you will learn about the clues to success that can be found in every deal if you know how to look and what to look for. You will read about what the opening lead tells you and how to sniff out the best line of play. Sometimes you have to assume an opponent's card is placed favorably for you, and in this chapter you'll learn whether that assumption should change your line of play.

Finally, you will read about perhaps the most important technical skill—one that takes practice, practice, practice—none other than counting.

Examining the Evidence

In the course of a deal of bridge, your opponents will present you with considerable evidence, so you must be on the alert at all times to collect your clues and put them to work for you. Occasionally, you will gain information from what your opponents don't do.

It's easiest when one or both of your opponents make descriptive bids, such as announcing a two-suited hand in an auction such as one of these:

West	North	East	South
		1♥	
2NT			

West is announcing at least five cards in each minor, so right off the bat you know ten of his cards.

West	North	East	South
		1♣	
2♣			

West is using the Michaels cue-bid, which shows at least five cards in each major.

West	North	East	South
1♥	Pass	1NT	Pass
3♣			

West is announcing a very strong hand (at least 18–19 high-card points) and at least five hearts and four clubs.

West	North	East	South
			1♣
1♠	Pass	1NT	Pass
2♥	Pass	2♠	Pass
3♥			

West must have a Michaels cue-bid hand that is of medium strength, perhaps the equivalent of good but not great opening hand.

The general practice with Michaels is to use the convention with a hand of less than opening strength or with significant extra values (the user simply wants to know which suit his partner likes best so that he can make a strong invitation to game or an actual game bid). Intermediate hands go more slowly: higher-ranked suit first, then second suit if appropriate.

This kind of bidding provides you with a lot of information that you can use as a defender or, should your side prevail in the auction, as the declarer.

Long but Weak

Another good source of information is an opponent's weak preemptive opening bid, anything from a weak 2♦ to four of a major or five of a minor.

Bridge Basics

If you think bidding to a high level in one fell swoop shows a lot of high-card points, it's time for a reality check. In general, preemptive bids are made on hands that are weak, not strong. Even a bid of 5 ♣ or 5 ♦ does not show a strong hand. Those bids show a long suit (usually at least eight cards in the suit) without much strength outside the suit and are intended to disrupt communication between the two opponents. With a strong hand and a long suit, you take it slow. Remember, when you blast away in the bidding, you are also taking bidding space away from your partner.

If you end up as the declarer after an opponent has opened at the three level, say 3 ♣ and you have to find a queen in another suit to make your contract, you have a good basis for playing the partner of the preemptor for that missing card.

Note that even opening bids of 4 ♥ or 4 ♠ do not show powerhouse hands. They, too, are preemptive. Here's an example:

> ♠ A K Q J 10 7 6 4
>
> ♥ A
>
> ♦ A Q 3
>
> ♣ 4

This hand is much too strong for an opening bid of 4 ♠. Look at all those tricks, for Pete's sake! There are eight spades, one heart, at least one diamond trick. Just think how you would feel if you opened 4 ♠ and your partner put down this hand:

> ♠ 2
>
> ♥ 6 5 4 3 2
>
> ♦ K 6 4
>
> ♣ 8 4 3 2

If you opened 4 ♠, usually promising about seven and a half tricks, your partner would never make a move with that collection. You should open that hand 2 ♣, strong, artificial, and forcing—your big bid. You plan to rebid 3 ♠ to show that you have enough or nearly enough for game in your own hand and a self-sufficient suit that is most definitely going to be the trump suit. Your partner is invited to bid any ace, king, or singleton he might have and to raise to 4 ♠ with none of the above.

This is what a 4♠ opener should look like:

♠ K Q J 1 0 7 6 4 3

♥ 6 5

♦ K 4

♣ 4

You have seven spade tricks after you knock out the ace, and you will take a trick with the ♦ K half the time. You don't expect to make your bid unless your partner can put down a useful value or two. Your main purpose with your jump to 4♠ is to take bidding space from your opponents.

Available Spaces

Okay, the lecture about preemptive bidding is over. Back to the idea that such bids can help you out a lot in the play. Observe:

♠ A J 6 4

♥ K Q J 2

♦ A 7 6

♣ 4 3

♠ 5 2

♥ A 1 0 9 8 7

♦ K J 1 0 9

♣ 7 5

West	North	East	South
3♣	Dbl	Pass	4♥
All Pass			

A word about the bidding: You, South, have only 8 high-card points, but they figure to be working opposite your partner's takeout double, and you can't afford to bid only 3♥, which you would do with a much weaker hand. The preemptive bid by your left-hand opponent put you under pressure, so you chose an aggressive action rather than the conservative path. Remember, your partner was also under some pressure. He might not have the ideal shape or lots of high cards, but he felt he was going to have only one shot at this. The dilemma under discussion is why people preempt.

Bridge Lingo

There is a principle in bridge regarding what is known as vacant spaces. The idea is that when one opponent shows up with a long suit, his partner is known to be short in that suit and therefore has more room in his hand—the vacant spaces—for other cards, including, perhaps, one you are trying to find to make your contract. There is some validity to that idea but it does not provide guarantees. It's a guideline more than a rule, and there are usually other clues you can sniff out to help you find your way.

Anyway, West leads the ♣K, you play low from the dummy and East overtakes with the ace. When the ♣10 is returned, you play low and West wins. West has now seen all the clubs in the deck, so he won't be so accommodating as to continue the suit and allow you to ruff in the dummy and discard a spade. Instead, West exits passively with a trump. You win in the dummy, play a heart to your hand, finding that trumps were 2-2.

You now know nine of West's cards: seven clubs and two hearts. You will have to lose a spade no matter what you do, so you play low from your hand and low from the dummy when West follows with the 7. East also contributes a low card. When West continues with a spade, you go up with the ace and ruff a spade, West following with the queen.

Your contract is now assured. Can you see it?

Thanks to the preemptive bid and the research you were able to conduct, you now know twelve of West's cards: seven clubs, three spades, and two hearts. All you have to do is play a diamond to the dummy's ace. If West follows low, you know he has just played his only diamond. You can take the diamond finesse with certainty.

♠ A J 6 4

♥ K Q J 2

♦ A 7 6

♣ 8 3

♠ Q 8 7   ♠ K 1 0 9 3

♥ 6 5   ♥ 4 3

♦ 2   ♦ Q 8 5 4 3

♣ K Q J 7 6 5 4   ♣ A 1 0

♠ 5 2

♥ A 1 0 9 8 7

♦ K J 1 0 9

♣ 9 2

It is true that after West opened 3 ♣, you would naturally be inclined to play his partner for the missing ♦ Q, but if you played East for that card without doing some detective work, West might have shown up with this hand:

♠ Q 8

♥ 6

♦ Q 8 5 3

♣ K Q J 7 6 5

Lots of players in today's world of aggressive bidding would start with 3 ♣ on that hand, especially at favorable vulnerability. With careful play, you might be able to determine that West had four diamonds, in which case the odds would favor playing him for the queen.

Got the Goods—or Not

An opponent's simple overcall also paints a picture of his hand, although not as clearly as some bids might. If, however, you are playing against experienced or even semi-experienced opponents and one of them overcalls at the two level when vulnerable, you can count on that person for the equivalent of at least a good opening hand.

On the other hand, some things the opponents don't say can also help you in the play. For example, if you open the bidding with 1 ♣ and your left-hand opponent passes but later shows up with five hearts to the K Q 1 0 , you can play his partner for just about all the rest of the high-card points.

If an opponent passes his partner's opening bid and later shows up with an ace or king, it's almost certain that the rest of his hand is barren, with at most another jack.

When an opponent opens 1NT, it usually shows a narrow range of high-card points: 12–14, 13–15, or 15–17, to name three. Even the 10–12 so-called mini-1NT, which you might encounter in a tournament, provides useful information.

The fact that you can find clues to the right plays—as declarer and as defender—means you must listen to the auction and pay attention to what goes on at the table.

It may seem like stating the obvious, but you have to train yourself to watch the cards. Even experienced players sometimes function on autopilot, barely paying attention. There is nothing more annoying than realizing you need to know what card was just played—this is especially true with non-face cards—but you can't remember because you never saw it.

Lefty Attacks

You know by now that when you are the declarer, it is your left-hand opponent's duty to make the opening lead. The card he selects—or doesn't select—can tell you a lot about his hand.

Consider this scenario (neither side vulnerable):

♠ 8 6 5 2

♥ 6 5

♦ A 7 6 4

♣ K J 2

♠ A K Q 7

♥ J 7 3

♦ K 10 3 2

♣ 7 4

West	North	East	South
			1♦
1♥	Dbl	2♥	2♠
3♥	Pass	Pass	3♠
All Pass			

This is a typical auction you might see at a tournament. You don't like being pushed around, but the bidding indicates there's a chance your partner has a singleton heart, which means you can use some of your partner's trumps to ruff hearts.

West surprises you by starting with the ♠10. What does that tell you about West's hand? East's hand?

First, West does not have the ♥AK. With that holding, he would have led the ace (or the king if he has not adopted the modern approach). Could he have the ♥KQ? Not likely. With that holding, he would be equally likely to start with a heart (the king) as he would with the AK.

So what does that leave? Most likely, West has the ♥AQ and does not want to lead from that holding in case you have the king. Just because East raised to 2♥ does not mean he has the king, so West reasonably shies away from starting with that suit.

You win the spade in hand and assess your chances.

You will have to lose two hearts no matter what you do, and the odds are against your avoiding a diamond loser. That's three losers already. You can afford only one more, which brings the club suit into focus.

Obviously, you must play the club suit for one loser. You pull trumps, noting that they break 3-2, West holding three to the ten. You play three rounds of diamonds, West showing up with a doubleton queen. East wins the third round of diamonds with the jack and plays the ♥K—making sure West knows where that card is—and continues with the ♥10 to your jack and West's queen. Now the ♥A forces you to ruff, and you are glad you have the ♦10 to get back to your hand for a play in clubs.

You lead a low club from your hand and West plays low. Now what? Do you play West for the ace and go up with the dummy's king, or do you play West for the queen and put in the dummy's jack?

Consider what you know about West's hand. Your assessment about the layout of your opponents' hearts was accurate—West holding the AQ and East the king. Now consider the bidding. West overcalled and bid again over your 2♠. With which of the following two hands do you think West would bid 3♥?

Hand 1	Hand 2
♠1 0 9 3	♠1 0 9 3
♥A Q 9 8 4	♥A Q 9 8 4
♦Q 5	♦Q 5
♣A 6 5	♣Q 6 5

Bidding 3♥ with Hand 1 is a bit of a stretch, but at least the hand has two aces. Bidding 3♥ with Hand 2 would be asking for big trouble. Only a truly inexperienced player would consider bidding. No experienced player would bid with either hand if his side were vulnerable.

Clearly, the right play is to play the dummy's ♣K, which wins when this is the full deal:

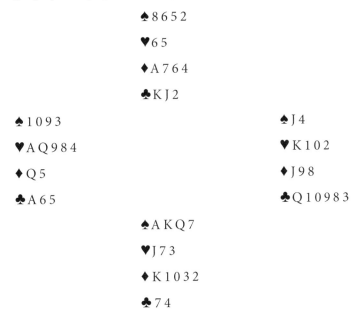

```
                    ♠ 8 6 5 2
                    ♥ 6 5
                    ♦ A 7 6 4
                    ♣ K J 2

  ♠ 1 0 9 3                       ♠ J 4
  ♥ A Q 9 8 4                     ♥ K 1 0 2
  ♦ Q 5                           ♦ J 9 8
  ♣ A 6 5                         ♣ Q 1 0 9 8 3

                    ♠ A K Q 7
                    ♥ J 7 3
                    ♦ K 1 0 3 2
                    ♣ 7 4
```

The fact that you could work out that West held the ♥A Q did not materially affect the play that ultimately decided whether you made your contract or went down. It's a good exercise, though, because it helps get into the habit of picking up on these clues—points that help you read your opponents' cards. Any information you scoop up will help you, and practicing this process will eventually make it second nature. It does get easier with practice.

There are other ways to put information to work for you.

♠ K 7 4 3

♥ A 10 6

♦ J 10

♣ A Q 9 6

♠ A 8 5 2

♥ K J 2

♦ 4 3

♣ J 10 5 4

West	North	East	South
1♦	Dbl	Pass	2♠
Pass	4♠	All Pass	

Your 2♠ bid is a bit aggressive, but 1♠ does not do the hand justice. You might bid 1♠ on 0 high-card points, but you have 9. Most players agree that in responding to a takeout double, one jumps with 9–11 support points.

West starts with the ♦A. Dummy plays the 10, East plays the 2, a discouraging signal (more on signaling in Chapter 15). West continues with the king and exits with the ♠J. You play the king in the dummy and then a low spade, on which East plays the queen. You win with the ace and, with no other choice, the ♣J. West covers with the king and you win the ace. When you play the ♣Q and another club to your 10, you find that West started with three clubs.

It appears that West has a balanced hand with three spades, three clubs, three or four, perhaps even five, diamonds, leaving him two or three hearts. Obviously, the key to this deal is finding the ♥Q.

Here are the facts: West almost certainly started with the ♠J109. By inference, he has the ♦AKQ. How do you know this? If East had the ♦Q, he would have signaled encouragement on the lead of the ♦A, which promises the king. West has also shown up with the ♣K, so he cannot have the ♥Q.

How do you know this? Count the high-card points he has shown up with: 1 for the ♠J, 9 for the ♦AKQ and 3 for the ♣K. That's 13. If he had the ♥Q as well, that would be 15, and West has a balanced hand. With a balanced 15 high-card points, he would have opened 1NT, not

1♦. So you confidently play a heart to the dummy's ace and another one to the jack in your hand. When the jack wins—you knew it would—you can claim. This was the full deal:

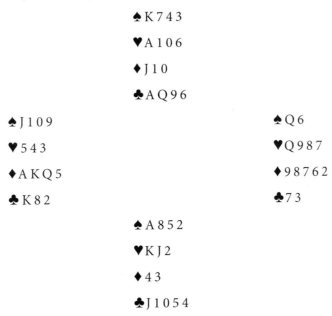

♠K 7 4 3
♥A 1 0 6
♦J 1 0
♣A Q 9 6

♠J 1 0 9
♥5 4 3
♦A K Q 5
♣K 8 2

♠Q 6
♥Q 9 8 7
♦9 8 7 6 2
♣7 3

♠A 8 5 2
♥K J 2
♦4 3
♣J 1 0 5 4

Lead Conventions

When it comes to selecting your opening lead, the first thing you look for is a sequence. No matter whether the contract is notrump or in a suit, you hope to have been dealt a nice robust sequence such as the following:

A K Q

K Q J

Q J 10

J 10 9

10 9 8

It's better, of course, if you have more than three cards in the suit, especially when you are leading against a notrump contract. You want to start developing a suit that will eventually— you hope—take the setting trick or tricks against your opponents' contract.

Of course, the stronger your sequence the better you like it. Following are some holdings with various combinations. The card in bold is the one you would lead. It makes a difference, by the way, whether the contract is in a suit or in notrump. The *x* is used to indicate an insignificant low card. Suits, of course, can be longer than the five depicted in the examples.

Here are some holding combinations for contracts in notrump (any of these could be any suit):

➤ A Q J 10 x

➤ A J 10 9 x

➤ A 10 9 x x

➤ **K Q J** x x

➤ K Q **10** 9 x (see note below)

➤ K J 10 9 x

➤ K 10 9 8 x

➤ **Q J 10** x x

➤ Q **10** 9 8 x

➤ **J 10** 9 x x

➤ **10** 9 8 x x

Regarding the K Q 10 9 x , leading the queen is a special lead that tells your partner to play the jack if he has it, and, if not your partner should give a count signal (more on that in Chapter 15). Of course, your partner can also play the ace, as he must do in a situation such as this:

♥6 5 4

♥K Q 10 9 3   ♥A 2

♥J 8 7

Can you see what would happen if East played low on the ♥Q? That's right, the next heart would go to the bare ace. If West didn't have a way to get in, the defenders would take only two heart tricks when they should have taken five.

You want your partner to play the jack on those situations because you want to guard against

Bridge Lingo

As the declarer, when your left-hand opponent leads the king and you have the AJ in that suit with at least one other card, you can play low, hoping to entice your left-hand opponent to lead from the queen into your AJ. This play—called the Bath Coup—dates from the days of whist and is believed to have been named for the English town of Bath.

having the declarer duck with the AJx, fooling you into leading into his tenace. Signals can help in some situations, but they can be hard to read. Say you lead the king from KQ109 and your partner is holding the J32. If you are not using the special conventional lead, your partner has to try to encourage with the 3, which may be hard to read. Equally, if your partner is dealt the 987, he will try to discourage by playing the 7, but that sometimes looks like a high card—a come-on signal. It's a lot easier if you just agree to lead the queen when you have that strong holding with your partner playing the jack if he has it.

Note the lead of the queen from a holding of AQJ10x. This is legitimate against notrump because although you may give up a trick to a king on your right, you establish tricks in the suit almost immediately, and if you can get in later, you can cash those tricks. You would never consider this lead against a suit contract because you might end up taking no tricks. In general, you would shy away from leading a suit headed by the AQ against a suit contract unless there were strong indications from the bidding that you should do so.

Here are some holding combinations for suit contracts:

The combinations headed by aces are left off because it is generally poor strategy to lead an unsupported ace (no king) against a suit contract. There are many exceptions, but in general you won't lead from a suit headed by an unsupported ace.

> ➤ A K x x (see note below)

> ➤ **K Q J** x x

> ➤ **K Q** x x

> ➤ **K J** 10 9 x

> ➤ K **10** 9 8 x

> ➤ **Q J** 10 x x

> ➤ Q 10 9 8 x

> ➤ J 10 9 x x

> ➤ 10 9 8 x x

The card you lead from AKxx (or longer) depends on your agreement.

Note that against suit contracts, you don't want your partner throwing his jacks under your kings and queens. That could easily cost a trick. Whereas against notrump, your lead of a king will generally include at least the 10 to go with the queen, but it is not unusual for the opening leader to select a suit such as KQ32. The queen is not led because it's not standard—and you are less interested in where the jack is. Your partner will do his best to show encouragement if he has the jack.

There are some other rules about sequence leads that you should know. These holdings show the minimum strength of a suit when you lead a high honor:

➤ K Q 10 x x

➤ K Q 9 8 x (in a pinch because of the 9 and 8)

➤ Q J 9 x x

➤ J 10 8 x x

➤ 10 9 7 x x

You may have noticed that for the most part the top two cards are backed up by a card only one removed from the next card in the sequence. For example, instead of the ideal QJ10, you have QJ9. Read on for what to lead when your sequence does not have proper backing.

Well Spotted

This review of the standard leads against notrump and suits is meant to help you understand what is going on. For example, if you get the lead of the ♠Q against your 4♥ contract, you can mentally place the ♠K in the other opponent's hand.

If the opening lead against your suit contract is an ace, you can generally also figure that the opening leader has the king—if you are playing in reasonable company, that is. Experienced players do not lead aces unless they have the king to go with them.

All this discussion about leading honors—and, remember, the 10 is considered an honor—may leave you wondering what to make of the opening lead if it's not a high card.

Well, this is where you get the rest of the story.

When you don't have a sequence to lead, your best option is usually, to quote an old bridge maxim, "fourth from your longest and strongest suit." Fourth best is the standard lead against suit and notrump contracts.

Sequences have been discussed, and you have seen some examples of strong sequences to lead from. What if your sequence doesn't quite measure up? That's when fourth best comes into play.

From QJ654, lead the 5—fourth best. From KQ87, lead the 7. From A10632 (against notrump), lead the 3. The reasoning is pretty logical: you need some help from your partner if you are to take tricks in this suit. If your partner does have that help, chances are it will be in a holding with fewer cards than you have. Leading a high one can cause the suit to block or worse, crash your high cards into your partner's, promoting winners for the declarer in that suit. Here's an example of what can happen:

♦ 6 5 3

♦ K Q 7 4 2   ♦ J 8

♦ A 10 9

If you lead the king and your partner plays low, the declarer can duck. Now if you continue with a low diamond, the declarer ducks again when your partner plays the jack. He has no more diamonds to lead, so the suit is not established. You may never take another trick in the suit. It would not be impossible for your partner to figure you for a stronger suit than you have, in which case it would be right for him to play the jack. Now a grateful declarer can win the ace because his 109 remains as a second stopper against your queen.

Now check out what happens if you lead low originally. Your partner plays the jack, and if you have a quick entry, it won't matter when the declarer takes his ace—first, second, or third trick—you will end up taking four tricks in the suit.

Bridge Facts

Although agreeing to lead fourth best from a suit not headed by a sequence doesn't sound like a convention—the word *convention* makes you think of Blackwood or Stayman—it does indeed fit the definition. In fact, leading fourth best is the oldest convention in bridge, dating back to the 1700s for card games that preceded bridge.

Why fourth best? The best answer is the Rule of Eleven.

Sounds like mumbo jumbo, you are thinking. Maybe, but the Rule of Eleven is one of the most useful tools in your arsenal—when you are the declarer and when you are defending.

Here's how it works:

When your partner leads a spot card—as distinguished from an honor, or face card—you can take the number of the spot (the 7, say) and subtract it from 11. The sum will tell you how many cards higher than the one led that you will find in the other three hands. Inasmuch as you can see your own hand and the dummy, you will often be able to figure out the declarer's exact holding in the suit.

Check it out:

North

♦10 9 2

East

♦K 8

West leads the ♦6 and the declarer plays the 10 from the dummy. Using the Rule of Eleven, what do you know about the layout of the diamond suit?

Subtracting your partner's spot card—the 6—from 11, we get five. That means there are five cards higher than the 6 in the other three hands. You can see four of them—the dummy's 10 and 9 and your king and 8—so the declarer has only one card higher than the six. It can be the ace, queen, or jack. If it's the ace, the declarer will probably duck when you play the king. It won't matter, of course, if this is the layout:

♦10 9 2

♦Q J 7 6 5   ♦K 8

♦A 4 3

When you play back the ♦8, if the declarer plays low, West overtakes with the jack and clears the suit.

If the declarer's card is the queen, that means your partner has led from the AJ and you are going to take three or five tricks in the suit. Your king will win and you will play your other diamond through the declarer's Qxx or Qxxx. If the declarer has three to the queen, your partner has led from five to the AJ. If the declarer has four to the queen, you will be limited to three tricks because of the dummy's 10 and 9.

If the declarer started with the jack, your king will win and you will send a diamond through to your partner's ace and queen.

Consider how things would have gone had your partner led the ♦Q, which he might have been tempted to do before he read this book. You are in a real mess now. If you play the king, the dummy's 109 will be a stopper in the suit (the declarer will gladly take two honors with the ace). If you play low, the suit will be blocked. When that happens, frustration sets in. You might not even know what happened, but you will know something went wrong. It's better to see ahead of time what could happen so you can prevent it and pass the frustration to the declarer, the victim of your expert defense.

The following is a classic example of the Rule of Eleven at work.

Dummy

♣K 4 3

East

♣A 1 0 9 2

West leads the ♣7. The declarer plays low from the dummy. What is your play? Did you apply the Rule of Eleven? If so, you can surprise your partner—and perhaps the declarer, too. Subtract 7 from 11 and you get 4—and you can see all four cards between the dummy and your hand: the king to your right and the A109 in your hand. You play low and your partner is soon putting the ♣Q on the table. The full layout:

♣K 4 3

♣Q J 8 7   ♣A 1 0 9 2

♣6 5

The Rule of Eleven can be observed and used by the declarer as well as by the defenders. The declarer can often take advantage of that knowledge to make an expert play—even if he's not an expert.

Need to Know

Many plays that might seem the sole province of experts can be made by mere mortals—if they only recognize them when they come up at the table. You don't have to be a world champion, for example, to execute a Bath Coup, the tricky play described earlier in this chapter. You don't have to be a professional to use the Rule of Eleven and make deductions from what someone led or didn't lead. If you study the game and pay attention, keeping a clear head at all times, you can do well. If you play the right cards, it doesn't matter how good your opponents are, you will prevail. Remember, even the experts can't turn your aces into deuces!

Check out this fine play that you would make only if you were thinking about what's going on at the table.

♥A 3

♥1 0 9 6 2

West, who overcalled 1♥, leads the ♥5 against your notrump contract. Stopping to take stock, you apply the Rule of Eleven. That tells you East has two cards higher than the 5 (11–5 = 6, and you have three higher, dummy has one). What do you think West has led from? Probably not KQJ—he would surely have led the king. How about QJxxx? Possible. KJxxx? Also possible. In either case, that means East has a doubleton honor. Do you see where this is heading?

Suppose you have to knock out an ace to make your contract and you are sure, because of his overcall, that West has that ace. If you play low from the dummy, East will win his king or queen and return the suit. When West gets in, he will have two high honors to pick up your 10 and 9 and cash his last heart for the setting trick.

It's a different story if you play the ace at trick one because this might well be the complete layout of the suit:

♥A 3

♥K J 8 5 4   ♥Q 7

♥10 9 6 2

If you play the ace and East plays low, when West gets in, if he cashes the ♥K, he will be dropping his partner's queen, giving you a stopper in hearts with your remaining 109. If East unblocks the queen and somehow gets in, he can play a heart through your hand, but West will not be able to take more than another two heart tricks. You play the 10 and West can win with the jack and cash the king, but you will still have the 9 left, and it will be good.

That's a nifty play, isn't it? And you thought only the big shots could do so well. All it took was using the tools at your disposal and applying some logic to the situation.

On Your Mark, Get Set ... Count!

Successful bridge play has many components. You must learn to bid accurately and hone your judgment for competitive situations. Getting to the right contract is not enough, however. You must also develop your skill in card play.

One of the key attributes of a skillful declarer is the ability to count—tricks and high-card points. Expert counting and application of its adjuncts will carry you far.

You have seen how counting can be critical when you are searching for a missing queen—and you saw how your counting task was made easier by your opponents' bidding, especially when one of them showed a long suit.

Here's an elementary exercise in counting:

♠ A Q 10 9

♥ J 6 4

♦ K 2

♣ Q 8 4 3

♠ J 7 6 4 3

♥ Q 9 2

♦ A Q J 5

♣ A

West	North	East	South
Pass	1♣	Pass	1♠
Pass	2♠	Pass	4♠
All Pass			

West starts with the ♥A, continuing with the ♥K as East plays the 10 and 5. West plays the ♥3, which East ruffs. You had the ♥2, so you know West's 3 is the lowest heart he had, indicating he wants East to return a club after he ruffs. The only reason he would want a club back is that he has the king and hopes to get in with it later.

Need to Know

In situations where you know you are giving your partner a ruff, you can send a message with the card that you play. In the parlance of bridge, it's called a suit-preference signal. So if the contract is spades and you are giving your partner a ruff, you can let him ruff a low card to say return a club—or a high card to say return a diamond. There are normally only two suits involved because the trump suit is not usually considered and it's obvious that if your partner is ruffing a suit, he can't return that one. You must learn this play and apply it in the appropriate situations.

You win the ♣A and consider your prospects. You have no losing diamonds and no losing clubs, so you turn your attention to the trump suit. You have already lost three tricks, so you must play the spade suit for no losers.

In isolation, the correct way to play trumps is to lead the jack or a low card from your hand and finesse against the king. In this case, however, you know the finesse cannot succeed. How? By counting, that's how.

Just the Facts

Consider what you know so far: West, who passed as dealer, has played the ♥A and ♥K and then requested a club return when he gave his partner a heart ruff. That means he is very likely to have the ♣K. By inference, you place him with an ace and two kings—10 high-card points. If he also held the ♠K, that would give him 13 high-card points. Would he have passed with that hand? Highly doubtful.

Your only chance, therefore, is to hope the full deal is as follows:

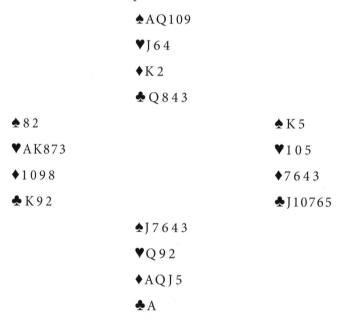

You will play a low spade from your hand and call for the ace, dropping East's now-singleton king. You were able to make that excellent play because you were counting.

There's another way to apply your counting skills that can be seen in changing the deal in question just a bit:

♠ A Q 10 9

♥ J 6

♦ J 7 6

♣ A Q 8 4

♠ J 7 6 4 3

♥ A K Q

♦ Q 4 3

♣ 5 3

West	North	East	South
Pass	1♣	Pass	1♠
Pass	2♠	Pass	4♠
All Pass			

Same auction, but this time West starts with two high diamonds, and noting his partner's high low (the 10 followed by the 5), he continues with the 6, which East ruffs. East exits with a heart, which you win.

Time to take stock. You now have two suits to consider: spades and clubs. Your line of play is marked by a principle called assumption.

You cannot make the contract unless West has the ♣K, allowing you to take a successful finesse against him and avoid a club loser. Therefore, you must assume West has that card.

Again, West has shown up with the ♦A and ♦K, and you are assuming he has the ♣K. That's 10 high-card points already accounted for. On that basis, West cannot also have the ♠K would have opened the bidding. You take your only chance by playing low to the dummy's ♠A. You will be rewarded if this was the full deal:

♠ A Q 10 9
♥ J 6
♦ J 8 7
♣ A Q 8 4

♠ 8 2
♥ 10 9 8
♦ A K 9 6 2
♣ K 9 2

♠ K 5
♥ 7 5 4 3 2
♦ 10 5
♣ J 10 7 6

♠ J 7 6 4 3
♥ A K Q
♦ Q 4 3
♣ 5 3

You gave yourself the only chance there was to make the contract. You were lucky, of course—the black kings might have been switched. If that were the layout, you would never have had a chance.

As you progress in your bridge game, you will notice that players who work hard to improve their card play technique are consistently "luckier" than most.

CHAPTER 14

On the Defense: Part 1

> ### In This Chapter
>
> ➤ Opening lead objectives
>
> ➤ Third-hand play
>
> ➤ Ducks are for defenders, too
>
> ➤ Listening to the bidding

In this chapter, you will learn about opening lead strategies—when to be active, when to go passive. You will find out your best strategy when it's your partner's lead. You will also learn that the ducking move—deciding not to win a trick when you could have—can be used by defenders as well as by the declarer. Every deal provides clues to the best—or least worst— opening leads, but you must pay attention and learn to accurately process the information.

Going for the Kill

As has been pointed out, the fact that a defender gets to make the opening shot against the declarer's contract can mean an advantage—if the lead is effective. There are few sure bets, but there are certain principles that can help you with your decision.

It does not hurt, of course, to have some help from your partner. Here are some road signs you can look for to help you find the killing opening lead. Ask yourself:

> ➤ Did your partner open the bidding? If so, a lead of his suit stands a decent chance of hitting the mark. Take care, however. A player would open 1♥ every time on the following hand:

♠Q 3

♥J 7 6 5 4

♦A K J

♣Q 10 9

If you lead the ♥A from A98 against, say, 4♠ and find your partner with the queen and four low cards, you probably have blown at least one trick. The conventional wisdom about leading unsupported aces against suit contracts—don't do it—applies even when your partner has opened the bidding in that suit. It's a different matter if you hold a doubleton ace in your partner's suit. You can lead the ace and continue the suit. Even if you blow a trick, your partner might have an early trump entry and be able to give you a ruff.

➤ Did your partner overcall? This is different from your partner's opening the bidding. Whereas an opening bid in a suit may be made on five cards to the 6, when your partner overcalls, it's almost always on a suit with some substance. Do not take that as a guarantee that leading your unsupported ace will work out, but it has a better chance.

It is worth noting that an astute player will be able to figure out what you have if your partner overcalls and you decline to lead his suit. Your partner will also know that the most likely reason you didn't lead his suit is because you have the ace. This is especially true if you raised your partner's overcall. You will, of course, lead your partner's suit if you have a holding such as the AK.

➤ Did your partner double an artificial bid? There are many opportunities for you and your partner to help each other with opening leads. If your right-hand opponent opens 1NT and lefty bids 2♣, Stayman, your partner can double to show a substantial holding in that suit—a lead-directing double. He doesn't necessarily have length in the suit, but your partner wants you to know that a club lead against the final contract could be a winner for your side.

The same can be applied to other artificial bids, such as transfers over 1NT and 2NT openings and other conventions such as splinter bids (unusual jumps to show good support for your partner's suit and shortness in the "jump" suit).

➤ Did your partner decline to double an artificial bid? Your partner's failure to double Stayman or a transfer or other artificial bid can help you eliminate the bid suit as a lead possibility, especially if your holding in that suit is tenuous—♦KJ43, for example. You would be delighted to lead that suit should your partner double a transfer bid of 2♦ (showing hearts), but you could easily blow a trick with that lead if your partner has a poor diamond holding.

The Sequence

Your job as opening leader is made easier, of course, when you have a strong suit with which to attack. Even a sequence such as J1098 is attractive because it won't blow a trick—and it's descriptive. Your partner will almost certainly know what you have led from—he will mostly likely see clues in his own hand or the dummy's, and the declarer's play may provide the answer. If your partner has a poor holding in that suit, he won't waste time and concede tempo to the declarer by continuing the suit when he gets in.

A suit headed by the AK will always be an attractive lead because whichever of the top cards you lead will likely hold up, giving you a chance to get a look at the dummy. It may be obvious that you should switch to another suit—as when the dummy has a guarded queen in the suit you led—and your partner may be able to help you.

In many cases, getting a look at the dummy is only modestly helpful. There are times, however, when your partner can play a major role in leading you to the killing defense.

When you start with an ace or king as the opening lead against a suit contract and the dummy hits with a singleton in the suit you have led, your partner can help you decide which suit you should switch to. In most cases, with the dummy now void in that suit, you will not play it again because the declarer can ruff and you might need to attack some other suit right away. Here's an example:

Dummy

♠ 2

♥ K Q 10 9 3 2

♦ K 7 2

♣ K 6 5

West

♠ A K 6 5

♥ 5 4

♦ J 6 3

♣ J 1 0 9 7

You lead the ♠A (ace from AK) against 4♥ by South, who opened 1♥. You can see that there is no chance you will be able to take another spade trick, and there's no chance of promoting a trump trick for your partner, who cannot possibly be out of spades because that would mean South started with seven spades but opened 1♥ anyway.

So now what?

Bridge Basics

When you lead a high card—one that is winning the trick—and the dummy has a singleton in the suit you led, your partner can give you a suit preference signal if that is your agreement about continuations. There will be times, however, when your partner simply wants you to continue the suit, as when the declarer is in six and the dummy has AKQ alone in trumps. If your partner has three trumps to the jack, he wants you to make the dummy ruff so as to promote the setting trick. This is an area of defense that you should discuss at length with your partner.

Well, you haven't seen your partner's card yet, and in this case you can expect that the spade he follows with will be meaningful. Your partner is aware that you desperately want to know which minor to switch to if, indeed, it makes a difference.

If your partner has a clear preference, he will tell you about it when he follows to trick one. Suppose your partner plays the 10, the declarer following with the 9. What does that mean to you?

If you and your partner are in tune, he is telling you to switch to a diamond, the higher ranking of the two relevant suits (spades and trumps are not in the discussion). If your partner had preferred a club, he would have followed with a low spade. If your partner had no preference, you might see the 6 or 7.

Need to Know

In this book and others, spot cards are often referred to a high or low. The relative "size" of a card is easy to see if it's a 2 or a 3, but sometimes even a 7 can be low in context. For example, if you can see most or all of the higher spot cards, when your partner plays the 7 you will know that it is his lowest card in the suit. That could have relevance for what you do next or how you plan the defense. Similarly, if your partner plays a 4, that might be the highest spot card he can afford. You must always consider all cards played—by your partner and your opponents—in context. That means you must be looking at all times. Failing to pay attention often has a high cost.

Now what? Switching to a diamond seems obvious, but which diamond? In this case, you must switch to the jack, hoping that the full deal is as follows:

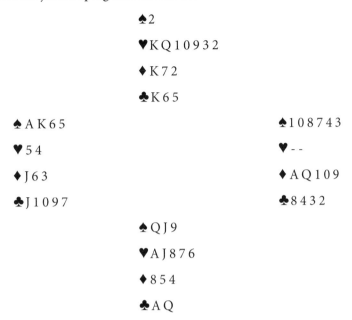

♠2
♥KQ10932
♦K72
♣K65

♠AK65
♥54
♦J63
♣J1097

♠108743
♥--
♦AQ109
♣8432

♠QJ9
♥AJ876
♦854
♣AQ

Do you see what happens if you play a low diamond at trick two? The declarer will simply play low. Your partner can win with the queen, 10, or 9, but two diamond tricks will be the limit for the defense. The dummy's king will be good if East cashes the ace; and if East exits with a club, the declarer will win, pull trumps, cash the other club in his hand, then go to the dummy with a trump to discard one of his losing diamonds on the ♣K. The declarer will lose a spade and two diamonds.

If you play the ♦J, the declarer has no chance. Whatever he does at trick two, you will collect three diamond tricks to go with the high spade you won at the first trick. Instead of recording a minus score, you will have a plus for your astute defense.

Your decision about what you are trying to do on opening lead often depends on what you know from listening to the auction.

Objectives Clarified

In theory, you are trying to make the opening lead that will result in the failure of the contract. An aggressive style in the bidding often carries over to aggressive tendencies as a defender. Many players make it a policy to always lead from something, meaning they don't make leads from a collection of low cards (non-honors). In essence, they are taking a chance that their partner has some strength in the suit. For example, the lead of the 2 from a KJ32 is a lead from something, whereas the lead of the 8 from 8654 is a lead from nothing.

The aggressive lead hits the jackpot when the partner has the ace and the declarer the queen. You might get three tricks and a ruff for your partner. The lead loses out, however, when the declarer has the AQ in his hand or the ace and queen in separate hands, either way. Leading the 2 into the AQ is obviously a loser, but the declarer can play low and win his queen if the ace is in the dummy—or the declarer can play the dummy's queen if the two cards are reversed between the two hands.

Your hand will often tell you whether to be active or passive with your opening lead. Here's an example:

♠ K J 5 4

♥ 1 0 9 6

♦ Q 6 5

♣ A J 1 0

As West, you hear this auction:

West	North	East	South
			2NT
Pass	3NT	All Pass	

What is your lead?

The books tell you to lead fourth best from your longest and strongest suit—in this case, a spade—but now is not the time to depend on maxims.

Consider the auction. South promises 20–21 high-card points for his 2NT opener. North probably has about 6 high-card points. That's 26. You have 11 high-card points, accounting for 37 of the 40 points in the deck. How much help do you think your partner is going to provide? He might have only 2 high-card points.

You can lead a spade and hope that it doesn't blow a trick even if your partner has no help in that suit. A famous football coach once said that he didn't like passing the football because "when your quarterback passes, three things can happen—and two of them are bad." He was referring to the pass being incomplete or intercepted.

When you select an aggressive opening lead, three things can happen:

1. Your partner provides just the card you were looking for.

2. You don't blow a trick but you lose a tempo.

3. You blow a trick and hand the declarer a game he couldn't make any other way.

You must consider all of these before putting your opening lead on the table. With the hand in question and the auction as presented, your best choice is probably the ♥10, which is unlikely to surrender a trick.

You will apologize to your partner if he was sitting there with the ♠Q. Chances are he wasn't. One of the top players of all time once had this admonition for his partner, "Don't play me for specific cards because I won't have them." Wise words to play bridge by.

Another time to go passive—and this one is probably more urgent than in the previous discussion—is when your opponents have had a tortured, tentative auction before landing in game, perhaps bidding it this way:

West	North	East	South
			1♦
Pass	1♥	Pass	1♠
Pass	2♦	Pass	2♥
Pass	3♥	ass	4♥
All Pass			

North-South clearly have nothing in reserve, and they may well be in a very shaky contract. The last thing you want to do in this case is to be aggressive with your opening lead. One blown trick could mean handing them a game they couldn't make on their own. Be very careful in these situations.

Swing for the Fences

There are times, of course, when the auction will tell you that it's now or never—a passive lead won't do. Here's an example:

West	North	East	South
	3♣	Pass	3NT
All Pass			

In most auctions like this, South has bid 3NT because he has a fit with North in North's long suit. That means that when South gets in, there's an excellent chance he's about to rip off seven tricks in clubs to go with a couple of other tricks. If you have your own suit to lead, perhaps KQJ109 in some suit with a potential entry, go for it. If you don't, you should try to find your partner's strength, if he has any. Passive won't cut it on bidding like this.

There's a saying that it's a good idea to lead an ace against a preempt, and there's some validity in that. You might even lead the ace from a holding of AQx, hoping to hit your partner with five or six to the king. Even if the lead isn't successful, you might be able to figure out a successful plan B when the dummy hits.

Another occasion when it is right to lead aggressively is when an opponent has landed in slam after his partner indicated a long, strong suit. Here's a sample auction:

West	North	East	South
			1♠
Pass	2♦	Pass	2NT
Pass	3♠	Pass	4NT
Pass	5♣	Pass	6♠
All Pass			

In the modern style, North's bidding shows a strong diamond suit, good spade support, and slam interest. South has enough to simply bid Roman Key Card Blackwood (see Chapter 16). When he finds out what he wants to know, South ends the auction with 6♠.

You are on lead holding

♠ 6 5 4

♥ K 7 2

♦ A 4

♣ 10 9 8 7 6

What is your lead? The ♥2 stands out. It's clear that the opponents have the ♥A, and North has a strong diamond suit. South no doubt is counting on that to make his slam. You hope the North-South hands are configured this way:

♠ K Q 10

♥ 10 5 4 2

♦ K Q J 10 8

♣ A

♠ A J 9 8 3

♥ A 8 3

♦ 9 2

♣ K Q 4

A low heart lead will defeat the slam. The declarer plays low from the dummy, and your partner plays the jack, knocking out the declarer's ace. The declarer can pull trumps, but when he leads a diamond—as he must—you jump in with the ace and cash the ♥K for the setting trick. If you went passive with the ♣10, which would be the choice of many players, the declarer would win the singleton ♣A in the dummy, pull trumps, and play a diamond. After you played your ace, the declarer would have four diamond tricks, using two of them to pitch losing hearts from his hand.

Even if you didn't have the ♦A, leading a heart would be right because your partner could have the ♥Q and the ♦A, and you would still beat the slam.

This may seem to contradict the previous advice about not playing your partner for a specific card, but the situations are different. In the first case, the auction told you that your partner had almost nothing in the way of high cards. In this case, you have only an ace and a king—and there are strong indications your opponents are counting on taking lots of tricks with a long suit. You must get busy.

If it turned out that the declarer had the ♥Q in the dummy and played it at trick one, you could console yourself with the certainty that you weren't going to beat this slam no matter what you did.

A Little Help from Your Friends

It's time to learn about the concept of playing third hand high to force out the highest card possible in the declarer's hand.

It's not unusual for an inexperienced player holding the king in a suit to be annoyed when his partner makes the opening lead in that suit. Players with that mindset feel as though the king is unfairly targeted, and some refuse to play it.

What they don't realize is how happy they should be that their partner has selected that suit—and that they can make a contribution to the defense. Suppose this is the layout of a suit led against a notrump contract.

♥54

♥QJ732   ♥K96

♥A108

West will properly lead the ♥3—fourth best—instead of the queen because he doesn't have the right cards to back up that sequence. If East, in a fit of pique, refuses to play his king, the declarer will take two tricks in that suit instead of one. Worse, the declarer will have gained a tempo. The defenders will have to get in again to establish the heart suit. What a mess!

If East plays the ♥K as he should, the declarer will take one trick in hearts. And if West has a fast entry, it won't matter if the declarer plays low a couple of times. The defenders will still take four tricks overall.

Here's another layout in which refusing to play the king would be a disaster for the defense. This time, the contract is 3NT, and you get to see a full deal:

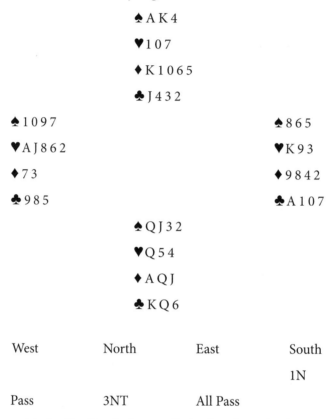

	♠ A K 4		
	♥ 1 0 7		
	♦ K 1 0 6 5		
	♣ J 4 3 2		

♠ 1 0 9 7			♠ 8 6 5
♥ A J 8 6 2			♥ K 9 3
♦ 7 3			♦ 9 8 4 2
♣ 9 8 5			♣ A 1 0 7

	♠ Q J 3 2		
	♥ Q 5 4		
	♦ A Q J		
	♣ K Q 6		

West	North	East	South
			1N
Pass	3NT	All Pass	

West will start with the ♥6. The declarer will play low from the dummy. If East does not play the king, South will win a trick with the queen that he is not entitled to. If East does the right thing and plays the king, it will win. When he continues the suit, South's queen will be trapped—West has the ♥AJ over the queen—so the defenders will take the first six tricks, consisting of five hearts and the ♣A.

It may seem silly to state a principle so basic, but it is difficult for some new players to get the picture.

Low or High?

One way to remember your responsibility as the player following to partner's opening lead is to remember this maxim: "Second hand low, third hand high." There is a logical basis to this guideline, which usually applies to defenders.

It means that when the declarer leads from his hand or from the dummy and you are the next to play, you generally play a low card if you have one. For example:

♠A 1074

♠J 65   ♠Q 8

♠K 932

When South plays the ♠2 from his hand and you are West, it would be folly to play the jack. North's ace will win. And when the declarer plays a low card from the dummy, East's queen pops up and the declarer has no losers in this suit because the 10 will pick up your last card.

If you play low as second hand, the declarer will always lose a trick in the suit.

Bridge Lingo

When you are playing to a trick—usually second or third hand—and you have two or more honors in sequence—KQx, QJ10x, J109x, etc—the play of one of the high cards is known as "splitting" your honors. It means you play one of them to keep declarer—or a defender if you are playing the contract—from winning a trick cheaply.

Now consider the play if the first lead is from the dummy. If East, playing second to the trick, comes up with the queen, the declarer can win with the king and play a low spade from his hand, inserting the 10 from the dummy. The ace will clear the suit and again your side will have no tricks when you should have taken at least one.

There are exceptions, of course, and some are rather obvious. Observe this combination from a suit contract:

♠ A J 7 4

♠ K Q 6 5   ♠ 1 0 9 8

♠ 3 2

When South leads the ♠2, if you play second hand low, the declarer can put in the dummy's jack and will lose no tricks in the suit. Put another way, you will get no tricks. If you want to win a trick in spades, you must play one of your honors—the queen or king.

Be careful, though. Playing an honor can be costly on occasion. The following is a common situation. South, the hand you can't see, opened 1♠ and landed in 4♠. In the dummy, he leads a low spade. It's your play.

Dummy

♠ 9 6 5 2

You

♠ K Q 4

You will regret it if you play your king or queen and find that this is the complete layout of the suit:

♠ 9 6 5 2

♠ J   ♠ K Q 4

♠ A 1 0 8 7 3

The declarer will take the ace, dropping your partner's jack and will then play a card high enough to force your other high honor. You will take one trick where you should have taken two.

But, you say, suppose South has the AJ873 and plays the jack? Well, you were getting only one trick in the suit anyway—and you will still get that trick. If you play the king or queen, South will win with the ace and later lead toward his jack. You will have to play your other high honor and the jack will be good. With four of the suit in one hand and five in the other, you will always get one trick. You win, of course, when the declarer has AJ873 and plays the ace, hoping the suit splits 2-2 or that a singleton honor drops on his left.

Message Sent

There is an important principle in third hand play that many new players violate routinely. It is not uncommon to see this happen:

♥6 5 4

♥K 7 3 2   ♥Q J 9

♥A 1 0 8

West leads low, the dummy plays low, and East plays the queen. Wrong! In that situation, if you are third hand you must always play the jack. Whichever card you play, you will send your partner—the opening leader—a message.

Say you play the jack and the declarer wins with the ace. West will know that you have the queen. How? Well, if the declarer had the AQ and you played the jack, wouldn't he win with the queen? It would not make sense for the declarer to win with the ace in that situation, making your partner's king a winner.

Bridge Basics

When you are dealt a sequence of cards in a suit and you are playing third hand, always follow with the lowest card in the sequence. Think of the cards as equals. When you have KQJ10, the play of the 10 will force out the opponent's ace just as effectively as the king—and it sends a message about how strong your suit is. There will be times when you don't want an opponent to know how strong your suit is, and when it won't hurt to be deceptive—e.g., you know your partner is never getting in. At those times, play any card you like according to your judgment. For most routine plays, however, you will follow with the lowest of your equals.

Following this logic, if you play the queen from your holding of QJ9, your partner will "know" that the declarer has the jack. He is expecting you, after all, to play the jack from QJ, not the queen.

Well Spotted

There will be times when you are playing third hand that you will withhold the highest card for a legitimate reason. Take this situation:

♣J 6 5

♣Q 10 8

Your partner leads the ♣4 against a notrump contract, and the declarer plays low from the dummy. It would be wrong to play the queen in this situation because it could easily give up a trick. The proper play is the 10. For starters, it is equal to the jack in the dummy.

Second, apply the Rule of Eleven to your partner's opening lead. Subtract 4 from 11 and you get 7. That means there are seven cards higher than the 4 in the other three hands. You can see six of them between the dummy and your hand. So the declarer has one card higher than the cards you can see. It has to be the ace or king. The layout of the suit is probably like this:

♣J 6 5

♣A 9 7 4   ♣Q 10 8

♣K 3 2

If you play the queen, South wins the king and will later be able to lead up to the dummy's jack and win a trick. It works the same way when South has the ace instead of the king.

When you play the 10, the declarer wins with the king. If you are the first to get in, you can cash the queen and play to your partner's ace. You will not be afraid to play the queen even

Need to Know

Many players use what they call attitude opening leads in an effort to clarify their holdings in the suit led. In this context, *attitude* means how you feel about your suit. Do you like it because you have some high cards, or do you hope that when your partner gets in he will play some other suit? The way to express attitude on opening lead is to start with a high card—a 10, 9, or 8—even from a holding of three or more cards, such as 852. If this is the agreement you have with your partner, he will know when you lead a low card that you have something in the suit—that your attitude toward that suit is positive, not negative. The upside is that your partner will know when you start with a high card to play a different suit if he gets in. The downside is that it is informative to the declarer as well. Be sure to discuss this with your partner before adopting this style.

though the jack is in the dummy because by using the Rule of Eleven you know that the declarer has already played the only card in his hand higher than the 4. You defend so well.

Here's another familiar situation you will see in defending against a notrump contract:

♣ Q 6 5

♣ J 9 7 4   ♣ K 1 0 3

♣ A 8 2

West again starts with the ♣4, and the declarer plays low. It will almost never be right to play the king in that situation. The 10 should be your choice just about every time.

Using the Rule of Eleven, you know that the declarer has two cards higher your partner's 4. If the two cards happen to be the AJ, putting up the king will give the declarer three tricks in the suit.

But, you say, what if the declarer has only the jack—as with J8 doubleton? If so, putting up the king will win the trick, but the declarer will still get a trick in the suit because the jack will knock out the ace and make the queen good. Consider this layout, where South does have a doubleton:

♣ Q 6 5

♣ A J 9 4 2   ♣ K 1 0 3

♣ 8 7

If you play the king, the dummy's queen will eventually take a trick. If you play the 10, it will hold, and you can follow with the king and then another club to your partner's ace for a total of five tricks.

Even seemingly insignificant combinations can have big implications. Observe:

West leads the ♦3 and the declarer plays low from the dummy. If you put up the jack, the declarer wins the ace, and the remaining diamonds in the dummy will serve as a stopper against your partner's ♦KQ4. When you insert the 9, the declarer must win with the ace. When your partner gets in, he knows you have the jack—the declarer would have won with that card if he had it—so he will play over to you so that you and your partner can take three tricks in the suit.

Applying Pressure

Here's another third hand play that is somewhat counterintuitive:

♣7 5

♣A Q 6

Your partner leads the ♣4 and the dummy plays low. What should you play? If this is a notrump contract, you should consider putting in the queen—really.

Think about what the declarer might have. If he has the king, unless it's singleton, he's going to take a trick with that card no matter what you do. But here's what happens when you play the ace and the layout of the suit is like this:

♣7 5

♣J 9 8 4 2   ♣A Q 6

♣K 1 0 3

If the declarer has to lose the lead to establish enough tricks to make his game, he will play low when you play the ♣Q at trick two. The declarer will win the third round of the suit, and if he can lose the critical trick to you instead of to your partner, he will do so and you will have no more clubs to lead to your partner's club winners.

When you play the queen, South is under some pressure. Do you have three to the AQ or three to the queen? If it's three to the queen, the declarer better take his king now or he won't get it. Do you see? If you have three to the queen, that means your partner has led from five to the AJ, so if the declarer plays low on your queen, you can push another club through his now-doubleton king and he won't take a single club trick.

If you think for a long time and play the queen, the declarer has a better chance of guessing your holding, so you must play your queen smoothly—in tempo as it were (there's that word again with a different meaning). If the declarer works it out anyway, give him credit.

Duck for Winners

You have seen how playing low when you can win a trick—known as ducking—can help you make your contract by cutting communication between two defenders. You have also seen that when you have a long suit that might or might not run—as with A K Q x x opposite two low cards—you can try the safety play of low from the hand and low from the strong suit to guard against a 4-2 split in the suit. In that way, you maintain communication between your hand and the important suit.

So you see, ducking can have the differing goals of maintaining communication and cutting it off, depending on the situation.

Return to Sender

Before you learn about ducking by defenders, it's important for you to know about your responsibilities after your partner has made the opening lead. When you win the opening lead and wish to continue the suit—or if you win a trick later in the play and wish to return the suit your partner led—there are rules about the card that you should play.

When your original holding was three cards, you will have a doubleton remaining. When you return that suit, lead a high one. Some examples:

➤ A 8 2

➤ K 7 3

➤ Q 4 2

➤ J 8 4

➤ 1 0 5 2

With all of these holdings, the next time you lead the suit, put the original middle card on the table assuming you played the high one the first time.

When you had a sequence and originally followed with the lowest of your equals, if you started with three cards, return the higher of the two remaining cards. That is, if you played the jack from your original holding of QJ4, when you get in again and lead the suit, play the queen, not the 4.

If you started with four or more cards and have three or four remaining when you play the suit the next time, lead back a low one. Your partner will be relying on you to let him know how many cards you have left. This will have application in notrump and suit play.

Staying in Touch

Now that you know what to return when you win the opening lead or get in later, here is what you need to know about maintaining communication with your partner.

A full deal will help illustrate this point.

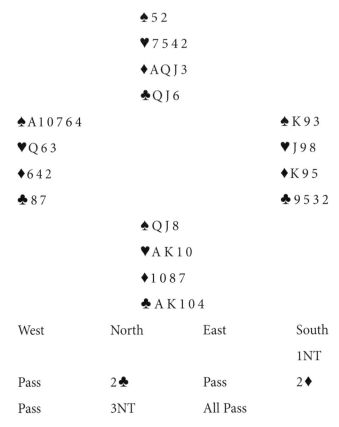

	♠ 5 2		
	♥ 7 5 4 2		
	♦ A Q J 3		
	♣ Q J 6		
♠ A 1 0 7 6 4			♠ K 9 3
♥ Q 6 3			♥ J 9 8
♦ 6 4 2			♦ K 9 5
♣ 8 7			♣ 9 5 3 2
	♠ Q J 8		
	♥ A K 1 0		
	♦ 1 0 8 7		
	♣ A K 1 0 4		

West	North	East	South
			1NT
Pass	2♣	Pass	2♦
Pass	3NT	All Pass	

Your normal lead is a spade, so you put the 6 on the table. The dummy plays low and your partner puts up the king, which holds the trick. His next play is the ♠9, on which South plays the queen. South is hoping to convince you that he started with a doubleton queen and that your suit is about to run. You know, however, from your partner's return of the ♠9 that he did not start with four spades. If he had started with four, he would not have returned the 9. At trick two, he would have played some other card.

It is tempting for you to take the ♠Q with your ace and clear the suit. After all, you saw the declarer play the 8 at trick one and your partner returned the 9 to the declarer's queen. Your 107 are good enough to drive out the declarer's jack.

Before you play, consider how you would play this card combination if you needed four tricks from this suit and the dummy had no outside entries:

♠ A 1 0 7 6 4

♠ K 9 3

You would play the king, and if everyone followed low, you would continue with either of your low cards, playing low from the dummy. If the suit splits 3-2, you will take four tricks because the ace will take the last outstanding spade, making your 10 and 7 good.

That is the situation you face in defending 3NT. You have no entry to your hand, so if you win the ace and play a third round, your 10 and 7 will be established, but they will die on the vine, so to speak. In the given deal, the declarer will take the losing diamond finesse, but your partner will have no spade to return, so he will end up with three diamonds, four clubs, two hearts, and a spade for an overtrick.

If you play low at trick two, the declarer is toast. He does not have enough tricks to make his contract without the diamond finesse, and when your partner gets in, he will shoot another spade through and your side will take four spades and a diamond for down one.

You might wonder what to do if your partner started with only two spades. Now you don't even get your ace. If your partner had only two spades, that would mean South had four. Remember the auction? North's 2♣ asked South if he had a four-card major. South's 2♦ said no. Even if you didn't have the information from the auction, if South had four spades and your partner had two, you simply were not going to defeat this contract.

Yes, in the given deal it would work for East to initially play the ♠9, driving out one of South's honors. When East gets in later, he could play the king and continue the suit to take four spades, tricks in all. That's a big position to take, however, and is a disaster if West's spade holding is five to the AJ.

Ears Open

At the beginning of this chapter, you were told that your partner can provide help with finding the best opening lead—with overcalls and doubles, for example.

Your opponents can also help you find the best opening lead—or avoid a bad one—by what they reveal in the bidding.

Listen in on this auction (you are West):

West	North	East	South
			1♦
Pass	1♠	Pass	2♣
Pass	3♣	Pass	5♣
All Pass			

This is your hand:

♠ 6 5 4 3

♥ A 8 7 2

♦ 6 4 3

♣ K 3

Although you have been lectured about leading unsupported aces, this auction screams for a heart lead. Most players don't bid game in a minor unless they have no choice, which usually means they are wide open in some suit. If either of your opponents had as much as the guarded ♥K, maybe even three to the queen, the contract would probably be 3NT. Expect to be able to cash a couple of tricks in hearts and hope that the ♣A doesn't turn up in the dummy.

A good time for a trump lead is when you have a strong holding in one of the declarer's long suits.

♠ K J 9 6

♥ 7 4 3

♦ Q J 10 9

♣ A 7

West	North	East	South
			1♠
Pass	1NT	Pass	2♥
All Pass			

It would not be a surprise to see the dummy looking like this:

♠ 5

♥ J 6 5

♦ A 8 4 3 2

♣ Q 9 8 6

South no doubt has a minimum with nine or ten cards in the majors. If you start with a trump, you can play another each time you get in—and you expect to be in at least once more. You might even get lucky and find your partner with the ♥A. Your main objective is to keep the declarer from using low trumps in the dummy to take care of his losing spades. Without such a strong holding in spades, you would normally start with the ♦Q.

Another auction that strongly indicates a trump lead is one in which an opponent shows an extreme two-suited hand, as with a Michaels cue-bid or the Unusual 2NT.

To refresh your memory, a direct cue-bid of a minor suit opening shows at least 5-5 in the major suits. A direct cue-bid of a major shows at least five cards in the other major and at least five cards in an unspecified minor. Over a major suit, a direct bid of 2NT shows at least 5-5 in the minors. Over 1♣, 2NT shows 5-5 or better in hearts and diamonds; over 1♦, 2NT shows hearts and clubs.

Here's a sample auction:

West	North	East	South
1♠	2NT	Dbl	3♣
Pass	Pass	Dbl	All Pass

You are West. Your partner's double told you that he has some high-card strength and the desire to penalize at least one of North's minor suits. Your partner confirmed his intentions with the double of 3♣.

Perhaps this is your hand:

♠ A K J 7 6

♥ K J 5

♦ Q 8 4

♣ 5 2

Now is the time for you to get off to the lead of a low club (when leading trumps from a doubleton, it is usually correct to start with the low one). The declarer, somewhat of an innocent bystander, might be short in both of his partner's suits. His 3♣ bid, after all, showed a preference, not an endorsement of either suit. He could easily have a singleton diamond and a doubleton in clubs or a doubleton diamond and three low clubs.

If you think of the South hand as the dummy, knowing that North has length in both minors, you would certainly play on trumps to keep North from ruffing his losers in the other suit. Envision the South hand and start your attack in trumps right away. Don't waste time leading spades.

CHAPTER 15

On the Defense: Part 2

In This Chapter

➤ Carding

➤ Lead conventions

➤ When to signal and when not to

➤ Other defensive conventions and tricks

Some combinations of cards send special messages. It takes just a bit of study to learn them. In this chapter, you will find out about how you can send legal messages to your partner solely by the cards you play. You'll also find out that it's not always a good idea to make a clear signal as a defender because the declarer is watching, too. You'll learn when to keep your secrets to yourself.

Everyone has agreements about cards to be led from certain combinations, and in this chapter you will read about which are the most common.

Sending Messages

It has already been established that the auction is very similar to a conversation:

"Good news, partner, I have at least five spades and about thirteen high-card points."

"Glad to hear it. I have three or four trumps for you, although my hand is modest."

"It sounds as though we have found the right place to play."

Of course, that's not what players say to each other. It would be more like:

West	North	East	South
	1♠	Pass	2♠
Pass	Pass	Pass	

Players are not allowed to make extraneous remarks that indicate approval or displeasure at what happens.

That said, there are perfectly legal, nonverbal, gesture-free ways to communicate approval or disapproval of events. This communication is always between defenders. The declarer is in charge of the cards that the dummy plays, and all he has to do is call a card or play one himself.

The art of communication between defenders comes under the heading of carding. This broad topic covers many different methods players employ to get messages across to each other—from the opening lead almost to the final card played. There are many different methods to consider. What follows are some of the most important.

Lead Conventions

The practice of leading the ace from a holding of AKx or longer.

Other honor leads, as when the lead of the queen usually promises the jack or the lead of the king promising the queen.

The agreement that, against notrump, the lead of the jack indicates that it is the highest card in the suit. Partnerships with that agreement lead the 10 from interior sequences such as KJ109 or Q1098. They call the style "jack denies, 10 implies."

Leading fourth best or, for advanced players, third- and fifth-best.

Defensive Signals

The standard defensive signals are *attitude* and *count*. *Attitude* applies to one partner's opinion about a lead or play by the other player. This is a classic example:

Dummy

♠ 8 5 4

West

♠ A K 2

West leads the ace and the dummy plays the 4. If East wants West to continue playing spades, as when East has the ♠Q, he will play the highest spade he can afford as a come-on to West. If East holds ♠Q109, he will play the 10, requesting a continuation of the suit. If East's holding is ♠763, East will not want to encourage West to continue with the spade suit in case South has the guarded queen. Playing another spade will set up South's queen as a winner. East expresses a negative attitude about the spade suit by playing the 3.

Bridge Basics

Many partnerships choose to signal attitude in a way that is opposite to standard. They play low cards to encourage, high cards to discourage. This method is called upside-down signaling. The theory is that using a high card may sometimes cost a trick, as when you have to play the 10 from Q1043 to encourage your partner to play that suit. At the same time, throwing the 9 from a holding of 954 can hardly cost because you are not likely to take a trick with those cards anyway. Upside-down signals can be effective, but you must discuss this with your partner.

You can signal attitude even if your partner is not winning the trick. For example:

Dummy

♦ A 6 3 2

East

♦ K 9 4 3

Your partner leads the ♦Q and the declarer plays the ace. You are East. Which card do you play? You should contribute the ♦9 to the trick. You want to let your partner know that you have the king. This is clearly an attitude situation.

Your partner might want to know if he can reach your hand so that you can play through the declarer's hand. If you carelessly play a low diamond on this trick, you are depriving your partner of information he may need.

These principles are applicable throughout the deal, not just on opening lead. Observe:

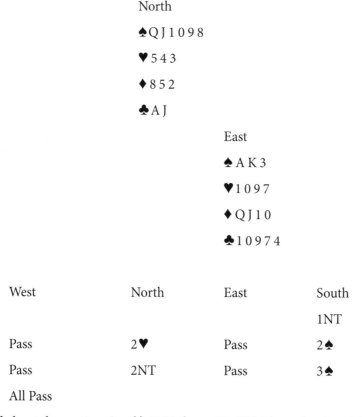

North

♠ Q J 10 9 8

♥ 5 4 3

♦ 8 5 2

♣ A J

East

♠ A K 3

♥ 1 0 9 7

♦ Q J 10

♣ 1 0 9 7 4

West	North	East	South
			1NT
Pass	2♥	Pass	2♠
Pass	2NT	Pass	3♠
All Pass			

A word about the auction: South's 1NT shows 15–17 high-card points. North's 2♥ is a transfer (see Chapter 5 for a refresher). South bids 2♠ on orders from North, and when North bids 2NT, he is inviting South to bid game in notrump or spades. If South has a maximum 1NT opener and at least three spades, he will bid 4♠. If he has a maximum without three spades (he must have at least two for his 1NT opener), he will bid 3NT. With a minimum and two spades, he will pass 2NT. In the actual case, he has a minimum but at least three spades, so he opts to play in the suit contract.

Your partner starts with a trump, and you are in at trick one. You do a quick count of yours and the dummy's high-card points and see 18. If South has only 15 high-card points, which is likely given the bidding, that means 33 high-card points are accounted for. Your partner has 6 or 7 high-card points over there and considering the weakness of the dummy's holdings in diamonds and hearts, you may be able to get something going in a red suit.

Your diamond suit looks promising—your partner needs only the ace for you to hit the jackpot: three fast diamond tricks. When you switch to the ♦Q, the declarer plays the ace and you look expectantly at West's card (you might still be on the right track if your partner has the ♦K).

Your helpful partner contributes the 3, however. You can see the ♦2 in the dummy, so you know the 3 is your partner's lowest card. You are using normal signals, so that means your partner was not excited about your switch to diamonds.

Fortunately, on this deal you get another chance because the declarer must play a second spade. He does not want to let your side score those low trumps.

Now, in with the ♠A. You follow your partner's lead and play the ♥10. Eureka! You have struck gold because this is the full deal:

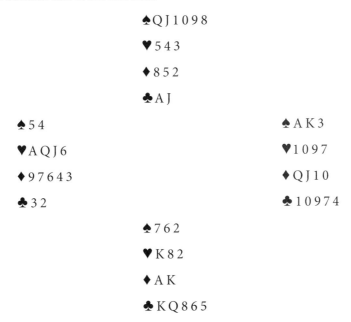

♠QJ1098
♥543
♦852
♣AJ

♠54
♥AQJ6
♦97643
♣32

♠AK3
♥1097
♦QJ10
♣10974

♠762
♥K82
♦AK
♣KQ865

If you and your partner had not discussed signaling, you would not have known what to do when you got in the second time. If the card your partner plays is meaningless, you will be guessing in every similar situation. Why guess when you can provide help through your signals?

Fresh Out

Another opportunity for signaling occurs when you have to discard. If the declarer is playing a suit that you are out of, you can discard to show interest—or lack of it—in a particular suit. When you discard a low card in a suit, an alert partner will look to another suit or suits to play should he gain the lead. A high card says you hope your partner will get in so he can lead the suit to you.

If practical, it is better to discard from suits you don't like so that you don't signal with a potential trick in the suit you do want your partner to play.

Reconfigure the deal just discussed and you can see how that would work:

North

♠Q 10 8 6 5

♥6 5 4

♦8 5 2

♣A Q

East

♠K 9 3

♥1 0 7

♦Q J 10 9 7 6

♣9 4

West	North	East	South
			1NT
Pass	2♥	Pass	3♠
Pass	4♠	All Pass	

Again, a word about the auction: When North bids 2♥ as a transfer bid, South is very pleased. North is showing at least five spades, so a fit of nine cards is certain. Further, South's hand is about as good as it could be—all aces and kings plus four spades. In such a situation, it is standard for South to make a bid known as super acceptance. Instead of bidding 2♠ as instructed, South jumps to show a maximum 1NT opener with so-called prime support (four cards) for North's suit.

With his dull shape and the weak holdings in diamonds and hearts, a pass of 2♠ by North would not be out of the question. It is annoying to make an invitation and find yourself one trick too high.

South's super acceptance takes the pressure off for North. Experienced players would get to game on these cards just about every time.

West leads the ♣ J, taken in the dummy with the queen. The declarer now plays a spade to his ace, his partner contributing the jack. When the declarer plays another spade at trick two, his partner discards the ♦ 2. Even beginning players should recognize this as a discouraging signal. So what does that leave? It looks as though the declarer has the ♣ K, so if you passively return a club to the dummy's ace, you are giving the declarer the chance to pull your last trump and get to hand to take a discard from the dummy on the ♣ K (he did announce the maximum for his 1NT opener, so he almost surely has that card).

Your only shot, therefore, is to play the ♥ 10 and hope that the full deal is like this:

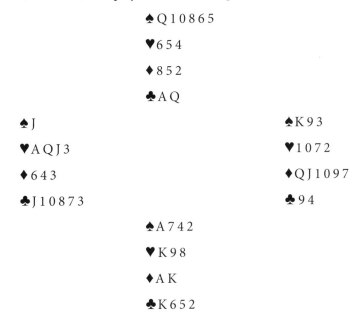

```
                    ♠ Q 10 8 6 5
                    ♥ 6 5 4
                    ♦ 8 5 2
                    ♣ A Q
  ♠ J                                  ♠ K 9 3
  ♥ A Q J 3                            ♥ 1 0 7 2
  ♦ 6 4 3                              ♦ Q J 1 0 9 7
  ♣ J 1 0 8 7 3                        ♣ 9 4
                    ♠ A 7 4 2
                    ♥ K 9 8
                    ♦ A K
                    ♣ K 6 5 2
```

Note that West could not signal encouragement in hearts because his spot cards are so low. Throwing the ♥ 3 or ♥ 2 would not get the job done, and signaling with the ♥ J or ♥ Q would have burned a trick for the defense. Say West plays the ♥ J at trick three. You get in and fire back the ♥ 10. South covers, West wins and can cash the queen, but now the declarer's ♥ 9 is good.

All would have been well had West been dealt AQJ98 in hearts. He would have been able to discard the ♥ 9 without giving up a trick.

Note also that the key card was your ♥ 10. If, for example, the dummy had held that card, you would not have been able to defeat the contract. The declarer would simply play low and you would be able to take only two hearts. Equally, if your partner held the ♥ 10, you could switch to a heart, but again South would play low. West would win the 10 but would not be able to get East in again to play another heart through, so West either cashes the ♥ A, making the king good, or exits with some other suit, allowing the declarer to eventually discard a low heart from the dummy on the ♣ K.

Bridge Lingo

When you play a high card followed by a low card as a count signal or as a come-on signal, it is known as an echo. In Great Britain, the play is known as a peter. The one exception to the high-low rule to show an even number occurs when you are following in trumps as a defender. With three trumps, you play high-low to show three. In most cases, echoing in trumps indicates that you are in a position to ruff one of the side suits. This is called trump echo.

Numbers Game

Another standard signal involves count, which is the number of cards you hold in a suit. This is often critical information for your partner.

Before you see an example of why giving count can be extremely important, here's how it works:

When you have an even number of cards in a suit, you play a high one, then a low one. With 102, play the 10 first, then the 2. With 8765, play the 8, then one of the others. Always play the highest spot card you can afford in order to make your signal as clear as possible for partner.

When you have an odd number of cards in a suit, you play a low one first, then a high one. With 643, play the 3, then the 4. With 87542, play the 2, then the 4 or 5.

Here's a deal to illustrate how important it can be to signal accurately.

```
              ♠ 8 3 2
              ♥ A 6
              ♦ K Q J 10 5
              ♣ J 6 4
♠ 1 0 5 4                      ♠ 9 7 6
♥ 1 0 9 7 5                    ♥ K 4 3 2
♦ 9 4 3                        ♦ A 8 2
♣ K 8 2                        ♣ Q 10 9
              ♠ A K Q J
              ♥ Q J 8
              ♦ 7 6
              ♣ A 7 5 3
```

West	North	East	South
			1NT
Pass	3NT	All Pass	

You, West, hit on the opening lead of a low heart, which turns out to be the killing lead. The declarer must play low from the dummy, desperately hoping you have led from the king, but your partner—bless him—wins the king and returns the suit, knocking the ♥A out of the dummy and effectively killing the contract.

If, that is, you continue to defend accurately.

The declarer has no choice but to go for the diamond suit, hoping one of the defenders has a singleton ♦A—or that one of you will err on defense.

At trick three, therefore, the declarer plays a spade to his queen (feigning a finesse) and then plays a low diamond from hand. If West is alert and aware of his responsibility, he will play the 3, giving count.

East has the ♦2, so when he sees West play the 3, he knows it is either a singleton or from a three-card suit. If West has a singleton ♦3, there is no hope. East cannot cut the declarer off from the dummy's diamonds by ducking. So East must play West for three diamonds.

If West has three diamonds, South has two, so East plays low when the declarer puts up the dummy's ♦K. East must not duck again, however, because a second duck will give the declarer his ninth trick. Count them: four spades, two hearts, the ♣A, and two diamonds. East must hold the declarer to one diamond trick. If he wins the second diamond and returns a heart, the declarer will have to go down. He will lose two hearts, two clubs, and a diamond.

Too Much Information (Sometimes)

Some partnerships have the agreement to signal count at all times so they can have as accurate a picture of the declarer's hand as possible. These partnerships are relying on the opponents not to be paying attention. The problem with this agreement is that the declarer is watching, too, and can use the information to his benefit.

Take the following suit layout for example:

♥Q 1 0 7 6

♥A K 4

If the declarer plays the ace then the king and sees both opponents playing high-low—one signaling to show four hearts, the other signaling to show two, he won't have any difficulty picking up four hearts to the jack when West follows to the third round of hearts. The declarer will confidently stick in the dummy's 10 and thank his opponents for their disciplined counting.

This may seem to be a silly example—why would West give such helpful information to the declarer?—but less-obvious situations come up all the time, and if your opponents are obligingly providing such helpful clues, you owe it to yourself to take advantage.

The best policy is to signal count only in situations such as the example with the long, strong suit in the dummy, when East needed to know how many diamonds West had so that he could take his ace at just the right time.

Not Enough Info

So, how do you know when to signal and when not to?

Some situations will be obvious, as when there is a long suit in the dummy with no outside entry.

Here's another situation where giving count is essential:

Dummy

♥Q 7 6 3

♥A K 5 4

Against 4 ♠, you lead the ace or king depending on your lead agreements, and the dummy plays low. This is a situation where you need to know how many cards your partner has in the suit. If you know that, of course, you know how many the declarer has (you *can* count to thirteen, right?). That knowledge could be the difference between defeating a contract or letting it make. Here's an example starting with this auction:

West	North	East	South
			1♠
Dbl	2♠	Pass	4♠
All Pass			

You lead the ♥A and these are the cards you can see:

Dummy

♠10876

♥Q76

♦854

♣KQ4

You

♠AQ

♥AK32

♦9762

♣986

You know you are going to win two trump tricks, so the question is how to get another couple of tricks to defeat 4♠. Your ♥K lives, the declarer playing the jack. The declarer's play could be honest, but he might also be falsecarding. If you try to cash the ♥A, you might find the complete layout to be as follows:

Deal 1:

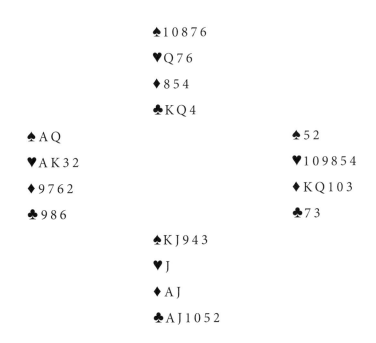

♠10876

♥Q76

♦854

♣KQ4

♠AQ   ♠52

♥AK32   ♥109854

♦9762   ♦KQ103

♣986   ♣73

♠KJ943

♥J

♦AJ

♣AJ1052

By trying to cash a second heart, you set up the dummy's queen, and the declarer will be quick to use the ♥Q to discard his losing diamond.

If you do not continue hearts, you might find that this is the full layout:

Deal 2:

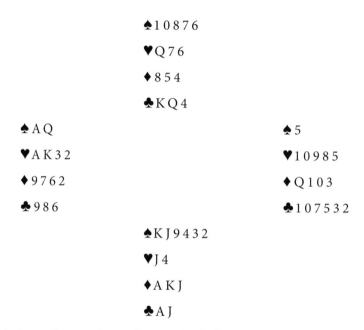

♠10876
♥Q76
♦854
♣KQ4

♠AQ
♥AK32
♦9762
♣986

♠5
♥10985
♦Q103
♣107532

♠KJ9432
♥J4
♦AKJ
♣AJ

Say you switch to a diamond at trick two. The declarer wins, cashes the ♣A, and plays the ♣J to the dummy's king. On the ♣Q, he discards his ♥4, suppressing a chuckle at having swindled you out of the setting trick.

That's galling, of course, but what can you do? You should look to your partner for help in this situation.

A good rule of thumb for defenders is that when the opening leader is going to hold the trick, as with the lead of the ace or king from AK, and the dummy has a stopper (e.g., three or four to the queen), third hand is obliged to signal count.

In deal 1, East must play the ♥4, his lowest heart, to show an odd number of hearts (three or five). West can read the 4 because he has the 3 and the 2. West must try to envision South's hand to determine his next play. West can infer that South's trump suit is not superstrong—West is looking at two of the top three honors. On the bidding, it is likely that South has a very shapely hand with a good second suit. Because West has trump control—he will get in twice more—he can risk not trying to cash his other high heart. West can switch to diamonds and see if anything good happens. If not, he can try the second heart when he gets in with the ♠Q.

Need to Know

As a defender, when you are switching to a new suit in the middle of the play, you can send a message to your partner about whether you have something good in the suit. Most experienced players agree that switching to a low card indicates that if your partner wins the trick, it's okay to return it. You might switch suits to lead from the KJ32 in the middle of the play with three low cards in the dummy. If your partner wins the ace, you want him to return the suit. Your 2 tells your partner that he can. On the other hand, if you have a poor holding and don't want the suit continued, you play the highest card you can afford, such as the 9 from 974. This tells your partner you have no high-card strength in that suit. This is related to the opening lead practice of leading low from something and high from nothing.

Still on deal 1, at trick two West switches to a diamond, which goes to East's queen and the declarer's ace. When West comes in with the ♠Q, he continues diamonds and East takes the king. The setting trick is the ace of trumps.

For deal 2, the defense is easier (recall that East held four hearts to the 10). When West leads the ♥A and the dummy follows low, East signals with the 10 to show an even number of hearts. This is almost certainly four (it can't be six because in that case South is void and will ruff), and it doesn't matter if it's a doubleton. In the case of a doubleton, West will be able to give his partner a heart ruff, so the contract will go down two. That probably won't happen, but knowing East has two or four hearts allows West to cash a high heart and sit back to wait for his trump tricks.

You can see how impossible it would be to defend if West had to guess what to do in situations like the one described. In situations where you have to guess—that is, you don't have many clues from the bidding or play—you will be wrong a certain percentage of the time. You could get on a losing streak of wrong guesses that would have you tearing your hair out and wondering if you know anything about bridge at all.

When partners cooperate and provide needed information, at least some of the guesswork is removed from the equation, making for much happier and more successful players.

Just Kidding

There are certain defensive situations in which it is mandatory to falsecard—to try to deceive the declarer and make his life difficult.

Here is a common situation:

♦ A J 3

♦ Q 1 0 4   ♦ 8 7 2

♦ K 9 6 5

South leads a low diamond to the dummy's jack. When North cashes the ace and follows low, you must play the queen. Do you understand why? The fact that the dummy's jack held the trick marks you with the queen, so if you follow with the 10, the declarer will have an easy time taking four tricks in the suit. He knows you still have the queen.

If you follow with the queen, however, the declarer may play your partner for an original holding of 10872, in which case the declarer will be able to take four tricks in the suit only by playing low to his 9.

Bridge Basics

One of the maxims of defensive play is to always play the card you are known to hold. Here's an example situation:

♣ A Q 1 0 9 8

♣ K J 2   ♣ 7 4 3

♣ 6 5

The declarer is in a heart contract and has only one entry to the dummy outside the club suit. The declarer plays a club to the queen and continues with the ace. If you follow with the jack, the declarer will comfortably ruff out your king and take two extra tricks. If you follow with the king, however, the declarer may play your partner for ♣ J 7 4 3 and run the 10. After all, the 4-2 split is more likely than the 3-3 split. The declarer will be chagrined when you win the jack but will acknowledge your good play. It might not work, but it's your only chance to take a trick in the suit.

There are other deceptive maneuvers you can make to try to create tricks that you would not get if you played normally.

This is another common situation:

♠ A J 8 4

♠ K 3   ♠ 1 0 9 5

♠ Q 7 6 2

You are East and the declarer is playing in a spade contract. He wins the opening lead and plays a low spade to the dummy's jack. If you follow with the 5, the declarer has no chance to go wrong. With the K109 still out against him, the only chance is to find a doubleton king on his left

Consider the declarer's view if you follow with the ♠9 instead of the 5. Now the declarer may decide you started with a 109 doubleton in trumps, in which case he should return to hand and play the queen, which blots out your 10 and picks up the suit for no loss.

An experienced player will look askance at your 9, and he may get the layout right anyway, but you at least you gave him a chance to go wrong, which wouldn't have occurred with your play of the 5.

Hidden Assets

Remember the discussion to always play the lowest of equals when playing third hand: the 10 from QJ10, the queen from KQx, the jack from QJx, etc.

There will be times when you do not want to be honest about your holdings. Usually this is when deceiving your partner won't matter, as when you can tell from the situation that your partner will never get in.

Suppose, after you (East) passed as dealer, that South arrives in a heart slam on this layout:

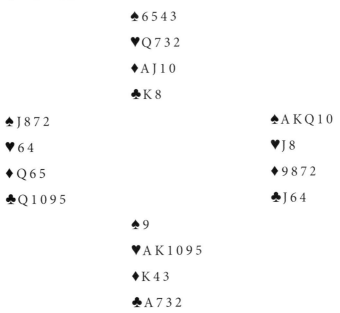

     ♠ 6 5 4 3

     ♥ Q 7 3 2

     ♦ A J 10

     ♣ K 8

♠ J 8 7 2   ♠ A K Q 10

♥ 6 4   ♥ J 8

♦ Q 6 5   ♦ 9 8 7 2

♣ Q 10 9 5   ♣ J 6 4

     ♠ 9

     ♥ A K 10 9 5

     ♦ K 4 3

     ♣ A 7 3 2

West hits on the opening lead of a low spade. If you play the queen, the declarer will know your exact holding in the suit. You would not play the queen from AQ because the declarer might have a singleton king. It is unthinkable for West to underlead an ace against a slam. So South will know you have the ♠AKQ, and West's lead of the ♠2 tells him you have four of them.

Do you see where this is going? You don't know for sure, but if the declarer has to decide how to play diamonds—he must locate the queen to make his contract—you don't want to provide clues he could use to get it right.

Bridge Basics

Falsecarding is an art and can be effective in sending the declarer—or for the declarer, the defenders—on the wrong path. A key to effective falsecarding is to keep it smooth. If you hem and haw before making your play, you will reveal a lot to an astute declarer or defender. Experience will help you to envision the deceptive plays so that you can make them without pauses that give away the show.

Before making his play in diamonds, the declarer will do some detective work to try to figure things out. He will play a club to the king, return to hand with the ♣A and ruff a club. Your ♣J will fall, and the declarer will stop to assess the situation. If the declarer knows you had the ♠AKQ and a couple of jacks (11 high-card points), he will reflect that you might have opened the bidding with another queen, giving you 13 high-card points. He will then play your partner for the ♦Q and score up his slam.

If, however, you play the king at trick one and follow with the ♠A, the declarer will not have so much information. If you are confident that the declarer has a singleton spade, you might even win the ace at trick one. That kind of deception can't hurt your partner, and he will see what you are doing when the declarer ruffs the second spade.

There are no guarantees, but playing deceptively improves the chances that the declarer will go wrong in the play.

Here is another familiar falsecard that almost always works.

♠KJ1098

♠65   ♠AQ743

♠2

If this is a side suit and the declarer needs to develop more than one or two tricks in the suit, you can gum up the works by winning with the ace when he plays the 2 to the jack. The declarer will certainly play your partner for the queen and may use valuable entries to the dummy trying to ruff it out. If you win with the queen, the declarer may return to the dummy and play to ruff out your ace and take four tricks in all.

High Tech

There are other defensive conventions and agreements that are worth consideration. Note, however, that these tools are recommended mostly for established partnerships. It is very important for two players to be on the same page when defending.

There are a few gadgets you could consider.

Rusinow Lead

Rusinow opening leads, named for Sydney Rusinow, one of the originators of the lead convention that was devised in the Thirites.

For players who employ this convention, there is no ambiguity regarding the opening lead of the king. It shows either the ace or shortness (doubleton or singleton). Similarly, the lead of the queen guarantees the king or shortness. In fact, the lead of an ace, king, queen, jack, or 10 shows the next higher honor or shortness.

Rusinow leads are used only for one's own suit. If the suit was bid first by your partner, you make your normal lead. That is, if you opened 1♠ and find yourself on lead with ♠QJ1096, lead the jack. If your partner opened 1♠ and it's your opening lead, start with the queen from QJ4.

Many players use Rusinow opening leads only against suit contracts—and only on opening lead. Some use them only against notrump. Some use the convention even in the middle of the play when switching suits. All such agreements are up to individual partnerships.

Bridge Basics

There are many bridge maxims that have limited validity, such as eight-ever, nine never, the old saw about whether to finesse for a queen or play for the drop (cash the top two and hope the queen is doubleton). There is a mathematical basis for this rule, but there are usually other factors to consider in deciding how to play.

Here's an adage that has withstood the test of time and should be on everyone's list: It is better to have a poor agreement than no agreement at all. In bidding and carding, your partnership will flounder if you do not have agreements to cover the many situations that will arise.

Here is how the system works, with the card to be led in the Rusinow scheme in bold (the x is included to denote a non-doubleton; the suit could be any length):

➤ **AK**: Top from a doubleton; the situation will be clarified at trick two

➤ AKx

➤ **KQ**: Top from a doubleton

➤ KQx

➤ KQJx

➤ **QJ**: Top from a doubleton

➤ QJx

➤ J10x

➤ **109**: Top from a doubleton

➤ 109x

➤ Interior sequences: AJ10, KJ10, K109, Q109

The leads are helpful to the defenders because they remove ambiguity, at least so far as the lead of an ace or king is concerned, but the declarer is also in on the secret. Then again, the same is true for the most part regarding standard leads.

Odd-Even Discards

This is one of the most popular defensive conventions in the tournament world. Basically, it works this way:

When you cannot follow suit, the discard of an odd-numbered card in a suit (3, 5, 7, 9) is encouraging in that suit. The discard of an even-numbered card (2, 4, 6, 8, 10) discourages in the suit played and carries suit-preference implications.

Need to Know

The use of odd-even discards is legal at clubs and tournaments only one time—the first time you fail to follow suit. You may not use this carding at any other time.

What that means is that when the declarer in a spade contract is pulling trumps and you cannot follow to, say, the third round of the suit, if you discard the ♣3, it means you have something useful in clubs. If you discard the ♥2, it would be discouraging in hearts but again indicative of some useful cards in clubs. The discard of the ♥8, on the other hand, discourages in hearts but encourages in diamonds.

The problem with the use of this method is that when a player is not dealt the correct card for the situation, there is usually a hesitation that more or less cancels the message sent by the discard. It is highly improper to communicate by the pace of your play or by any gesture.

Smith Echo

This sophisticated convention—credited to I. G. Smith of Great Britain—is recommended only for serious partnerships willing to work at it. Basically, against notrump, when the declarer begins playing on a suit, the defender can indicate whether he believes it would be fruitful to continue the suit that the opening leader selected for his attack.

For example, say West leads the ♠2 against 3NT by South. East plays the queen and South wins the ace. At trick two, the declarer plays a heart to the dummy. This is the heart suit:

♥ A K 6 5

South has played the ♥3. If West follows with the 10, he is indicating to his partner that it would be good for East, if he gets in first, to continue the attack on spades. If, however, West plays the 2, he is suggesting that unless East has a compelling reason from looking at his own hand, East should not continue playing spades if he is the first defender to gain the lead.

Similarly, if West follows with a middling heart and East follows with a low one, East is saying he doesn't have anything else to contribute to the defense in the spade suit. If, however, he plays a high heart, he is saying that West hit the jackpot with his opening lead, so the attack on spades should continue.

These signals are canceled when it is necessary to make a bridge play—that is, signaling count when the declarer is attacking a suit that can be isolated if a defender takes his control (usually an ace) at the proper time.

PART FOUR

Advanced Play

CHAPTER 16

Advanced Bidding Conventions

In This Chapter

➤ Roman Key Card Blackwood

➤ A new kind of Stayman

➤ Passed-hand bidding

➤ When they open 1NT

In this chapter, you will learn how to play the variation of Blackwood that has nearly supplanted the original version, and you will discover a variation of Stayman that will surprise you. You will read about how bidding after a partner has opened in third seat—possibly light—confounded players for years until Doug Drury came along. And you'll find out what he contributed to bidding theory.

Finally, as an enthusiastic competitor, you are not intimidated by an opponent's opening of 1NT, but you must be sure you take the best weapons to the fight. This chapter will help with that quest.

Favorite Convention

The world's most popular convention no doubt is Blackwood, named after its inventor, the late Easley Blackwood. It's interesting to note that when he submitted his idea to a prestigious bridge magazine in the thirties, it was dismissed as a silly idea. No doubt Blackwood, who died in 1992, was gratified to know that in time his invention was embraced by virtually every player in the world.

There have been, of course, many variations on the theme, including a mind-numbing version called Byzantine Blackwood that has stipulations about "key suits" and "half-key suits," those being side suits bid and raised or any suit bid by a player who first bid notrump. You don't want to know.

The most popular version of the ace-asking convention (see Chapter 9) is known as Roman Key Card Blackwood—RKCB for short.

The convention grew out of the ace-asking methods employed by the Italian Blue Team, the most successful international group in the history of world championship play. The ace-asking bid is still 4NT, but in Roman Blackwood, the responses are not what players familiar with regular Blackwood would expect.

These are the responses to Roman Blackwood 4NT:

➤ 5♣: Zero aces or three aces

➤ 5♦: One ace or four aces

➤ 5♥: Two aces of the same color or rank—*i.e.*, the ♥A and ♦A; the ♠A and ♣A; the ♠A and ♥A (major suits), or the ♦A and ♣A (minor suits)

➤ 5♠: Two aces of unlike color and rank—*i.e.*, the ♠A and the ♦A or the ♥A and the ♣A

This convention is meant to pinpoint particular aces but is not perfect and might be too complicated for inexperienced players.

RKCB, which has overtaken regular Blackwood in tournament play, includes the king of trumps as a fifth ace. This may sound complicated, but it really isn't. You do have to know what suit you are asking about, and it's usually best to restrict it to the suit that has been supported.

Here are the responses to RKCB:

➤ 5♣: Zero or three key cards

➤ 5♦: One or four key cards

➤ 5♥: Two key cards without the trump queen

➤ 5♠: Two key cards with the trump queen

Bridge Basics

Technically, when you use RKCB, the 5♥ and 5♠ responses show two or five key cards, but if the responder held five key cards, that would mean that the 4NT bidder used the convention with no aces or even the trump king. Such a situation would almost never come up.

Here's a deal and a sample auction with RKCB thrown in:

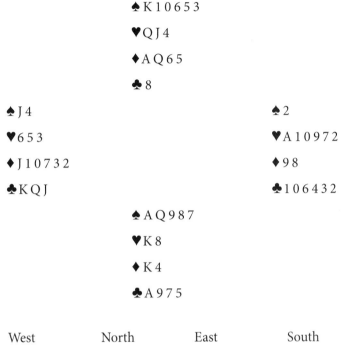

♠ K 10 6 5 3
♥ Q J 4
♦ A Q 6 5
♣ 8

♠ J 4
♥ 6 5 3
♦ J 10 7 3 2
♣ K Q J

♠ 2
♥ A 10 9 7 2
♦ 9 8
♣ 10 6 4 3 2

♠ A Q 9 8 7
♥ K 8
♦ K 4
♣ A 9 7 5

West	North	East	South
			1♠
Pass	4♣	Pass	4NT
Pass	5♥	Pass	6♠
All Pass			

Here are the meanings of the bids:

➤ 1♠: Opening hand

➤ 4♣: A spade raise showing at least four trumps and a singleton or void in clubs

➤ 4NT: RKCB for spades

➤ 5♥: Two key cards—two aces or an ace and the trump king—without the queen of trumps. This is no surprise to South, of course, because he is looking at the trump queen.

➤ 6♠: As far as South wants to go while missing one of the key cards. In this case, South doesn't know if the missing key card is the trump king or an ace, but even if he knew his side had all the aces, he would not want to bid a grand slam needing to pick up the king of trumps.

As you can see, information about the trump queen is included in the responses because that is an important card when you are exploring for slam.

Just as you do not want to bid a grand slam when your opponents have the king of trumps—they meanly have it offside (behind the ace) more often than you would like—you also do not want to bid a small slam when you are known to be missing a key card and the queen of trumps. That card, too, can be elusive. You do not want to bank your contract on being able to find the queen of trumps—and there will be times when you cannot pick up the queen—that is, play the suit for no losers—even if you know where it is, as in this situation.

♠A J 5 4

♠7   ♠Q 1 0 3

♠K 9 8 6 2

You will always lose a trick if that is the layout.

Whither the Lady

As you probably noticed, the trump queen is not mentioned in the first two responses to 4NT: 5♣ and 5♦. There is a way, however, to ask about the trump queen in case that is the last piece of information you need to decide whether to bid slam or stop at the five level.

It works this way: After a response to 5♣ or 5♦, a bid of the next highest non-trump suit asks about the trump queen. Here is an example:

West	North	East	South
			1♠
Pass	3♠	Pass	4NT
Pass	5♦	Pass	5♥
Pass	5♠	All Pass	

In this example, 3♠ shows an opening hand with good spade support.

North launches into RKCB and admits to one key card (he will rarely have four).

South still wants to know about the trump queen, possibly as a probe to bid a small slam but also possibly because he is interested in a grand slam. The bid of 5♥ expresses no interest in that suit. It is the lowest non-trump bid available and in this context is asking whether North has the trump queen.

Bridge Facts

You learned about the Gerber convention in Chapter 9. Instead of bidding 4NT to ask for aces, you start with 4 ♣. The responses are in steps, just like Blackwood: 4 ♦ shows no aces or all the aces, 4 ♥ shows 1 ace, etc. The 4 ♣ convention can also be played as Roman Key Card Gerber (with the trump king as the fifth key card). After 4 ♣, 4 ♦ shows zero or three key cards, 4 ♥ shows one or four key cards, 4 ♠ shows two key cards without the trump queen, and 4NT shows two with the trump queen. Then 5 ♣ asks for kings, which are bid up the line as in RKCB.

In this case, when North retreats to the trump suit—which tells his partner he does not have the ♠Q—South gives up. The partnership is obviously missing a key card—almost certainly an ace—and South does not want to speculate by bidding a slam missing the queen of trumps and an ace.

In the given auction, if South bid on to 6 ♠, it would mean that he was inquiring about the trump queen because he was interested in a grand slam. After learning that his partner did not have the queen of trumps, he settled for a small slam.

Here is the queen-ask structure and the responses. After 4NT—5 ♣ or 5 ♦, the next highest non-trump suit asks about the queen, and:

➤ A retreat to the trump suit at the five level denies holding the queen of trumps.

➤ In response to a queen-ask, if the responder has the queen but no outside kings, he bids 5NT.

➤ With the trump queen, the responder bids a king if he has one, even if he has to bid at the six level. With more than one king, the responder bids them up the line, meaning clubs first, then diamonds, etc. If the responder skips over a suit, it means he doesn't have that king.

Here's an example auction:

West	North	East	South
			1 ♠
Pass	2 ♥	Pass	3 ♥
Pass	4 ♣	Pass	4NT
Pass	5 ♣	Pass	5 ♦
Pass	6 ♣	Pass	7NT
All Pass			

After South raises North's response in hearts, North makes a control bid (cue-bid) in clubs. South then bids RKCB with the heart suit as the anchor. North shows three key cards, which must be the ace and king of trumps and the ♣A. South is still concerned about the trump queen, however, so he asks via 5♦. North admits to holding the queen of trumps and the ♣K. South can now count thirteen tricks: five hearts, four clubs, three top spades, and the ♦A.

These might be the two hands:

> ♠ 6 5
>
> ♥ A K Q 5 4
>
> ♦ 1 0 9 8
>
> ♣ A K 5

> ♠ A K Q 1 0 9
>
> ♥ J 1 0 9
>
> ♦ A
>
> ♣ Q J 8 7

A well-practiced pair might get to the grand slam without RKCB, but the convention makes life a lot easier.

Need to Know

Some pairs playing RKCB switch the meanings of the 5♣ and 5♦ responses to 4NT in a scheme known popularly at 1430. It's sort of a mnemonic because 1430 is the score for a vulnerable small slam in a major. It gets the 1430 tag this way: instead of 5♣ showing zero to three key cards, in the 1430 version, the bid shows one or four (the "14" part), and 5♦ then shows zero to three (the "30" part). The one advantage apart from ease of memory is that when the trump suit is hearts and the responder shows one or four key cards with a bid of 5♣, the queen ask can be made with a bid of 5♦. Playing the other way, when the trump suit is hearts and the responder shows one or four by bidding 5♦, the queen ask (5♠) forces the side to slam.

Fresh Out

You may wonder what you should do if your partner bids 4NT, asking about key cards, and you have a void in a side suit.

In that case, with two key cards and a void, bid 5NT. With one key card and a void in a suit ranked below the trump suit—*e.g.*, a void in clubs when your partner is asking about key cards for a heart contract—jump to six of your void suit. If you have one key card and a void in a suit ranked higher than the trump suit, jump to six of your agreed suit.

Bridge Facts

There is an extension of RKCB known as Exclusion RKCB, also sometimes called Voidwood. It is an unusual jump in a suit that asks the partner to show key cards, excluding the suit in which the asker jumped. For example:

West	North	East	South
1♥	Pass	2♦	Pass
4♠			

There is no reason for West to jump—2♠ would never be passed—unless the bid had a special meaning. In this case, it is asking East to show key cards with diamonds as trumps but not to include the ♠A if that is part of East's hand. This convention is used because the ♠A opposite a void is a wasted card, and the presence of the ♠A would not necessarily be uncovered by regular Blackwood or RKCB.

When your agreed suit is a minor, things can get tricky. You can use RKCB, but you must take care.

For example, if you have only one key card yourself, you should not employ RKCB because the response is likely to push you too high. Say you have agreed on clubs as the trump suit and bid 4NT with only one key card. If your partner shows two key cards with a bid of 5♥, you will be forced to bid 6♣ and you might be off two aces. At best you will be off an ace and the trump king. Not a good situation.

The solution is a convention known as Kickback, where the suit directly above four of the agreed minor is RKCB—4♦ when the agreed suit is clubs and 4♥ when the agreed suit is diamonds. Responses follow the same pattern as with 4NT: the first step shows zero or three key cards; the second step one or four; the third, two without the queen; the fourth, two with the queen. So if you bid 4♦ to ask about key cards for clubs, 4♥ shows zero or three, 4♠ shows one or four, 4NT shows two without the queen, and 5♣ shows two with the queen.

Using these lower-level bids to ask about key cards allows you to stop below slam when it's appropriate.

When there is no agreement on the trump suit, RKCB is not used. You can use the same responses used in regular Blackwood:

> ➤ 5♣: Zero or four aces

> ➤ 5♦: One ace

> ➤ 5♥: Two aces

> ➤ 5♠: Three aces

Some experts use this scheme when 4NT is employed with no agreement on the suit:

> ➤ 5♣: Zero or three aces

> ➤ 5♦: One or four aces

> ➤ 5♥: Two aces

All this may seem too complicated to seriously consider, but a bit of study should make the logic of it clear enough to convince you that RKCB should be part of your bidding agreements.

Noisy Opponents

Most of the time when you employ RKCB, you and your partner will have a substantial edge over your opponents in high-card strength. That will not keep them from interfering with your conversation, especially when they have located a big fit in some suit. You must be prepared to cope with these busy opponents who are trying to mess up your RKCB auctions.

For example:

West	North	East	South
		1♠	
2NT	4NT	5♦	?

West's 2NT shows at least ten cards in the minors. North's 4NT is Blackwood (agreeing spades by inference), and 5♦ is thrown in by East to gum up the works. What should South bid?

The two most popular methods for coping with interference are known as DOPI and DEPO.

DOPI stands for Double 0, Pass 1. That is, double by South shows no aces, pass shows one. In this method, a bid of 5♥ would show two aces, 5♠ would show three.

DEPO stands for Double Even, Pass Odd. That is, double shows an even number of aces, pass shows an odd number.

DEPO is used when bidding over the interference would put you past five of your trump suit, as in this auction:

West	North	East	South
			1♥
2♥	4NT		5♠

West's 2♥ shows at least five spades and at least five of an unspecified minor. As with the previous example, 5♠ is East's attempt to wreak havoc on your auction. In this case, if you have two aces, you cannot bid without forcing your side to the six level, and that may be too high. You can double, however, to show an even number of aces, and your partner can convert the informative double to a penalty double by passing if he so chooses. Likewise, if you pass to show an odd number of aces, North can double if he knows slam is out of the question for your side.

It is possible to use RKCB responses to 4NT when your opponents interfere as in the two examples. Using Roman DOPI, double would show zero or three key cards, pass would show one or four, and the next two bids up the line would show two key cards without and with the queen, respectively. This could just as easily be one or four, zero or three (1430).

More High Tech

In Chapter 5, you learned about two important conventions that you should play after your partner opens 1NT—Stayman and Jacoby transfers.

The idea behind the transfer is to keep the strong hand concealed and to make sure the opening lead goes into rather than through the strength.

There is a pretty cool convention invented by the late Mike Smolen that combines the two concepts. One of the key features of the convention is the ability to locate 4-4 fits. Read on to see why this is important.

When your partner opens 1NT and you have five cards in one major and four in the other, it's best to try to play in your 4-4 fit. Consider these two hands:

♠ A K 10 9

♥ Q 7 6

♦ A 4 3 2

♣ Q 6

♠ Q J 8 7

♥ A K J 4 3

♦ K 7 6

♣ 7

There are eight-card fits in both majors, but you can take twelve tricks in the 4-4 spade fit but only eleven in hearts. Can you see how it works?

In spades on normal splits you will be able to ruff a club in the South hand, pull trumps, then play five rounds of hearts, discarding two low diamonds from the dummy. In the end, you will have one good spade and the ♦ A 4, with the ♦ K in your hand to cover the dummy's 4. That's four trumps in the North hand, one in the South hand (a club ruff), five hearts, and two diamonds for twelve.

In hearts, you get four spade tricks, five hearts and two diamonds. You don't gain a trick by ruffing a club with the long heart suit, and with both hands having four spades, you can't get a discard, so you are limited to eleven tricks.

Now here's how Smolen—officially called Smolen transfers—works:

When your partner opens 1NT and you have enough to force game (10 high-card points, or a really good 9) plus five cards in one major and four in another, bid 2♣, ostensibly the Stayman convention, asking about four-card majors.

If your partner has a major and bids it, you simply go to game in that major.

If your partner bids 2♦, indicating no four-card major, your next move tells the story—you jump in your four-card suit, showing five of the other suit at the same time. Here's a sample auction:

West	North	East	South
			1NT
Pass	2♣	Pass	2♦
Pass	3♠		

This shows a game-forcing hand with four spades and five hearts. If the declarer has three hearts, he can bid 4♥, otherwise he bids 3NT.

The goal of finding a major suit fit and keeping the strong hand concealed has been achieved.

You can use Smolen transfers with 6-4 in the majors just as easily:

West	North	East	South
			1NT
Pass	2♣	Pass	2♦
Pass	3♥	Pass	3NT
Pass	4♥	Pass	4♠
All Pass			

North's jump to 3♥ shows four of that suit and at least five spades. South, with only a doubleton in spades, opts for 3NT, but North continues with a transfer bid of 4♥, allowing South to be the declarer in the spade contract.

Knowing his partner's unbalanced shape thanks to the Smolen transfer, the 1NT opener can even show slam interest over his partners' jump (implicitly accepting the responder's long suit as trumps) by cue-bidding with a suitable non-minimum.

Puppet Master

One of the dilemmas of owning a five-card major in a strong, balanced hand is what to open. Here's an example:

      ♠ A Q

      ♥ A K Q 8 7

      ♦ Q 3

      ♣ K J 4

You have 21 high-card points, so you have high hopes for the hand. How should you open the bidding? It's a good hand, sure, but not quite good enough to open 2♣ and rebid 2♥.

If you open 2NT—the high-card points are right, for sure—your partner might bid 3NT and put down this dummy:

♠ K 8 7

♥ J 10 6

♦ 6 4

♣ Q 9 8 7 2

Your opponents rattle off the first six tricks with five diamonds and the ♣ A, and you notice that unless someone can get a club ruff, you are cold for 4♥. Ouch!

Okay, so you have to open 1♥. Now your partner bids 1NT, leaving you with two choices: bid 3NT, which makes the wrong hand the declarer—the opening lead will go right through all your power—or make up a jump shift rebid of, say, 3♣. Yuck!

Bridge Lingo

A contract is said to be **wrong sided** when there is a major disparity between the strengths of the two hands of a partnership and the stronger hand ends up as the dummy. Many modern bidding tools are aimed at keeping the strong hand concealed so that the opening lead goes into the strength rather than through it. It is also best to keep the opponents in the dark as much as possible about the features of the strong hand. It's a lot easier to defend when two-thirds or more of a partnership's assets are on view in the dummy.

Even if your partner bids 1♠ instead of 1NT, you have a problem with your rebid. Showing 18–19, 2NT is inadequate. With your strong five-card suit, your hand looks more like 21 high-card points.

Rebidding 3NT over 1♠ shows a different kind of hand, something like this:

♠ J

♥ A K Q 10 9 8 7

♦ A 3

♣ K J 4

So, what can you do?

The answer lies in a convention with the curious name of Puppet Stayman. It is meant to help you find 4-4 and 5-3 major suit fits whenever they exist. Using this convention will ease your mind about opening 2NT with a five-card major and missing your major suit fit. Here is how it works:

When your partner opens 2NT and you have enough high-card points to go to game, you bid 3 ♣, which asks your partner if he has a five-card major.

The opener's responses are as follows:

> ➤ 3 ♥ / 3 ♠ indicates five of the suit bid

> ➤ 3 ♦ denies a five-card major but promises at least one four-card major

> ➤ 3NT describes a hand with no five-card or four-card major

If the responder has one four-card major, he bids the major he doesn't have:

West	North	East	South
			2NT
Pass	3 ♣	Pass	3 ♦
Pass	3 ♠	Pass	4 ♥
All Pass			

> ➤ 3 ♣: Asks about majors

> ➤ 3 ♦: No five-card major; at least one four-card major

> ➤ 3 ♠: Four hearts (not four spades)

> ➤ 4 ♥: The 4-4 fit is found and game is bid from the right side (strong hand concealed)

If South's major had been spades, he would have bid 3NT, knowing there was no major suit fit.

If the responder has two four-card majors, he would bid 4 ♦ over the opener's 3 ♦, so the opener could select the major. There is a variation of this aspect of the convention that allows the responder to bid 4 ♣ with both majors and slam interest, reserving 4 ♦ as a way to sign off in the partner's major.

This convention was originally devised by veteran California expert Kit Woolsey to be used with 1NT openers. It's called Puppet Stayman because in the original, 2 ♣ was not an inquiry; it was a directive for the opener to bid 2 ♦ if he didn't have a five-card major. The responder then bid the major he didn't have or 2NT with both majors. The opener could then pick the correct contract without revealing information about his distribution.

Staying Low

When two partners agree to play sound opening bids, it becomes vitally important for the player in the third seat to protect against your partner's having passed with a near opener.

Consider that if your partner as opener declines to open a 12-point hand and you are sitting in the third seat after two passes with 10 or 11 high-card points, your side has the larger share of the high-card points and can probably make at least a part-score contract (a bid below the game level—e.g., 2♠). If you pass and your partner did have the near opener, the player in the fourth seat will be too weak to keep the bidding open and the deal will be passed out. That could be a terrible result for you in a club or tournament game.

Bridge Basics

When there are three passes to you and you are trying to decide whether to keep the bidding open—if you pass, it's over—there is a formula that has some tactical validity. It's called the Rule of Fifteen (also known as Pearson Point Count). It works this way: Add the number of your high-card points to the number of spades. If the total is 15 or more, open the bidding. With less, pass it out. The theory is that if you keep the bidding open and your opponents have more spades than your side does, they will be able to outbid you and collect a plus by making their contract or pushing you too high. As with most aspects of bridge, judgment is important.

Need to Know

The term *limit raise* is somewhat vague and technically could apply to any raise that has a bottom and a top in terms of high-card strength. In bridge parlance, however, it has come to mean a hand with invitational strength, usually 10 to 11 support points, which can include high cards and distributional values when a trump fit has been established.

In the old days, if the opener had passed a near opener as the dealer and his partner bid in the third seat, the opener faced a dilemma: does he jump to show his values and risk a minus when the partner had opened light in third seat, or does he make a simple raise and risk missing game when his partner in the third seat had a full opening bid?

Doug Drury came to the rescue with his popular convention. When a partner opens a major in the third seat and the opener has 10 to a poor 12 high-card points, he can bid 2♣ to show support and limit-raise values without having to jump.

In the original version of Drury, the opener bid 2♦ to say he had opened light in the third seat and his partner, without some unexpected asset, would sign off in the partner's major.

Nowadays, the third-seat opener responds to Drury with no interest in going higher by simply rebidding his suit:

West	North	East	South
	Pass	Pass	1♥
Pass	2♣	Pass	2♥

This is known as reverse Drury, although this way of using the convention is overwhelmingly preferred by most users.

South's bid of 2♥ shows that his third-seat opener was light and that he has no interest in trying for game opposite his passed-hand partner. Any other bid by South would show at least mild game interest and, according to the partnership agreement, could be a game try, as in this sequence:

West	North	East	South
	Pass	Pass	1♥
Pass	2♣	Pass	3♣

South is interested in game and is making a help-suit game try in clubs. A help-suit game try asks the partner to accept the game invitation with honors in the suit bid. If South knows he wants to be in game and does not have sufficient assets to explore for slam opposite a passed-hand partner, he can just bid 4♥ and avoid giving information to his opponents.

Drury Refined

It is possible to use the convention simply to show 10 or 11 (or a poor 12) high-card points without promising a fit for the partner's major, but most partnerships agree that using reverse Drury shows at least three-card support.

A refinement of revised Drury devised by many-time national champion Marty Bergen allows the convention's user to distinguish between three- and four-card (or better) support for the partner's major suit.

With two-way reverse Drury, a response of 2♣ by the opener's partner shows three-card support, and 2♦ shows at least four-card support (some pairs reverse the meanings of those bids). This provides some comfort for the third-seat opener, who may prefer to open a four-card major as a lead-directing bid, perhaps with a hand such as this:

♠ A K J 10

♥ Q 7 4

♦ 7 4 3 2

♣ J 4

If you open this hand in third seat after two passes—and you certainly should—you would never consider 1♦ for your bid. That is definitely not the suit you want led. An opening of 1♠, on the other hand, could get your partner off to a dynamite opening lead if your opponents buy the contract.

Using two-way reverse Drury, you might even feel like competing if your partner shows four-card spade support and your opponents get into the auction.

Don't Back Down

In the old days of bridge, when a player opened 1NT—usually with a range of 16–18 high-card points—he pretty much had the auction to himself. Only in rare cases did the other side enter the fray.

Attitudes are vastly different today, and competitive players view a 1NT opening—in this era, 15–17 HCP—as a challenge. That is why there are so many different conventions for competing after an opponent opens the once-feared 1NT.

There's another factor at work, too. Many 1NT openers these days are of the weaker variety with several different ranges: 12–14, 11–14, 13–15, 14–17, and even a mini or kamikaze 1NT opener of 10–12.

What that means is that there are now more opportunities for players to open 1NT, so you must be prepared to cope with all the 1NT flavors that might come along. Let's look at a few of the popular defenses to 1NT openings.

DONT (Disturb the Opponents' Notrump)

DONT comes from the fertile mind of Marty Bergen, once an active and highly successful player who now concentrates on writing and teaching.

Here's how DONT works:

In the direct seat (the next player to bid after someone opens the bidding):

> ➤ Double: A one-suited hand, preferably six or more in the long suit

> ➤ 2♣: Clubs and a higher-ranking suit

> ➤ 2♦: Diamonds and a major suit

> ➤ 2♥: Hearts and spades

> ➤ 2♠: Spades (six cards or more preferred)

This convention is designed to make it easier for you to get into your opponents' 1NT auctions, with each bid structured so that you can stop at the two level with two modest hands. You can see that except for spades, any bid shows that suit plus one higher-ranking suit.

Here are some important points about bidding by the partner of the DONT bidder.

> ➤ When your partner doubles and the next player passes, the advancer (the partner of the DONT bidder) can pass with better than opening values, converting the double to penalty. Most of the time, the advancer will bid 2♣ to tell his partner to name his long suit or pass if that suit is clubs.

An important note about the spade suit: If the DONT bidder starts with a double and bids spades over the advancer's 2♣, the bid of 2♠ shows a better hand, possibly as good as an opening bid.

Also after your partner doubles, if the next player takes action, perhaps bidding a suit or transferring to a suit, double by the advancer sends the message that he has support for whatever the DONT bidder's long suit might be. For example:

West	North	East	South
	1NT	Dbl	2♥
Dbl			

That double says, "I want to compete and, except for hearts, I have support for all suits." The same message would be sent if South bid 2♦ as a transfer to hearts.

Need to Know

DONT can be used in the direct seat and in the pass-out seat (1NT has been followed by two passes; if you pass, the auction is over). All of the bids are the same. The convention can also be used against opening bids of 2NT, although that would be a rare occasion and almost always with extreme distribution such as 6-5 in two suits.

➤ When the DONT bidder starts with a suit, the advancer can pass with three-card support for the suit bid, and raise the suit bid with four or more of the partner's suit. If the advancer does not have a fit for the partner's bid suit (two or fewer cards), he bids the next higher suit to tell the partner to name his other suit. For example:

West	North	East	South
	1NT	2♣	Pass
2♦			

West's bid says, "I don't like clubs because I have two or fewer in that suit. If your second suit is diamonds, you can pass. Otherwise, bid your major."

West might have this hand:

♠ J 7 6

♥ Q 9 8 3

♦ K J 5 4 3

♣ 3

West does not expect East to pass 2♦, but even a 4-3 spade fit would be better than letting East play in clubs with only one card for support.

➤ If the advancer skips the next higher suit for his response, that shows a long suit and is to play. For example:

West	North	East	South
	1NT	2♣	Pass
2♥			

West's 2♥ shows a long, at least semi-strong heart suit and does not invite East to correct.

➤ When the advancer has an opening hand or better and the partner enters the auction directly over 1NT, a bid of 2NT shows the good hand and lets the partner know that game is possible.

Here are responses to 2NT after a DONT bid:

➤ If the DONT bidder originally overcalled 2♣, he bids 3♣ in response to 2NT to show a minimum. The advancer can then either pass if he fits clubs or bid 3♦, asking the partner to pass with diamonds as his second suit or correct to his major.

> ➤ If the DONT bidder started with 2♦, a response of 3♣ to 2NT shows a minimum and that his second suit was hearts; 3♦ shows a minimum with spades. A response of 3♥ or 3♠ would show the original suit (diamonds) with the bid suit and a maximum.

Need to Know

Some partnerships vary the system they play against 1NT openers depending upon the range of the opener. The weak 1NT, for example, can cause problems for the side that has the preponderance of the high cards. In that sense, the weak 1NT opener is a preemptive bid that takes away some of the opponents' constructive bidding tools. For that reason, many pairs agree that a double of a weak 1NT is penalty oriented, showing high-card values. In that way, they have a better chance of getting to game if that's where they belong.

> ➤ If the DONT bidder started with 2♥, a response of 3♣ to 2NT shows a minimum but with better hearts; 3♦ shows a minimum with better spades; 3♥ shows hearts and a maximum; 3♠ shows spades and a maximum.

Do You Dare?

You may be wondering what kind of hand you should have to get involved when an opponent opens 1NT.

Occasionally, it will be a close decision, and there is a way of deciding whether to jump in there or pass and wait for a better opportunity.

The first part of the formula is to determine how many losers your hand has, a loser being every missing ace, king, and queen in a suit of at least three cards (no suit has more than three losers).

That means AQ65 has one loser (missing king), A543 has two losers (missing king and queen), 87 has two losers (only two cards), K43 has two losers, AKQ5 has no losers, and a void has no losers.

Once you determine your losers for the entire hand, subtract that number from the sum of the cards in your two longest suits. If the answer is zero or one, wait for another chance to bid—just pass. If the sum is two or more, jump right in.

Here are some example hands. Your right-hand opponent has opened 1NT. What is your bid with these hands?

Hand 1	Hand 2	Hand 3
♠ A Q 7 6	♠ A 10 7 6 5	♠ 5
♥ K J 4 3	♥ K J 4 3 2	♥ Q J 8 7 3
♦ J 3	♦ 6	♦ A J 10 7
♣ Q 8 6	♣ 4 3	♣ K 7 6

> ➤ Hand 1: You have seven losers and eight cards in your two longest suits. Despite your 13 high-card points, you should pass.

> ➤ Hand 2: This hand has only eight high-card points, but there are seven losers and ten cards in the two longest suits. Do not hesitate to bid 2♥, showing the majors.

> ➤ Hand 3: This hand is a bit awkward because to get into the bidding you must start with the shorter of your two suits, which is counterintuitive. Still, the hand qualifies for a bid with seven losers and nine cards in the two longest suits. Suck it up and bid 2♦. No convention is perfect.

If you feel frisky and the vulnerability is in your favor (they are, you aren't), you can shade these requirements somewhat in the interest of annoying your opponents.

Hamilton/Cappelletti/Pottage

This convention has three names. The one you use depends in large measure on where you live or where you first heard about it. Cappelletti (named after Mike Cappelletti) has more of an East Coast orientation, Hamilton (named after Fred Hamilton) has more of a West Coast origin. When used in Great Britain, the convention is known as Pottage (named after Julian Pottage).

The key difference between Hamilton and most other defenses to 1NT is that double is for business (or at least showing a decent hand, starting with about 14 high-card points).

Here are the features:

> ➤ Double: Penalty oriented, showing a good 14 or more high-card points
> ➤ 2♣: One suit (should be six cards or more)
> ➤ 2♦: Majors
> ➤ 2♥: Hearts and a minor
> ➤ 2♠: Spades and a minor
> ➤ 2NT: Minors

Double and all the bids apply in the direct or balancing seat.

After a 2♣ overcall (showing one suit), 2♦ by the advancer asks the 2♣ bidder to pass with diamonds or correct. A direct bid of 2♥ or 2♠ would show a long, strong suit.

After an overcall of 2♥ or 2♠, 2NT asks the bidder to show his minor. When the advancer then returns to the bidder's major, that is an invitation to game in the major.

If the advancer's hand is weak and he has six or more clubs, he can pass the overcall of 2♣. If the 2♣ overcall is doubled, a redouble by the advancer is for rescue (short in clubs), but a pass shows a club suit, and 2♦ shows length in diamonds.

Hamilton is often the preferred defense to weak 1NT openings.

There are at least two dozen defenses to 1NT openings listed in the latest (7th edition of the *Official Encyclopedia of Bridge*, published by the American Contract Bridge League, and there are many other homemade or hybrid versions of existing conventions. It is up to individual partnerships to decide which suits them best.

CHAPTER 17

Advanced Declarer Play

In This Chapter

➤ Visualization

➤ Take your best shot

➤ Elimination

➤ Squeeze basics

In this chapter, you will be introduced to some plays you might think are beyond you. Such plays are easier than you imagine, but you must pay attention and use your brain. You will discover some counterintuitive plays that represent your best chance at making a difficult contract—or defeating one that is seemingly secure. You will also find out about a play you can make without any expert intentions—and you will see how it can help you score tricks you didn't think were possible.

Finally, the mystery-shrouded squeeze will come into your life—and you will see that it's not as complex as you think.

Eye on the Ball

A key to successful play is forming a picture of your opponents' cards and how they are laid out against yours. That can help a lot as you formulate your plans. On many occasions, getting it right is just a matter of putting the last piece of the jigsaw puzzle in place.

Your opponents' actions often present you with lots of clues—the bidding or the opening lead and subsequent play, for example.

Sometimes you have to go after the clues yourself. Consider this situation:

♠ K 6 3 2

♥ Q J 4 3

♦ Q

♣ A Q 8 5

♠ - -

♥ A 10 9 7 6 5

♦ A K 8 7

♣ 5 4 3

West	North	East	South
Pass	1♣	Pass	1♥
Pass	3♥	Pass	6♥
All Pass			

West leads the ♦10, and the dummy's queen wins.

You have to decide how to play the heart suit. Taken in isolation, the finesse is the percentage play, but you do have a chance to gain a bit of information. First, you consider that West passed as dealer and East declined to enter the bidding over 1♣.

At any rate, you can make a no-risk play at trick two if you put the ♠K on the table. East will be hard pressed to duck if he holds the ace (if he has the ace and plays low, you're in a tough game). If East covers the king with the ace, you ruff and take the club finesse. If it wins, you are home. You take the heart finesse for an overtrick, and even if that finesse loses you will be able to discard the dummy's two low clubs on your top clubs. It's when the club finesse loses that you must continue processing the information you have gained.

Okay, East played the ♣K on the queen when you took the finesse. Now you know that East started with the ♠A and ♣K. Based on West's lead of the ♦10, East also has the jack in that suit. Further, if West's spade suit was headed by the QJ, he might have led that suit.

You can therefore at least tentatively place East with the ♠AJx(x)—with five or six he probably would have overcalled 1♠ or maybe even 2♠)—the ♣K and the ♦J. That's 9 high-card points. If he also had the ♥K, it is highly likely that he would have entered the auction.

You now have a lot of evidence to indicate the anti-percentage play of a heart to the ace.

Need to Know

One of the key elements of successful play, especially as a defender, is to anticipate situations so that you can be ready when the declarer makes his move. For example, you hold four diamonds to the king and the declarer has three to the ace in the dummy. The declarer bids diamonds along the way to a heart contract, so you know he probably has four of them. When the declarer plays over to the dummy's ♦A and calls for a low diamond, you must be ready to play low smoothly. The declarer might have four diamonds to the Q10, giving him a guess about how to play the suit. If you fumble before following low, the declarer will most likely put up the queen and easily make his contract. If you follow low smoothly, it's a pure guess, and some of the time he will go wrong. All it takes to give the declarer the maximum problem is to anticipate the situation.

East played low smoothly when you played the ♠K at trick two. Your best bet would be to take the heart finesse and, if it loses, rely on West to start with the ♣K as well.

Playing the ♠K from the dummy at trick two is known as a discovery play. You are hoping to discover information that will help you make the winning decision in the play.

Make Them Help

Here's another type of discovery play that relies on the opponents to be diligent signalers:

♠ Q 7 3

♥ K Q 6 4 2

♦ 6 5

♣ 7 5 3

♠ A K 4

♥ A 5

♦ K 8 7

♣ K Q J 10 4

West	North	East	South
		2NT	
Pass	3NT	All Pass	

North might have transferred to hearts and then bid 3NT to give you a choice of games, but his hand is balanced and he figured the high-card strength between the two hands—at least 27 high-card points—should be good enough to take nine tricks. It turns out to be the best decision because you were going to land in 3NT anyway, and now your opponents don't know about the layout in hearts.

West leads the ♦3 and East puts in the 10. South can't afford to duck, so he wins the king. The ♦3 could have been led from a four-card suit, but it could also be a five-bagger (if you or the dummy had the ♦2, you would know). If you knew for sure West had led from a four-card suit, you would simply play the ♣K and let someone take the ace. The opponents would have at most three diamonds to cash and you could go on to the next deal.

Or try hearts first, and finding they don't break 3-3, turn your attention to clubs, you might still be defeated even if diamonds were 4-4 all along because one of your opponents will have a good heart at that point.

Anyway, because you can't be sure about the diamond suit, you must do a bit of detective work.

Bridge Basics

You are told to always lead fourth best, and in general it's a good policy. There will be times when you want to deceive the declarer into thinking your suit is safe. Consider that you are on lead against 3NT with this hand:

♠ Q J 7 6 2

♥ 7 6 4

♦ Q 8 3

♣ 10 9

You hope to find your partner with the ace or king of your long suit, but if you start with the ♠6, the declarer might hold up with a single stopper. The declarer may have to take a finesse into your partner's hand, and in case the finesse loses, the declarer wants to make sure that when you start with a five-card suit, your partner won't have any of your suit left.

If you start with the deceptive ♠2, a declarer who is watching the cards will play you for a four-card suit and may not hold up when your partner plays the king. The declarer will think the suit is safe—that no matter what, you won't be able to take more than three spade tricks. Imagine his surprise when your partner gets in and returns your suit and you cash the setting trick.

Put yourself in the place of the defenders, who are looking at the dummy and are unsure about how many hearts you have. If you start with the low heart from your hand, it is very likely that each opponent will signal count in case the other has the ♥A and needs to know how long to hold it up.

Say you play the ♥5 from your hand and West follows with the 3. That's a good sign. He would play low from a three-card holding, and if that's what he has, East also has three so you will be able to run five hearts to go with your three spades and one diamond. You won't need to risk playing on clubs.

Onward with the discovery work. The ♥K wins, East following with the 8. Now when you play a heart back to your hand, East follows with the 9 and West the 7. Both opponents have played up the line, so it is very likely they both have three hearts. Forget about clubs. Just play over to the dummy's ♠Q, run your hearts, and return to your hand with spades to take your nine tricks because this was the full deal:

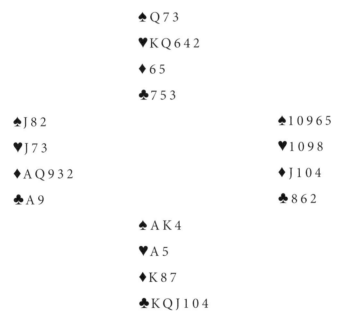

          ♠Q 7 3

          ♥K Q 6 4 2

          ♦6 5

          ♣7 5 3

♠J 8 2   ♠10 9 6 5

♥J 7 3   ♥10 9 8

♦A Q 9 3 2   ♦J 1 0 4

♣A 9   ♣8 6 2

          ♠A K 4

          ♥A 5

          ♦K 8 7

          ♣K Q J 1 0 4

You can see that playing on clubs would have led to defeat. West wins and cashes four diamonds.

If your opponents' count signals indicated that the heart suit was breaking 4-2, you would have abandoned the heart suit before you set up a winner for the opponents and tried your luck in clubs. If diamonds weren't 4-4, you were always going down anyway.

Go the Other Way

Here's a situation you see all the time:

♦A 5 2

♦K J 9

The right way to play this suit for no losers is to play low to the ace, followed by low to the jack unless East plays the queen.

Now and then, you will find yourself with this combination when you know the queen cannot be on your right.

♠Q 10 9 6

♥Q 8 7

♦A 5 2

♣Q 5 4

♠A K J 4 3 2

♥6 4 3

♦K J 9

♣A

West	North	East	South
	Pass	Pass	1♠
Pass	2♣	Pass	4♠
All Pass			

West leads the ♥J, which you duck, East plays the 9. The ♥10 goes to East's king, followed by the ♥A with West discarding the ♣2. East exits with a trump, which you win in hand with West following.

Your contract depends on playing diamonds for no losers, and clearly the percentage play is low to the ace then low to the jack. Something in the back of your mind is telling you not so fast. It was that signal in clubs by West. With the ♣K, West would surely have played a high club.

The diamond finesse can still be taken later, but there's no rush at this point.

At trick five, you cash the ♣A and play a second spade to the dummy, East follows. Now you try a discovery play by calling for the ♣Q. East covers, you ruff, and now you know the routine play in diamonds cannot win.

Think about it: East has shown up with five hearts to the AK and the ♣K. If he also had the ♦Q, that's 12 high-card points plus two and a half quick tricks. Almost everyone would open that hand in the second seat with a bid of 1♥. That means West almost certainly has the ♦Q.

So what can you do? You could play the ♦A and ♦K, hoping the queen drops, but that would work only once in a blue moon. Your opponents have seven diamonds between them and a 5-2 split occurs only 30 percent of the time—and even at that the queen is two and a half times more likely to be in the five-card holding than to be sitting doubleton.

If you did not have the ♦9 in your hand, you would have to rely on a miracle in the suit. Because you do have that lucky card, you have an option. It's called the backward finesse.

You have just ruffed when East covered the ♣Q with the king, so you are in your hand. Here's the diamond combination again:

   ♦A 5 2

   ♦K J 9

Your correct play is the jack from your hand. If West plays low, you will let the jack run. If West covers, you win and play the ♦2, inserting the 9 if East follows low. If the cards are as you hope, this will be the full layout:

                    ♠ Q 1 0 9 6
                    ♥ Q 8 7
                    ♦ A 5 2
                    ♣ Q 5 4

    ♠ 5   ♠ 8 7
    ♥ J 10   ♥ A K 9 5 2
    ♦ Q 8 7 6   ♦ 1 0 4 3
    ♣ J 8 7 6 3 2   ♣ K 1 0 9

                    ♠ A K J 4 3 2
                    ♥ 6 4 3
                    ♦ K J 9
                    ♣ A

Obviously, if West started with the ♦Q and the ♦10, you were not going to make your contract. Once you knew that the normal finesse in diamonds could not work, you took advantage of your luck in having the ♦9 to take your best shot.

Losers Go Away

There's an old saying about not being able to see the forest for the trees. In bridge, you can sometimes overlook a winning play by taking too wide a view. Observe:

♠ 4 3 2

♥ 8 3

♦ A 7 6

♣ A 9 8 3 2

♠ A K Q J 9 6

♥ 1 0 9 2

♦ K 4 3

♣ 7

West	North	East	South
2♥	Pass	3♥	3♠
Pass	4♠	All Pass	

A word about the auction. West's 2♥ shows a six-card suit and East's raise is meant to further the preemptive action of the opening bid. In a sense, East is sending a message to South: "This deal may belong to your side, so I'm going to make it tougher for you to get involved."

East might be trying to set a trap for you with a good hand, but if he really had the goods he might have bid 2NT to try to find out more about his partner's opener.

In any event, you had your bid of 3♠ and your partner could hardly do less than raise to game with his trump support and two aces.

West started with the ♥K, which is overtaken by East with the ace. East fires back a heart to West's jack, and West continues with the ♥Q. Now what?

Unfortunately, your partner's trump support is not robust, so it is very likely that if you ruff the third round of hearts in the dummy it will be overruffed? Do you have any options?

Bridge Basics

When there is an opening bid to your left that is followed by two passes, a jump bid by you in the pass-out seat is not a weak bid. It shows a better-than-minimum opening hand and a good suit, usually with at least six cards. The same applies whether it's an opening at the one level (normal opener) or a weak bid such as an opener of 2 ♦. The jump by the player in fourth seat should have intermediate strength. When 2 ♦ on your left is passed to you, this is what a 3 ♥ bid by you should look like:

> ♠ A Q J
>
> ♥ K Q 10 9 8 5
>
> ♦ A 3
>
> ♣ 6 5 4

Take away the ♦ A and the proper bid in fourth seat is 2 ♥.

This is a trump contract, remember? Did you count your losers before you played to the opening lead? Well, even if you didn't, it's not too late.

Look at your diamond suit. There's a certain loser there, right? Why not lose that trick now? You know you are going to lose the third trick because the dummy's trumps are so weak. Instead of futilely ruffing the third heart, just discard the dummy's ♦ 6. You are home and dry if this is the full deal:

♠ 4 3 2
♥ 8 3
♦ A 7 6
♣ A 9 8 3 2

♠ 8 5   ♠ 10 7
♥ K Q J 7 6 5   ♥ A 4
♦ Q 10 5   ♦ J 9 8 2
♣ J 4   ♣ K Q 10 6 5

♠ A K Q J 9 6
♥ 10 9 2
♦ K 4 3
♣ 7

If West continues with a fourth round of hearts, ruff in the dummy, and if East does not overruff, discard a losing diamond from your hand. If he does overruff, you overruff him. You then follow with two rounds of trumps. When they split 2-2, you can claim because you can play a diamond to the ace in the dummy, then a diamond to your king, and ruff your losing diamond. You get six trumps in your hand, one trump in the dummy, two high diamonds, and the ♣A for ten tricks. If West plays a diamond at trick four, just win the ace and cash a couple of trumps, eventually ruffing your losing diamond in the dummy.

The play you just executed is called a loser on loser play.

Here's another variation on that theme:

♠ K Q 5 4

♥ 8 4 3

♦ Q 9 4

♣ 9 7 3

♠ - -

♥ A K J

♦ A K 8 7 6 5 3 2

♣ A 4

West	North	East	South
1♣	Pass	Pass	Dbl
Pass	1♠	Pass	3♦
Pass	4♦	Pass	6♦
All Pass			

When you double in the pass out seat and later bid your own suit with a jump, you show a hand much too strong to simply bid 2♦, which would show an intermediate hand of a good 13 to 16 high-card points. Your partner recognizes that you are showing a powerhouse and is happy to be able to raise. You bid what you think you can make and hope your assessment is accurate.

West leads the ♣K to your ace. Can you back up your optimistic bid with accurate play?

Start by considering your losers. West has knocked out your ♣A, so you have a loser there. You also have a potential loser in hearts. You can take care of that if East has the ♥Q, which would allow you to finesse the jack to make your slam.

You will reject that idea if you remember the bidding, however. Between your hand and the dummy there are 27 high-card points, leaving only 13 for your opponents. If East has the ♥Q, that means West opened the bidding on 11 high-card points. That's not impossible, but it is unlikely—and you can be nearly certain that West has the ♠A. If he does not have that card, it means he opened on 9 high-card points.

The solution should be coming to you. After winning the ♣A at trick one, play the ♦A, West showing out. You then play a diamond to the dummy's queen, pulling the last trump. Now you are ready for the key play: call for the dummy's ♠K. When East follows low as expected, discard your low club. West wins but cannot cash another club, and you still have the ♦9 left in the dummy to get to the now-established ♠Q, which you can use to get rid of the ♥J. It is no surprise to you when this turns out to be the full deal:

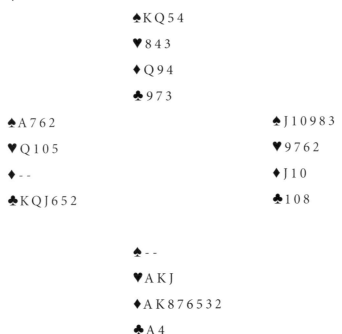

Even if West had not opened the bidding, giving you clues as to where the missing high cards were located, you would play the same way because it guarantees the contract with eight diamonds, one spade, two hearts, and one club. If your opponents had not bid and East had covered the ♠K with the ace, you could ruff, return to the dummy with your diamond, discard the losing club on the ♠Q, and take the heart finesse for an overtrick.

Here's one last example of a far-sighted loser-on-loser play:

♠ J 8 2

♥ Q J 10

♦ 3 2

♣ A 7 6 5 4

♠ 4

♥ A K 9 6 5 4 3

♦ K 5

♣ K 3 2

West	North	East	South
1♠	Pass	2♠	3♥
Pass	4♥	All Pass	

When your opponents hold the spade suit, especially with a nine-card fit, you can expect to be outbid on many occasions. At unfavorable vulnerability, however, they might not be so ready to step in there—and they will often like their chances on defense. No one wants to sacrifice against a non-making game.

At any rate, West starts with the ♠A, on which East plays the 7. This is a come-on, so West continues with the ♠K. You are at the crossroads now. What is your play?

You have already lost one trick and you have a certain loser in clubs. You can establish two club winners in the dummy by playing three rounds of the suit—ace, king, and a low one—but if East wins the third round of clubs, he will certainly push a diamond through your king. On the bidding, it is likely that the ♦A is in the West hand. Do you have a plan B?

Actually, plan B should never enter the picture. Plan A is the only choice: Just discard a low club from your hand on the second high spade. Now you can win any continuation—unless West sees the handwriting on the wall and cashes him ♦A—play a couple of trumps, then play to the ♣K, followed by a club to the ace and a club ruff in your hand. You can get back to the dummy with the last trump and make an overtrick by discarding your two diamonds on the good clubs.

You will succeed when this is the full deal:

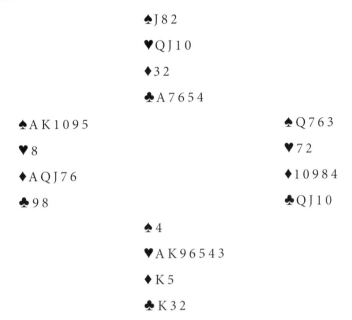

West, of course, may not be so accommodating as to continue with a second high spade. He might be able to envision the situation and decide to make you work for your ten tricks. Say West switches to a trump at trick two. You win and in dummy still have a chance to make your contract via a loser-on-loser play. Just continue with the dummy's ♠8. If East is alert, he will put the queen on that trick, hoping to hold the lead so he can play a diamond. If he does play the queen, ruff and return to the dummy with a trump and try the ♠J. When East cannot cover, you discard a low club from your hand. West wins but will have to cash the ♦A to keep you from making an overtrick.

You were lucky, of course, to have spot cards in spades good enough to let you execute this plan—and you will not always face such tough defense.

Good Riddance

When the bidding tells you that your finesses are not going to win, one of your best options to make your contract anyway is the endplay. To prepare for a successful endplay, it is often necessary to eliminate any suit the opponent might be able to use for a safe exit. Here is a classic end position that requires eliminating certain suits.

♠ A K 5

♥ Q 9 8 4

♦ A K 3

♣ 5 4 3

♠ 8 7

♥ A K J 1 0 5

♦ Q J 4

♣ A Q 1 0

You reach 6 ♥ from the South seat. West leads the ♠ Q.

You have eleven top tricks and need to hold your club losers to one. Taken in isolation, playing a club to your 10, and if that loses, a club to the queen gives you a 76 percent chance of success. That's all well and good, but why not go for the 100 percent chance. The only fly in the ointment might be a 4-0 trump split.

Bridge Lingo

When you go about the job of eliminating suits to set up an endplay, you are said to be stripping the hand. This can be in preparation for a situation in which the player who is endplayed is forced to offer a ruff and sluff—you ruff in one hand and discard or "sluff" a loser from the other hand—to return a suit that the declarer desires.

Win the ♠ A and play a trump to your hand. If everyone follows, you have a 100 percent line of play. Do you see it?

Here's what you do: Cash another high heart from your hand. If both opponents follow, play a spade to the king and ruff a spade, eliminating that suit. Now play the ♦ Q and a diamond to the ace. The ♦ K completes the elimination of another suit and you are ready to apply the coup de grâce. Simply play a low club from the dummy and cover East's card. West may win with the jack, but it's all over at that point when this is the full deal:

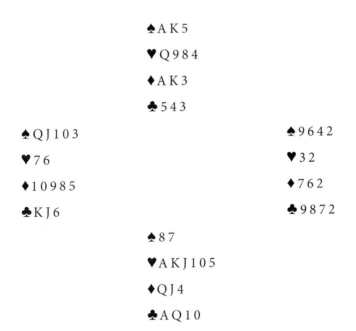

West will be down to the ♣K6 plus a diamond and a spade. If he returns a club, it's right into your AQ. If he plays either of the other suits, you ruff in the dummy and discard the ♣Q from your hand. Easy, right?

As you can see, if you had not eliminated the other suits, he would have played a diamond or a spade after winning the ♣J, and you would have had to take another club finesse and gone down in a cold contract.

Note that having the ♣AQ9 is just as good as the AQ10. Check it out:

The declarer is in the North hand and plays a low club. If East tries to help his partner by inserting the 10, the declarer covers with the queen. When West wins in a situation where the other suits have been eliminated, he must play from the ♣J into the declarer's ♣A9 or give a ruff and sluff. This works also when East has the ♣J10x. If he plays either of his high clubs, South covers and has the A9 left for West to lead into.

Take No Chances

You may have noticed that a lot of the elimination plays involve finesses. That's not always the case. Sometimes elimination helps you avoid making a guess in a key suit. Here's an example:

♠ K Q 7 6 4

♥ A 4

♦ A J 4

♣ K 10 5

♠ A J 10 3 2

♥ 5 3

♦ K 10 5

♣ A Q 4

You land in 6 ♠ with no bidding by the opponents. West leads the ♥ Q. You win the ace and pull trumps. It looks as though you must find the ♦ Q to make this contract. If that's your thinking, try again.

Even if you find the ♦ Q with a lucky guess, you will still have a heart loser.

Bridge Lingo

Sometimes your hand and dummy will have the exact same shape—five spades opposite five spades, two hearts facing two hearts, etc. In such a case, the two hands are said to have *mirror distribution*. This is occasionally problematic for the declaring side because no discards are available on any of the suits.

The 100 percent play in this case is to pull trumps, then cash your club winners, eliminating that suit, then exit with a heart from either hand. You don't care which opponent wins the trick, your troubles are over. If either one plays a diamond, your worries are over in that suit. If the player who wins gets out with another heart, simply ruff in one hand and discard a diamond from the other.

Your Best Shot

There will be times when you cannot guarantee your contract as with the elimination plays discussed so far, but that doesn't mean you should give up. Here's a deal where you can succeed if you give if your best shot.

♠ J 1 0 9 8

♥ A K 5

♦ A 6 4

♣ K 3 2

♠ A K 7 6 5

♥ Q 8 6

♦ K 8 7

♣ A 5

You reach 6 ♠ from the South seat and West starts with the ♥ J. You win in the dummy and play a spade to your ace. You return to the dummy with the ♥ K and play a second spade, East discards a low heart.

Drat! It looks like you are going down because you are certain to lose a spade, and it looks like you will have to lose a diamond, too. Is there anything you can do? Think about it before reading on.

There is a chance if you envision a layout of the cards that will see you home.

What if West has a doubleton diamond? That will work if played correctly.

First turn your attention to clubs. Play the ♣ A and a club to the king, then ruff a club. Now cash the ♦ K and play a diamond to the ace. If that holds up, you can now play a heart to your queen and exit with a low spade. You hope this is the full deal:

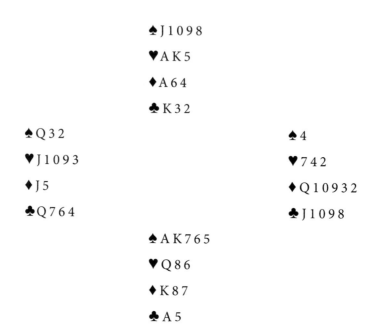

♠J1098
♥AK5
♦A64
♣K32

♠Q32
♥J1093
♦J5
♣Q764

♠4
♥742
♦Q10932
♣J1098

♠AK765
♥Q86
♦K87
♣A5

West will be on lead with only a heart and a club left. When he plays either one, you can ruff in the dummy and discard your losing diamond from your hand. Note that even if West had a singleton diamond, it would not have profited him to ruff when you played the second diamond from your hand. He would have been ruffing your loser with his natural trump trick—not a good move.

If West started with three diamonds, you will go down, but you took your best shot. Some players would simply concede down one when East discarded on the second round of spades. Not you.

Tighten Up

Most new players have the mistaken notion that only an expert can execute a squeeze. That is a myth, plain and simple. Check this out:

♠AKQ2
♥KJ
♦10976
♣A32

♠765
♥AQ5
♦AKQ
♣Q764

West	North	East	South
			1NT
Pass	2♣	Dbl	2♦
Pass	4NT	Pass	6NT
All Pass			

Your 1NT opener shows 15–17 high-card points, and when North bid 2♣, asking if you have a four-card major, East doubled to show a strong holding in clubs. With 17 high-card points, your partner has more than enough to invite a slam, which he does with his bid of 4NT.

For those who may not have been paying attention to earlier discussions, in this situation 4NT is not Blackwood. It is what is known as a quantitative raise. South is asked to bid 6NT with a maximum for his range. South is on the top of the 15–17 range, so he bids the slam.

West does as he is told and leads his club—the 8. You know where the ♣K is, so you might as well just play low. As expected, East wins the ♣K and returns the jack to the dummy's ace. On the second round of clubs, West discards a low heart. Now you know that East started with five clubs to the KJ109. He had his double of 2♣, that's for sure.

The Abacus Effect

It's time to take stock. First, count your tricks. You have two club tricks, three spades, three hearts, and three diamonds. That's eleven tricks—one short. There are possibilities for trick number twelve in spades and in diamonds. Spades could break 3-3 or the ♦J might fall under one of your high diamonds, making the dummy's 10 good for your twelfth trick.

So what should you do?

On this deal, it is very important not to touch spades (you will see why in a minute). If the spade suit is splitting 3-3, you are always going to make this contract. Don't worry about spades right now.

Bridge Basics

When you are a trick short of your contract and have a long suit to run, it is usually right to cash all the winners in that suit. Sometimes a squeeze will operate, but even if the cards are not lying just right for a squeeze, your opponents may fall victim to what is known as a pseudo squeeze. That is, an opponent may envision a lie of the cards that does not exist, causing him to make pitches that turn one or more of your losers into winners. Even expert opponents will occasionally form the wrong impression and hand you an unmakeable contract via a pseudo squeeze. Contracts made that way count just as much as the ones you bring home legitimately. It pays not to give up.

What you should do after winning the ♣A in the dummy is play a club from the dummy. East will play the ♣9 to force your queen. You know he still has the ♣10, which beats the ♣7 still in your hand. You will remember that East has the ♣10 because that will be important later on.

Now you cash three high diamonds, hoping the jack will fall, but East follows only twice, with the 8 and 2 before discarding the ♣5. Too bad—the ♦10 is not going to be a trick for you. So, you think, maybe it's time to try spades.

Hold your horses. You still have three winners to cash—your hearts. Now is when you must be on the lookout for East's ♣10. You can forget about West. Just concentrate on East.

You play a low heart to the dummy's king. East follows. He follows again when you play the ♥J from the dummy to your ace. When you play the ♥Q, you can get rid of the ♦10, which is worthless anyway, and watch for the ♣10. On the third round of clubs, East discards the ♠4.

So far, you have done everything right. When the ♣10 does not make an appearance, you finally have to try the spade suit. So you play over to the dummy's ace, everyone following, East with the 9. The ♠K is next. East plays the 10, you follow, and West plays another low spade. Finally, you cash the ♠Q, on which East plays the jack. You don't even have to remember that East had already played a spade (on the third round of hearts). The only card left is the ♠2, so you have to play it and—Eureka!—it's good.

You have just executed a squeeze without even knowing it. This is the full deal:

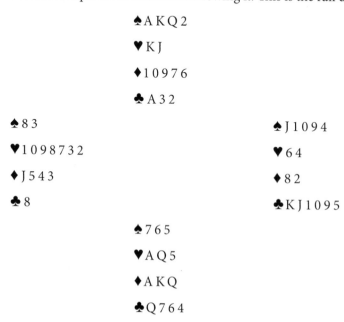

As you can see, East had to make two discards—one on the third diamond and one on the third heart. He had an extra club he could spare, but when he had to make the next discard, he had to pick between poisons. If he tossed his last club—the 10, the one you were looking out for—your 7 would have been good. So East had to get rid of one of his spades. That made your ♠2 good in the end.

Now, here's why it would have been wrong to play your spades first. If you had cashed three high spades and discovered they didn't split favorably, you could still have tried the diamonds, hoping the jack would drop, and when that hope was lost you would then have cashed your hearts, but this would have been the end position with your third heart to be played:

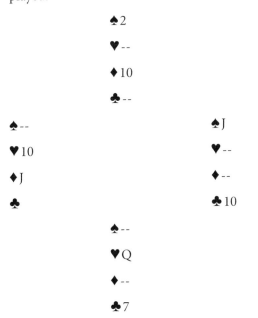

```
            ♠ 2
            ♥ --
            ♦ 10
            ♣ --
♠ --                    ♠ J
♥ 10                    ♥ --
♦ J                     ♦ --
♣                       ♣ 10
            ♠ --
            ♥ Q
            ♦ --
            ♣ 7
```

You cash the ♥Q and discard the ♦10 from the dummy, but East is in no discomfort. He can discard the ♠J, making the 2 good, but you can't get to it, so you have to concede a trick to East's ♣10 in the end for down one.

It was vitally important to maintain the link to the spade suit so that when East had to make the discard that gave you the contract, you were able to take advantage of it.

Bridge Basics

Clyde Love, author of the most authoritative book on squeezes, offers a mnemonic for remembering what you need in order to make squeeze work. It's called BLUE:

➤ B: Busy. An opponent must be busy in two suits, meaning he must hold the only guards in those suits.

➤ L: Loser. Only one loser remaining.

➤ U: Upper. At least one potential winner, known as a threat, in the upper hand.

➤ E: Entry. An entry to the threat card.

If you keep the following general guidelines in mind, the squeeze might work for you just by running your tricks:

➤ You must be within one trick of your contract. That is, if you are in 3NT needing nine tricks, you must have eight winners.

➤ You must have lost as many tricks as you can afford. That is, if you are in 3NT with eight winners, you must have already lost four tricks.

➤ You must have links between your hand and the dummy. Winners that materialize when you cash your tricks are useless if you cannot get to them.

Role Reversal

This chapter ends with an advanced play that is not easy to spot. It's called the dummy reversal. It is so named because, in general, you gain tricks only from ruffing in the hand with the shorter trumps, which is usually the dummy. Check out this combination:

♠ J 7 6

♠ A K Q 5 4

If you ruff in the long hand, you don't really gain tricks. You could just as easily cash the trumps and throw losers on them. When you ruff in the short hand, you get the five trump tricks in your hand plus any ruffs you take in the other hand.

With a dummy reversal, the longer hand does the ruffing and the shorter hand draws the enemy trumps. You need good spot cards to be able to accomplish this, but sometimes a dummy reversal is the only way to make a contract. Here's one:

♠ A 6 5 3

♥ J 10 9

♦ Q 5 4

♣ J 7 6

♠ 2

♥ A K Q 5 4

♦ A K 3 2

♣ 9 5 4

You land in 4♥ from the South seat and get the ♣K opening lead from West. East signals with the ♣10 and West continues with the ♣Q and a club to East's ace. East plays the ♠K at trick four, and you win the ace.

You have nine top tricks and the possibility of ten if diamonds turn out to be 3-3. If the diamonds do not split favorably, you have two chances to make your contract. One is to cash two heart tricks, then play three rounds of diamonds. If everyone follows, the suit is splitting and you can pull the last trump and claim. If the diamonds go 4-2, you have to hope that the hand with only two diamonds started with only two hearts. When six cards are missing, they will divide 4-2 48.45 percent of the time versus 35.53 percent for a 3-3 break.

A better line of play relies only on a 3-2 split in trumps, which occurs 67.83 percent versus 28.26 percent for a 4-1 split. The 3-2 split is two and a half times more likely than the 4-1.

So here's what you do:

Win the ♠A and ruff a spade with your trump ace. Now play a low trump to the dummy's jack and ruff another spade with your trump king. A second low spade from your hand puts you in the dummy again—you are pleased to see both opponents follow—and you ruff the dummy's last spade with your trump queen. You play a low diamond to the queen, leaving this position:

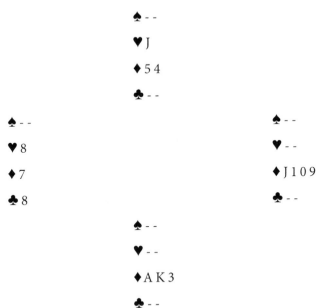

You use the dummy's ♥J to pull the last trump as you throw the ♦3 from your hand. You take the last two tricks with the top diamonds. The full deal:

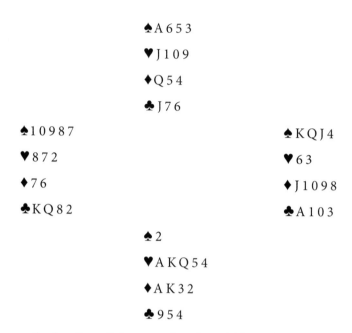

As you can see, the first line of play considered would have failed because West would have ruffed the third round of diamonds. Simply pulling trumps would have left you a trick short when the diamonds proved to be 4-2.

Had trumps turned out to be 4-1, which you would have learned on your second trip to dummy, you would have had to pull trumps and rely on the diamonds to split.

The dummy reversal in this case was clearly the best line of play, and you were rewarded with good luck in the key suits.

CHAPTER 18

 **Your Bidding Toolkit**

In This Chapter

➤ New minor and fourth-suit forcing

➤ Coping with competition

➤ More advanced concepts

➤ Other useful tools

In this chapter, you will be introduced to some more modern-day bidding conventions and discover they aren't as complicated as their high-tech names may sound.

Busy opponents can cause headaches and gum up your bidding system, so you will be introduced to gadgets to help you fight their gadgets.

Many players are creative when it comes to bidding innovations, some so logical you will wonder why you didn't think of them. No matter, just read about them and use them.

You Gotta Bid

There are different approaches to bidding. Some players like simple bidding systems with very few frills. Many of these players say they play the mythical KISS system—for Keep It Simple, Stupid—but what they are really playing is known to most others as mom and pop style.

There's nothing wrong with preferring a bidding system with features that are easy to remember, but a significant number of competitors like to be precise when they communicate with their partners.

Then there is the crowd who are like collectors of model airplanes or stamps—when they see a new convention, they want to play it, regardless of whether it comes up more than once a year or even has any value.

Some innovations, however, are worth their weight in gold. One of them is known as new minor forcing (NMF). It comes up frequently and is highly effective in helping partnerships get to the correct spot.

NMF is used in auctions like this:

West	North	East	South
			1♦
Pass	1♥/♠	Pass	1NT
Pass	?		

If North now bids 2♣, that is the new minor—South's 1♦ is the old minor. North's bid of 2♣ cannot be passed, hence the forcing part. You will find out more about what North is trying to convey if you continue reading.

NMF was created to help the responder clarify his holdings and intentions. Consider the following hand. You are South:

♠ 4

♥ K Q 10 9 5

♦ A Q 3 2

♣ 10 6 5

West	North	East	South
	1♦	Pass	1♥
Pass	1NT	Pass	?

South has a bit of a dilemma. North's 1NT rebid shows 12–14 high-card points, so with 11, South has enough to invite game, but he doesn't have a satisfactory course of action. He could bid 3♥ as an invitational bid, but that shows a six-card suit. If South bids 2NT, North might pass with a hand such as this:

♠ Q 7 6

♥ A 8 2

♦ J 6 5

♣ A J 7 2

Now a spade lead would probably give your opponents the first five tricks in the suit, and in the diamond finesse loss, your side would be minus on a deal where 2 ♥ would be relatively easy. North would not want to prefer hearts over 2NT for a couple of reasons: South might have only four hearts, and preferring hearts would put the partnership at the three level, which might well be too high.

That's where NMF comes in handy. Look at the auction again:

West	North	East	South
	1♦	Pass	1♥
Pass	1NT	Pass	?

If North-South are playing NMF, South bids 2 ♣, which shows at least invitational values—roughly 11 high-card points—and at least five hearts. South is not interested in spades because North's rebid of 1NT denied four spades. If North did have four spades, he would have rebid 1♠ instead of 1NT. It hasn't been said, but 1NT also denied four hearts, with which North would have rebid 2♥.

Here are North's obligations when South bids 2♣ as NMF after responding 1♥:

> ➤ 2♥: Minimum (12 to a bad 13 high-card points) with three hearts

> ➤ 2♠ : Minimum with two hearts (the 1NT rebid promised a balanced hand and therefore at least two-card heart support)

> ➤ 2NT: Maximum (14 or a good 13 high-card points) with a doubleton heart

> ➤ 3♣ : Maximum with diamonds and clubs, probably exactly 3=2=4=4 shape (use of the equal sign means that the hand is precisely three spades, two hearts and 4-4 in the minors)

> ➤ 3♦ : Maximum with five diamonds, doubleton heart

> ➤ 3♥ : Maximum with three hearts

If the responder's first bid was 1♠, here are the opener's bids after NMF 2 ♣:

> ➤ 2 ♦: Five-card diamond suit, doubleton spade

> ➤ 2 ♥: Natural four-card suit; partners can agree that three-card spade support is still possible

> ➤ 2 ♠: Minimum with three spades; partners can agree that this does not deny four hearts

> ➤ 2NT: Doubleton spade, less than four hearts

> ➤ 3 ♣: Maximum with clubs and diamonds, doubleton spade

> ➤ 3 ♦: Maximum five-card diamonds suit

> ➤ 3 ♠: Maximum with three spades

These bids are logical and descriptive. When the responder has a six-card major and less than invitational values, he simply rebids the suit. With invitational values, the responder jumps. With enough to force game—*i.e.*, an opening hand—he bids game in his suit knowing that the opener has at least two of his majors because of the 1NT rebid.

Some pairs takes the refinement of NMF a bit further, stipulating that the responder's bid of 2♣ shows invitational values only, with 2♦ reserved for hands with enough strength to force game. This is known as two-way new minor forcing.

Bridge Basics

The predecessor to new minor forcing was known as Checkback Stayman, and the checkback was always 2♣, even if the opening bidder had started with 1♣. The drawback, of course, was that 2♣ was never a possible contract after the opener rebid 1NT, but that's a small sacrifice to make for the benefits of being able to locate 5-3 major suit fits. Some pairs still play Checkback Stayman, but NMF has surpassed that convention in popularity.

The main feature of NMF is that use of the convention allows you to make a forcing bid without jumping. If you have to jump to express your invitational values, you risk getting too high when your partner has a minimum.

It is wise for partners to establish a protocol for responses to NMF, especially when the responder's first bid is spades and the opener has three spades and four hearts.

Some pairs consider raising their partner's major to be the opener's primary responsibility. With five spades and four hearts, a responder might well be looking for a 4-4 heart fit. To address this issue, some pairs agree that when the responder's first bid is 1♠ and his NMF bid is 2♣, a rebid by the opener of 2♦ shows both three spades and four hearts.

When your partner opens and you are dealt an opening hand, you can still use NMF as long as you have established the means to force to game after your partner shows a minimum.

West	North	East	South
	1♦	Pass	1♠
Pass	1NT	Pass	2♣
Pass	2♦	Pass	2♠
Pass	?		

South's bidding shows at least six spades and is forcing to game, usually with slam interest in light of the fact that he did not simply leap to game.

The responses to NMF previously described are meant to be general guidelines for use of the convention. Partnerships may adjust or augment any of the features of this convention to suit their preferences. Some sort of forcing checkback that can be used without jumping is recommended to keep the bidding low and to allow more space for exploration with strong hands.

Need to Know

Many bridge players are keenly aware of the principle of fast arrival and what the pace of the auction reveals about a bidder's hand. Consider this auction:

West	North	East	South
	2 ♣	Pass	2 ♦
Pass	2 ♠	Pass	4 ♠
All Pass			

South's 4 ♠ is a fast arrival bid that indicates trump support for North but nothing else—no ace, no king, no singleton or void. A slow 3 ♠ by South would have shown at least one of those features. Bidding just 3 ♠ allows North to make a cue-bid if he has slam interest, with the expectation that South will start showing why he went slow instead of fast.

Four to Force

If you have learned one thing in the discussion of various ideas and concepts about bidding, it's that jumping around to show extras is frowned upon as a waste of bidding space. You saw that new minor forcing allowed for the exchange of information at the two level, which is much more efficient in the decision-making process.

It is the same with fourth-suit forcing (FSF), a convention that allows you to make a two-level bid that tells your partner your side has the assets to play game in a suit or notrump. Nobody has to jump to get the message across.

A key objective of NMF and FSF is usually to try to uncover an eight-card fit in a major, but there are two big differences:

1. NMF is used only over the opener's 1NT rebid, and without specific agreement can show only invitational values.

2. FSF is used whenever three suits have already been bid—the fourth suit is the unbid suit at that point—and it is 100 percent forcing to game.

Here are some samples:

West	North	East	South
1♥	Pass	1♠	Pass
2♣	Pass	2♦	

East's 2♦ is the fourth suit. It is artificial and forcing to game and asks West to further describe his hand, perhaps by showing three-card spade support, bidding 3♣ to show at least 5-5 in that suit and hearts or by bidding 2NT to show a diamond stopper.

In this sequence, East might actually have enough values in diamonds to be able to bid notrump himself, but 2NT is not forcing and 3NT uses up a lot of bidding space. Being able to force to game with a bid of 2♦ may be critical to getting to slam. These may be the two hands:

♠5	♠A 8 7 6
♥A Q J 5 4	♥K 3
♦7 5	♦A 1 0 8
♣A J 1 0 3 2	♣K Q 7 4

The auction continues after FSF:

West	North	East	South
1♥	Pass	1♠	Pass
2♣	Pass	2♦	Pass
3♣	Pass	4♣	Pass
4♥	Pass	4♠	Pass
5♣	Pass	6♣	All Pass

Once West shows at least 5-5 in hearts and clubs, East can envision a slam. Without FSF, he would not have had a good bid over West's 2♣.

2NT would not have been forcing and 3NT would have ended the auction. West might have had the urge to bid 4♣ over 3NT, but although he has two good suits, he has a minimum opener in terms of high cards. Further, 3NT does not invite West to contribute any more to the auction without substantial extras.

Using 2♦ as a game force made for a much smoother auction that gave East the information he needed to get to a slam many other pairs would not have been able to reach. If East could find out how good West's hearts were, he could have bid the excellent grand slam in clubs. (On all but a 4-0 trump split and/or some horrible split in hearts, East's two low diamonds can be discarded so that trick thirteen is taken as a diamond ruff in East's hand.)

Need to Know

There is a convention similar to FSF that is something of a hybrid between NMF and FSF. It is called XYZ. It was first described by California player Joe Kivel in *Bridge Today* magazine. The basics are that after three natural calls at the one level, 2♣ and 2♦ are artificial bids. In XYZ, 2♣ shows invitational values; 2♦ is game forcing. Responses and objectives are similar to FSF.

Here's another auction:

West	North	East	South
1♦	Pass	1♥	Pass
1♠	Pass	2♣	

East's 2♣ is initially taken as artificial, although East could have the suit well stopped.

For his third bid, West will support hearts if he has three of them, or bid notrump if he has stoppers in clubs. West may have this hand:

♠ Q J 4 3

♥ A 2

♦ K Q J 4 3

♣ 8 5

Over 2♣, West can bid 2♦. East will know it shows five or six diamonds, but not three hearts and without a stopper in clubs. It is comforting to know there is no rush—that you can make descriptive bids to help you find the right contract.

Sometimes, the responder will use FSF when he has a fit for the opener's second suit. Observe:

West	North	East	South
1♣	Pass	1♥	Pass
1♠	Pass	2♦	

East's hand:

♠ K Q J 5

♥ A K Q 4

♦ K 4 3

♣ 7 2

East is certainly interested in slam, but what can he do to get information? A jump to 3♠ is invitational, a jump to 4♠ will end the auction, and 4NT is out of the question with the low doubleton in clubs, not to mention the fact that West might wonder which suit is in play for the 4NT bid.

The solution is FSF. Suppose West bids 2NT in response to 2♦. Now when East bids 3♠, his intentions become clear. He has a game-forcing hand with slam interest or he would not have gone through FSF—he would have just jumped to 4♠. Now if West can muster up a cue-bid in clubs, East can bid Blackwood, confident that West will know which suit East is asking about.

FSF can keep you out of trouble and get you to the best spot possible. Suppose this is your hand (you are East):

♠ A Q 4

♥ K Q 10 9

♦ 5 4

♣ Q J 5 4

West	North	East	South
1♣	Pass	1♥	Pass
1♠	Pass	2♦	Pass
2♥	Pass	?	

You have enough for game and apparent 4-3 fits in both majors, but notrump may still be a possibility. Remember, West will show three-card support first. Thanks to FSF, you still have room to explore.

Bid 2♠, which shows three-card support and expresses concern about diamonds. Your partner may have this hand:

♠ 10 9 3 2

♥ A 6 5

♦ A Q

♣ K 10 9 3

If this is West's hand, he can bid 2NT over your 2♠ and you will have found a good spot. You will go a different route, however, if West's hand looks like this:

♠ J 10 3 2

♥ A 6 5

♦ J 3

♣ A K 10 9

Now you will opt for the 4-3 spade fit (5♣ goes down when the spade finesses loses).

FSF has the advantage of being simple to use, and except for the bid that forces to game, completely natural. You make the bid that best describes your hand, allowing both sides to identify the optimum contract.

Fighting Back

Bridge Basics

If you and your partner have two 4-3 fits and decide to play game in one of them, do your best to play in the spot that will allow for ruffs in the hand with the three-card trump holding. If you have to take ruffs in the hand with four trumps, you may go down when trumps divide 4-2, which they will do nearly half the time, 48.45 percent versus 35.53 percent for a 3-3 split. An opponent with four trumps to the 5 can ruin your contract by forcing you to ruff in the long hand.

Some opponents love to jump into your auctions and wreak havoc, and one of the most popular conventions for annoying you this way is known as the Unusual 2NT.

Unusual 2NT can be used over any opening bid of one of a suit as follows:

➤ Over 1♥ or 1♠, 2NT: The minors, at least 5-5, typically weak but not necessarily

➤ Over 1♣, 2NT: The two lowest unbid suits: diamonds and hearts

➤ Over 1♦, 2NT: Clubs and hearts

Obviously, a bid of 2NT uses up our precious bidding space. Worse, it makes it difficult for the opener's partner to accurately describe his hand. Some bids become more than a little ambiguous because of the interference.

Here's a case in point. You are West and this is your hand:

♠ A K 8 7 6

♥ K J 9 3

♦ 3

♣ K J 4

West	North	East	South
1♠	2NT	3♠	Pass
?			

You like your hand, and with an unimpeded auction you might have made a game try by bidding 3♥. There is no room now for that. Any bid you make will be at the four level, so you must guess.

So you pass and find that this is your partner's hand:

♠ Q J 3 2

♥ A 8 7 6 2

♦ 8 6 4 2

♣ 1 0

Even with the expected bad splits, game in either major looks solid.

Perhaps you took the bull by the horns and bid 4♠, fearful that your opponents were jacking you out of your game. In that case, your partner will put down this hand:

♠ J 3 2

♥ Q 6 5 4 2

♦ K 1 0 6 5

♣5

It's an awful game to be in, with trumps probably breaking badly—and it wouldn't be surprising to see your left-hand opponent get a couple of heart ruffs. You aren't upset at your partner—he did have support for your suit and it's natural to want to compete.

The key question is whether you can do anything to help distinguish between just competing and a good, constructive raise.

Bridge Facts

The Unusual 2NT overcall is well known as a way to show a hand with both minor suits. What is not as well known is that 1NT can mean the same thing in the right context. Consider this auction:

West	North	East	South
Pass	1 ♥	Pass	1 ♠
1NT			

West is a passed hand, so he can hardly have the 15–18 high-card points expected for a 1NT overcall. The only meaning this bid can have is to show both minor suits.

Other difficult situations are created by the interference of 2NT over a major suit opening. Here are two hands you might have when the bidding goes 1♠ by your partner and 2NT by your right-hand opponent:

♠ 7	♠ 5 4
♥ K Q J 8 7 6 5	♥ A K Q 1 0 7 6
♦ 7 6	♦ 1 0 9
♣ 5 4 2	♣ A Q 2

Your natural inclination is to bid 3 ♥ with either one, but how can that be right? One has 6 high-card points, the other 15. You can't make the same bid with two hands that are so far apart in high-card strength. How would the opener ever know which was which?

The solution to this and the other problems created by the Unusual 2NT can be found in a convention known as Unusual over Unusual, often written as Unusual/Unusual. There are different ways to play the convention. Here is one scheme:

After 1♠—2NT

> ➤ 3♣: A good hand with hearts
>
> ➤ 3♦ : A limit raise or better in spades
>
> ➤ 3♥ : Natural, non-forcing, no spade fit
>
> ➤ 3♠ : Weak, simply competing

After 1♥—2NT

> ➤ 3♣ : A limit raise or better in hearts
>
> ➤ 3♦ : A good hand with spades
>
> ➤ 3♥ : Weak, simply competing
>
> ➤ 3♠ : Natural, non-forcing, no heart fit

Note that in this scheme, clubs always relate to hearts, diamonds always relate to spades. With the 2NT bidder advertising at least five cards in each minor, you will never want to play in either of his suits.

Another scheme attaches different meanings to the cue-bids.

After a major suit opening and an overcall of 2NT,

> ➤ 3♣: A limit raise or better in the partner's suit
>
> ➤ 3♦: A good hand with the fourth suit (spades if the opening was 1♥; hearts if the opening was 1♠
>
> ➤ 3♥: Weak raise if the opening was 1♥; natural and non-forcing over a 1♠ opening
>
> ➤ 3♠: Weak raise of 1♠ opener; natural and non-forcing over a 1♥ opener

If the opening bid is one of a minor, the same principles apply:

After 1♣—2NT (diamonds and hearts)

> ➤ 3♣: Weak, competitive
>
> ➤ 3♦: A limit raise or better in clubs
>
> ➤ 3♥: A good hand with spades
>
> ➤ 3♠; Natural, non-forcing

After 1♦—2NT (clubs and hearts)

➤ 3♣: A limit raise or better in diamonds

➤ 3♦; Weak, competitive

➤ 3♥; A good hand with spades

➤ 3♠; Natural, non-forcing

This concept can apply to other opponents' bids that show two suits, such as the Michaels Cue-bid. In that case, your cue-bids would be in the majors instead of the minors.

Where the opening bid was one of a minor, a cue-bid of one of the majors would show a stopper in that major and invite the opener to bid game with a stopper in the other major. A direct bid of 2NT would be invitational and show stoppers in both majors.

In all these situations, a double of 2NT or of a Michaels cue-bid shows a good hand with a desire to penalize at least one of the suits shown by the overcaller.

More High Tech

If no one ever opened with a weak two-bid or at the three level, bidding would be much easier. If no one ever interfered with your auctions, you would probably get to the right spot almost every time.

Bridge is such a fascinating, challenging game because it's not easy. If it were, who would want to play?

That said, you don't want to enter the fray completely on your own. You need some help, and that means some gadgets.

One of the handiest conventions for dealing with weak two-bids is known as lebensohl over Weak Twos.

Here is the dilemma addressed by lebensohl over weak twos.

Say your right-hand opponent opens 2♥ and you double for takeout. Your hand might be as follows:

♠ A K J 10

♥ 6 5

♦ A 9 8

♣ A Q 6 2

Bridge Facts

Many conventions are named for their inventors. Others are named for the writers or other personalities who popularized them. Blackwood, named for creator Easley Blackwood is an example. In those cases, the name of the convention is capitalized. There is one convention that does not start with a capital letter. It's called lebensohl. It got the name because its invention was initially—and incorrectly—credited to a player whose last name is Lebensold. Lebensohl is probably the only convention not capitalized except at the beginning of a sentence.

Your auction goes this way:

West	North	East	South
		2♥	Dbl
Pass	3♣	Pass	?

You want to make a move here, but what should you do? Your partner may have been bidding his best suit in an extremely poor hand. Unless he had a heart stack and a decent hand to boot, he did not have the option of passing, so in theory he could have 0 high-card points. He probably doesn't have a hand that bad, but it could be pretty weak.

That means anything you do other than pass could put you in a minus position, if you aren't there already despite your 18-point hand.

So what's your next move? Raising your partner's bid does not appeal. If he has some useful cards, you do not want to go past 3NT. That makes a cue-bid of 3♥ your best bet, but that, too, puts you at 4♣ if your partner does not have a heart stopper.

It's a tough position to be in, and anything you do could be wrong. You could pass, and your partner might turn up with this hand:

♠ 4 3 2

♥ Q J 4

♦ 1 0 9

♣ K 8 7 5 3

Your side is an odds-on favorite to make 3NT, but your partner could hardly bid more than 3♣. Your double did not promise a hand as good as the one you actually have.

If you cue-bid 3♥ in a move toward game, your partner's hand might look like this:

♠ 4 3 2

♥ J 4 3

♦ Q 7 6

♣ J 7 5 3

Then your partner would have no choice but to bid clubs again, and you are headed for a minus. And it wouldn't be a big surprise if West added to your partner's misery with a double.

Lebensohl over weak twos will help you with this problem. Here's how it works:

After any weak two-bid by an opponent and a double in the direct seat, if the advancer (the partner of the doubler) bids directly at the three level, it promises a hand with 8–10 high-card points or the equivalent (extra length in the suit bid, for example).

With 0–7 high-card points, the advancer bids 2NT, which requires the doubler to bid 3♣. The advancer then passes with club length or bids another suit to play.

When the doubler's hand is very strong, perhaps with a long, strong suit of his own, the doubler can ignore the request to bid 3♣ and bid his own suit. This would signal to the advancer that his partner has extra values and is interested in game even opposite a weak hand.

When the opening bid is 2♦ or 2♥ and your partner doubles, a bid of 2♠ is the same as if you were not playing lebensohl. Obviously, when the opening bid is 2♠ and your partner doubles, any direct suit bid will have to be at the three level.

Bid the following hands as South in this auction:

Bridge Lingo

It is well known that queens and jacks are not on par with aces and kings. In fact, the QJ combination, particularly when doubleton, is often known pejoratively as a quack. Some authorities upgrade hands without quacks.

West	North	East	South
2♥	Dbl	Pass	?

Hand 1	Hand 2	Hand 3
♠Q 7 6 3	♠K 10	♠K J 9 8 7
♥Q 7 6	♥6 3 2	♥7 6 2
♦J 8 5 4	♦K 7 6 4 3 2	♦A Q 7 6
♣9 7	♣J 10	♣3

Hand 4	Hand 5	Hand 6
♠ J 6 5	♠ A K 10	♠ J 5 4
♥ Q 7 6	♥ Q 3 2	♥ 7 6
♦ J 8 5 4 2	♦ K Q 6 4 3	♦ A Q 7 6
♣ 9 7	♣ 4 3	♣ K 8 7 3

Here are the explanations for these hands:

1. Bid 2♠: You have a poor hand, but you don't want to bid 2NT and put your side at the three level. A bid of 2♠ indicates 0–8 high-card points.

2. Bid 3♦: You have only 6 high-card points, but the six-card diamond suit could come in handy if your partner can bid notrump. The ♠K should also be a working value. This hand is worth an upgrade, in part because your points are in two kings rather than in queens and jacks.

3. Bid 4♠: Your partner should have more than an average hand for his double of 2♥. Bid what you think you can make. It might even turn out to be an underbid.

4. Bid 2NT: If your partner bids the expected 3♣, bid 3♦ to show your weakness and preference for diamonds.

5. Bid 3♥: If your partner has anything useful in hearts, even just a doubleton jack, you want to be in 3NT.

6. Bid 3♦: You aren't crazy about your balanced shape, but you have the values.

This convention helps enormously with competitive judgment, and when your partner invokes the 2NT bid showing a poor hand, the player who doubled a weak two-bid with hope can sign off quietly without reservation about possibly missing a game.

More on Weak Twos

The modern style in competitive bidding is to get in there and mix it up, especially in the first seat, with preemptive bids, especially weak two-bids.

A weak 2♠ based on ♠Q 9 8 6 5 is subject to a serious penalty if one of your opponents has the good spades you are missing, but the bid makes it that much more difficult for them to bid accurately.

The problem is that an aggressive preemptor often throws a spanner into the works for his partner, who might have a hand good enough to consider game or slam. When an opening 2♠ bid might be made on a pile of proverbial tram tickets—or something close to an opening bid—accuracy suffers.

To solve this problem, Harold Ogust created a conventional response to an opening bid of 2♦, 2♥, or 2♠.

The Ogust bid is 2NT, and the opener responds in this fashion:

> ➤ 3♣: Minimum hand, poor suit, or bad hand, bad suit

> ➤ 3♦: Minimum hand, good suit, or bad hand, good suit

Bridge Lingo

When you make a frisky bid—perhaps described less charitably by your partner as insane—and your opponents double you for a big penalty, you are said to have been caught speeding. Your partner may tell your teammates that you would have won the match except that you went for a telephone number. It's good partnership to remember that your flyers affect more than just you.

> ➤ 3♥: Maximum hand, poor suit, or good hand, bad suit

> ➤ 3♠: Maximum hand, good suit, or good hand, good suit

Players remember the responses this way, in order: Bad-bad, bad-good, good-bad, good-good.

A good suit can be defined as six cards with two of the top three honors or perhaps 5 high-card points in the suit, making five or six to the AJ the worst holding for a good suit.

An overall poor hand would probably be one in the minimum end of the range (usually 5–10 high-card points) or in the middle range with more queens and jacks than aces and kings.

Using Ogust allows the partnership to be more aggressive with weak two-bids, although if the opening is truly dreadful the three-level may be too high even opposite a good responding hand. He who lives by the sword . . .

Minor Suit Slams

The opening bid of 2NT is sometimes known as the slam killer because starting at such a high level leaves precious little room for exploration. Knowing that the 2NT opener has a powerful hand helps only marginally because it's tough to tell if particular cards are working or wasted.

Getting to a major suit slam is easier thanks to transfer bids, but most partnerships do not use minor suit transfers or the seldom-used Minor Suit Stayman over an opening of 2NT.

Creative minds have, however, addressed the problem. One of the solutions is presented here. The basics are that after a 2NT opener, a bid of 3♠ is a relay to 3NT. This is the structure after the opener rebids 3NT:

> ➤ 4♣: Slam interest with long clubs
>
> ➤ 4♦: Slam interest with long diamonds
>
> ➤ 4♥: Singleton or void in hearts with both minors, usually 5-5
>
> ➤ 4♠: Singleton or void in spades with both minors, usually 5-5
>
> ➤ 4NT: Both minors, 5-4 either way, with doubletons in the majors. This bid is not forcing.

After 4♣ or 4♦, if the opener fits the responder's suit, he answers key cards in steps (0-3, 1-4, etc.) skipping 4NT.

If the opener does not have a fit with the responder's single suit, he bids 4NT to play.

Another scheme for following up after the relay to 3NT is as follows. It is geared to make the strong hand remain hidden:

> ➤ 4♣: Slam interest with long diamonds
>
> ➤ 4♦: Slam interest with long clubs
>
> ➤ 4♥: Singleton or void in hearts with both minors, usually 5-5
>
> ➤ 4♠: Singleton or void in spades with both minors, usually 5-5
>
> ➤ 4NT: Both minors, 4-4 or 5-4 either way, with doubletons in the majors. This bid is not forcing.

If the opener has a fit in diamonds after 4♣, he can bid 4♦ as RKCB for diamonds. That makes the 2NT opener the declarer in a diamond contract, which likely will be to his advantage. If the opener's best course over 4♦ is Blackwood (4♥), the lesser hand might end up as the declarer in a club slam.

These methods improve your chances of getting to a minor suit slam with some confidence, but there is still guesswork to do. In many cases, one or the other partner may just have to blast into the slam and hope for the best.

CHAPTER 19

 **Duplicate Bridge**

In This Chapter

- ➤ How it works
- ➤ Why it's more fun
- ➤ Different formats
- ➤ Duplicate strategies

In this chapter, you will find out about duplicate, an exciting, intriguing way to play the game of bridge with the luck factor reduced in a setting where you can gauge your progress and improve your game in leaps and bounds. You will learn about the social aspects of duplicate, how much fun it can be to attend a big tournament, and how to meet new friends and partners at more than 3,200 bridge clubs in North America.

Duplicate is played in a variety of formats, and you will learn how each one works. Just as formats change, so do strategies. It pays to know how to handle each one.

Over and Over

The game of bridge is an offshoot of the game of whist, whose origins date back to the 1500s. The focus of both games is taking tricks, but in whist, there is no bidding. The trump suit is determined by the last card turned up at the end of the deal.

There were duplicate whist games in the late 1800s, but it wasn't until the early 1900s that anyone thought of organizing a duplicate bridge game.

Bridge Lingo

The term *duplicate* refers to the playing of a deal more than once and by different pairs at different tables. Through the years, there have been duplicate forms of the games of whist and auction bridge, the two predecessors to contract bridge. That form of the game is now dominant around the world. Whist or auction bridge games are rare nowadays.

In regular bridge, each deal is separate. You sit down to play a rubber, and someone shuffles and deals the cards, distributing the fifty-two cards one at a time until everyone has thirteen. When the bidding is over and a contract is determined, the player to the left of the declarer makes the opening lead. The dummy puts his hand down on the table, and the declarer pulls each card as play progresses.

Each player contributes a card to the trick, played face up and usually thrown into the middle of the table. The side that wins the trick scoops up the four cards to keep as a record of tricks won.

Bridge Facts

Non-duplicate bridge is usually referred to as rubber bridge or party bridge. Those who are unfamiliar with the differences between rubber bridge and duplicate sometimes refer to duplicate as contract bridge. In fact, rubber, party, and duplicate are all forms of contract bridge, which was invented by industrialist Harold Vanderbilt in 1925. Practically overnight, contract bridge replaced auction bridge as the most popular card game.

When play is completed and a result has been agreed to by both sides, the cards are put back into one pile to be shuffled and dealt later. The deal just played is gone forever.

In a duplicate pairs game, the deal just completed will be played again at another table, and another table, up to twelve more times. East-West pairs move from table to table, always to the higher-numbered table as the boards are passed to the lower-numbered table. Each table has a guide card with the table number on it, so if you bought East-West entry No. 8, you start at table 8. North-South pairs are stationary—they do not move during the game.

No Mingling

In duplicate, you play to a trick in a fashion much different than that of how you play to a trick in rubber or party bridge.

First of all, the cards are shuffled just once at the table where you start and before the game gets under way. The cards will not be in a single deck but in the pockets of a tray known as a board. That rectangular device is used to keep each card of a hand intact so that when the tray is passed to the next table at the end of the round, the exact same deal can be played again.

The pockets of the board are labeled with the compass directions. North and South, who play as partners, are on the long ends of the tray. East and West pockets are on the sides of the tray. Each board indicates which player is dealer. On board one, it is North, followed by East on board two, South on three and West on four. Then it starts again with North as dealer on board five, etc. Each board also indicates which side, if any, is vulnerable.

When the game begins, the players take their cards from their respective pockets and sort them. After the auction, play begins as it does with rubber bridge: the player to the left of the declarer makes the opening lead.

The dummy goes down at that point, and after the declarer studies the dummy for a few seconds, he plays to that trick. Instead of pulling the card himself, the declarer calls a card, which the dummy picks up from the cards laid out in front of him . The declarer may tell the dummy to play the king or to play low, which directs the dummy to select the lowest card in the suit that has been led.

Bridge Lingo

The term *dummy* originated with a form of whist called dummy whist. In that game, if there were only three players, the fourth hand would be exposed as an imaginary, and, naturally, silent (or dumb) player. The term in no way implies that the dummy is lacking in intelligence, but in bridge, the dummy is required to remain silent in all but one case: in North America, if the declarer shows out of a suit, the dummy may ask about the play to prevent a revoke.

The cards are put in front of each player as each contributes to a trick, instead of in the middle of the table as with rubber bridge. The side that wins the trick places the just-played card vertically on the table. If the trick is lost, it is placed horizontally.

When play is over, any player at the table can make a statement about the result: "Down one?" "Making five?" If the declarer or the defenders agree to the statement about the outcome of the play, the four players pick up their cards and put them back in the board, careful to put them in the correct pocket. This is important because the deals are played over and over, and if after, say, round four the board goes to the next table with the East hand in the North pocket and vice versa—this does happen, however unlikely it might seem—the board is no longer the same as it was when the game started.

Comparisons

You may be asking why it would matter if the hands in a board got mixed up—the technical term would be *fouled*—and it's a good question. It all comes down to the way a duplicate game is scored.

In rubber bridge, the objective is to get 100 points below the line—that is from bidding and making part-scores, games, or slams. If you bid and make 3 ♥, you get 90 points below the line. If you bid 3 ♥ and make four, you get the extra 30 points above the line, meaning it does not count toward the 100 points you need to win that game.

Bridge Lingo

Rubber bridge is so called because in a typical game, the objective is to win the best two out of three. The winning side receives a bonus of 500 points for winning two out of three and 700 for winning the first two. The first side to win two games wins the rubber, hence the application of the term *rubber match* to the third and deciding game.

In rubber bridge, if you get a string of good cards—lots more high cards than your opponents—you will almost certainly win. Similarly, if you are cursed with a series of hands with few face cards, you will be drubbed. All in all, if you play a lot, this kind of thing evens out over time, but it doesn't feel good while you are going through an unlucky streak—and if you are playing for money, as is the case in many rubber bridge games, it can be costly.

In duplicate, you can win with bad cards so long as you get the most out of what you are dealt.

The reason for this is that the scoring is based on comparisons, not on raw scores. You can score well even with a card full of minus scores if those minuses are smaller than other players' minuses.

The reason the deals are kept intact and moved from table to table is so that valid comparisons can be made when the game is over. In the end, the scoring comes from comparisons—how each pair did on each board compared to how the other pairs playing the same direction did on those boards.

Real Opponents

If you and your partner are sitting East-West, you move from table to table as the game progresses, facing a series of North-South partnerships. The North-South pairs are your opponents because you are playing against them, but your real opponents—the ones you want to beat—are all the other pairs playing East-West.

So how are scores—and, ultimately, the winners—determined?

It's by a commodity known as matchpoints.

At the end of the game, your scores on each board are matched against the scores achieved by the other pairs sitting your direction. You receive one matchpoint for every score you beat and half a matchpoint for every score you tie.

An illustration will make this more clear, but first a word about the basic scoring.

In duplicate, when you bid and make a part-score, you are awarded a bonus of 50 points. Trick scores are the same as in rubber bridge: Minor suit tricks are 20 each, majors 30 each, and notrump is 40 for the first trick and 30 for subsequent tricks.

If you bid game and make it, instead of the 50-point bonus for making your contract, you get a game bonus: 300 if your side is not vulnerable, 500 if you are vulnerable. So bidding and making a non-vulnerable 4 ♥ is worth 120 for the trick score plus 300 for the game bonus, for a total of plus 420. If you make an overtrick, that is tacked onto your score, making it plus 450. This can be of paramount importance in duplicate scoring.

If you bid and make a slam, you get your game bonus plus a premium score for the slam: 500 points for a non-vulnerable small slam, 750 for a vulnerable small slam, 1000 for a non-vulnerable grand slam, 1500 for a vulnerable grand slam.

Bridge Lingo

If you score more tricks than your contract requires—e.g., 3 ♥ making four—you get credit for the so-called overtricks. If you fail to make your contract or keep your opponents from making theirs, each trick short of the contract goal is known as an undertrick. Overtricks and undertricks can be the keys to scoring well in duplicate games.

You can also score well by defeating your opponents. Each non-vulnerable undertrick gives you plus 50, so if you defeat your opponents by two tricks and they are not vulnerable, you get plus 100; if they are vulnerable, it's 100 per trick.

Doubling overly optimistic, foolhardy, or unlucky opponents can reap big bonuses for you. Down one non-vulnerable is minus 100; second and third undertricks, 200 each. After that, each undertrick is minus 300. So down one is minus 100, down two is minus 300, down three is minus 500, down four is minus 800, then 1100, etc. If the doubled side is vulnerable, down one is minus 200, and it's 300 per trick after that.

If this seems complicated, don't worry. Just about every bridge club nowadays uses bidding boxes for silent bidding. This is vastly superior to spoken bidding and a real boon to players who are hard of hearing. On the back of each bidding card are scores for all possible contracts. It's easy to look up any score. Before you know it, they will all be second nature to you anyway.

Precious Points

Now that you know how you get your raw scores—the actual scores at the table—here's how the winners are determined.

Need to Know

Every score achieved at every table is recorded in some way—on a paper ticket or via a wireless electronic device—and posted to a computer program that will almost instantly produce final scores for all competitors, and overall standings as soon as the last score is entered.

Suppose you are playing in a nine-table game. That means there will be eight comparisons for your scores, one with each of the other pairs playing your direction.

You are pair No. 1 and you are looking at scores from board No. 1 to see how you did.

On the first board of the session, playing against North-South pair No. 1, you bid and made 4♠ with an overtrick for a score of plus 450. Scoring overtricks can be very good for your game. Check out the scores for yourself to see how you did.

Pairs	Contract	Plus	Minus	E-W matchpoints
1	4♠ - E	450		7
2	3♠ - E	170		2
3	3NT - W	400		3
4	5♠ - E		50	.5
5	4♠ - E	420		5
6	5♦X - N	500		8
7	4♠ - E	420		5
8	5♠ - E		50	.5
9	4♠ - E	420		5

As East-West pair No. 1, you scored 7 out of a possible 8 matchpoints because of the overtrick you made. Review it so that you can see where the matchpoints came from. You got one matchpoint for every score you beat. On this board, your plus 450 outscored all but one—the plus 500 that pair No. 6 achieved.

Note that the number of matchpoints will always be the number of times the board is played, minus one (you). You can see that the board was played nine times, so the best available score—known as a top—is 8. If you have a true disaster and your score neither beats nor ties any other score, you get no matchpoints—a zero.

The top score on this board went to pair No. 6, whose opponents took an ill-advised save of 5♦ and were doubled—that's represented by the X next to the contract—for down three and minus 500. Say pair No. 6 had been left to play the first board in 4♠ and, like you, managed an overtrick. Then you would have been tied with them and your score would have been 7.5 instead of 7, and theirs would have been 7.5 instead of 8.

Pair No. 3, as you can see, got mixed up in the bidding and landed in 3NT, which made only nine tricks for plus 400, which did not compare well to all the spade games. Pair No. 2 did worse by not bidding their game, stopping in 3♠.

The worst scores, as you can see, were reserved for the pairs who apparently tried for slam—or didn't double when the opponents took a save—and ended up too high, going down in 5♠. They tied for the bottom score, so they received 1/2 matchpoint each.

Little Can Be Big

It doesn't matter how much the margin is—if your score is better than someone else's, you get a matchpoint. A difference of 10 points, if it outscores all others, is just as much of a top as plus 1700 down six in a doubled, vulnerable contract. In the same way, if you have a minus that is smaller than the minuses of your competitors, you can score a top.

For example, suppose board No. 10 in a duplicate game is played in 4♠ by North at every table (this is a normal occurrence in duplicate). At eight of the tables, North scores plus 650—both sides are vulnerable on board 10—for making an overtrick. Suppose also that somehow you managed to hold the declarer to ten tricks. Your score of minus 620 would be better than all the other pairs sitting your direction, so you would get a top—all the available matchpoints on that board.

Here's another example of how you can score big even while going minus. On board No. 8, everyone gets to a rather routine 3NT. Because of a bad break in a key suit, the contract has no chance and almost everyone goes down a couple of tricks. At your table, your opponent makes a dubious opening lead and you manage to go down only one. At every other table, your competitors are minus 100 for going down two. Your score of minus 50 for going down one is another top.

Now you can see why it is important to avoid returning your hand to the wrong pocket in the board when play is completed. This happens occasionally when players cannot resist going over a board just played, pulling other players' cards out to look them over. If they have to rush to put them back in because the next round has been called, confusion can result and hands can be misplaced.

Bridge Facts

There have been some games at major tournaments with so many competitors that they have been divided into multiple sections. When all the results at all the tables in all the sections are scored as though they were one big section, that is known as matchpointing across the field. In such cases, the matchpoints available on each board can be in the hundreds. Woe unto any pair who gets a zero when top is 200. Ouch!

If a board has been fouled in this way, comparisons on that deal become impossible—it is no longer the same deal. Fortunately, the computer program that does the scoring includes adjustments for fouled boards, and usually a penalty for the player or players responsible.

When the game is completed, the final score will reflect the number of matchpoints you earned on every board. You won't get a top every time no matter how well you play, but a score of 60 percent will usually do quite well, and 65 percent or better will usually win.

If you played in a nine-table game, you would normally play nine rounds of three boards each. On each board, 8 matchpoints would be available, or 24 per round. Multiply 24 times 9 and you get 216. Half of that—average—is 108. If you managed to string together enough good results to get to 130, you would have a game just a bit better than 60 percent. If you scored 65 percent, that would be about 140 matchpoints.

In a larger game, say thirteen tables, you would most likely play thirteen two-board rounds, or twenty-six boards. With twelve comparisons, 12 matchpoints would be available on every board, 312 in total. The average would then be 156.

A Piece of the Pie

Most duplicate club games are set up to reward the top performers in each direction—North-South and East-West. In general, the top 40 percent of the pairs in each direction will scratch, that is place in the section. If, for example, you play in a nine-table game, the top four pairs in each direction—40 percent of nine, or 3.6, rounded up to 4—will scratch.

In some club games and at most tournaments, even when an event has only one section, there will be an overall winner from among North-South and East-West pairs.

The payoff for people who scratch in games sanctioned by the American Contract Bridge League is the highly sought-after masterpoint.

The ACBL is the world's largest bridge organization with roughly 166,000 members. Headquartered in the Memphis, Tennessee, area, the ACBL began issuing masterpoints—the measure of achievement in bridge competition—in 1936. Players seek masterpoints to advance in rank through several levels, the primary objective being to earn status as a Life Master.

There are about 3,200 clubs in North America affiliated with the ACBL, and the organization sanctions about 1,200 tournaments at various levels each year. Club games have modest masterpoint payoffs for doing well. At each higher tournament level, the potential for winning masterpoints increases.

Luck Factor

When all players play the same deals again and again, some of the luck factor in the game is removed. This is especially true when considering the distribution of high-card points.

As stated previously, if the high cards are running your way in rubber bridge, you will win. In duplicate, you can win with poor cards. In fact, even if the cards are running North-South, in a nine-table game, there will still be a winning pair East-West—plus second through fourth—even if their results are not stellar.

The luck factor is not totally eliminated, of course. In fact, there is quite a bit of luck in pairs games. For example, say board No. 11 lands North in a very difficult slam. When you play that deal as East-West, North at your table happens to be the club's best player and he lands the contract while North-South at other tables are either not bidding the slam or going down in it. That's bad luck for you.

On the next round, however, you and your partner have a bidding misunderstanding and stop in a part-score on a board that should be bid to game. In fact, every other East-West pair does get to game. The only problem for them is that trumps are 5-0 and they all go down. You get a top from your bidding misunderstanding. Luck was on your side this time.

Over the long haul, luck evens out and the best players usually come out on top. No one is immune, however, to the vagaries of luck. Even the best players in the world don't win every time—and they have stinkers just like the regular folks.

Improved Product

Now that you know how duplicate works, perhaps you have considered whether it's a game for you.

Make no mistake, duplicate is a competitive game. It is a highly social activity, especially postgame, but players can be intense when trying to work out complicated end positions or to decide whether to bid slam and in what denomination.

Players do not chitchat during the bidding and play as they might at home with their friends on a Saturday night. There are rules you must observe, and the games are run by directors who intervene when there is an irregularity or a dispute.

That said, duplicate is great for a number of reasons:

➤ You get to compare yourself against good players in the same game.

➤ You can measure your progress as you strive to improve.

➤ You will have access to more experienced players, most of whom are willing to give you tips for improvement.

➤ Duplicate is the one sport in which you can compete head-to-head against the best in the business. You might not be ready for that when you start out, but when you get a few tournaments under your belt and start feeling confident, you can buy an entry in a game that also includes world champions. You won't get the better of them very often, but it's not impossible.

Suppose your hobby is golf. Do you think you would ever have a chance to play against Tiger Woods or Phil Mickelson in a serious game? Do you think you would ever—even once—beat one of them in a game? How about playing tennis against Roger Federer? You might not even be able to return one serve.

In duplicate, if you play against the best player in the world and make the correct plays, you can prevail. No matter how good your opponent is, he must still follow suit and can still be endplayed just like the duffer at your club. All you have to do is play your cards in the correct order.

> ➤ The competitive atmosphere of a duplicate game is not for everyone, but in recent years serious efforts have been made to make the game more friendly and welcoming to new players. More than a decade ago, the ACBL officially adopted a policy known as Zero Tolerance, which provides penalties for rude behavior. This policy and other efforts have significantly improved the atmosphere at duplicate clubs and at tournaments.

> ➤ In today's tournament world, especially at large gatherings, there are games for players of just about every level of experience, from brand-new players to intermediates to top-ranked experts. The goal is to provide a comfort level for all players, enhancing their enjoyment as they move up in rank and skill.

Review, Please

One of the best features of duplicate is the availability of hand records.

At just about every tournament nowadays, the deals you play are created by a computer program that randomly deals the cards. Because the cards come from a computer, it is easy to make printouts of every set of deals. These printouts are copied and distributed to players at the end of each session so that they can see every hand and go over them for learning purposes.

Bridge Facts

The number of different deals that can be created is represented by a twenty-nine-digit number. Even if you could play one deal per second, 24 hours a day, 365 days a year, it would still take thousands of years to play every possible deal.

In most cases, the printouts also have small notations with each deal that indicate possible makeable contracts. This information is provided through a program called Deep Finesse, which is part of the random deal programming.

An increasing number of bridge clubs have purchased computer programs for randomly dealing the cards and have added dealing machines so that players just have to sit down at the start of a game and take their hands out of the boards. Wherever the dealing program is used, there are also printouts of the hands for players to go over at the end of the game.

Knowing that there will be hand records available makes it more fun to play because if a particularly difficult board comes along, you don't have to try to remember it so you can ask someone about it later—or make notes in your score card. You simply grab a copy of the hands at the end and go over the relevant deal (or deals) with your partner or one of the experts at your club.

Different Strokes

This chapter has concentrated mostly on pairs play, by far the most common form of the game at clubs.

There are, however, two other types of games in the duplicate world. The first is Swiss teams, the other is knockout teams.

Swiss Teams

In this form of the game, players form teams of four to six members, although only four play at a time. When the final entry is sold and the number of teams in the event is ascertained, teams are randomly paired for the first round. The game is set up in matching sections—A and B, C and D, and so on depending on how many sections are needed.

Teams 1 and 15 may be assigned to play at A1 and B1 in the opening round. So North-South for team 1 will play at table A1, and their teammates will go to B1 and play East-West. East-West for team 15 will play at A1, while North-South for 15 will play at B1.

Bridge Facts

Swiss teams in bridge is so-called because the progress of the event is modeled on the Swiss movement in chess. In chess, after the first round all winners play each other while losers are matched up. In the second round, undefeated players are matched, players with 1-1 records are paired off, as are those who have not won a match. In Swiss teams in bridge, the same scheme is used. It is managed by a computer program that randomly matches teams with like records.

In most Swiss teams, there will be seven to nine boards in play, and in most events the pairs at the table will be charged with shuffling and dealing the cards. Both pairs for team 1 will start at the home table, and when it's time to start, the East-West pair will take three or four of the boards with them to B1 to be made. The East-West pair from B1 will move to A1 to help make the boards, and play will begin.

Scoring in Swiss teams is by International Matchpoints (IMPs). IMPs are determined by the difference in the result for the same board played at both tables. For example, if the East-West pair at table A1 bid and make a vulnerable game on board 1, they score plus 620 as they would in a pairs game. If North-South at the other table defeat the same contract, they get plus 100.

When the match is over, the teams reunite at their home tables and compare scores. On the board in question, North-South at A1 are minus 620 because their opponents bid and made the game. On that same board, their teammates are minus 100 because they went down. The net result is minus 720 because both pairs on that team were minus.

In IMP scoring, minus 720 gives 12 IMPs to the other team. Here is the IMP scale in use in North America:

Score Difference	IMPs		Score Difference	IMPs
20–40	1		750–890	13
50–80	2		900–1090	14
90–120	3		1100–1290	15
130–160	4		1300–1490	16
170–210	5		1500–1740	17
220–260	6		1750–1990	18
270–310	7		2000–2240	19
320–360	8		2250–2490	20
370–420	9		2500–2990	21
430–490	10		3000–3490	22
500–590	11		3500–3990	23
600–740	12		4000+	24

Losing 12 IMPs on one board is not good, but with six or more boards to play, you are not out of the match by any means. You could easily recover those IMPs by defeating your opponents' vulnerable game while your teammates make theirs.

You can see that swings can be as low as 1 and as high as 24. Don't hold your breath for the big one. That almost never happens. If the comparison of a board results in a difference of less than 20 points, the board is considered to be a tie—a push in the vernacular—as with plus 110 at your table and minus 100 at the other table on the same board.

When all the comparisons are done and one team is determined to be the winner, the captain of the winning team will go to the other team's table and, after making sure the other team agrees with the score, will report the result to the tournament director. The TD enters the score for both teams in the computer, which will convert the IMP result to victory points.

VPs versus Win-Loss

In the early days of Swiss teams, winners were determined by wins and losses. In a large field, however, it is possible to end up with two or three undefeated teams, all of whom would be tied for first. This is unsatisfactory for all the "winners."

The prevalent method of determining winners nowadays is known as victory points, which puts a premium on the margin of victory. The major complaint about VPs is that a team can go undefeated but still not win because of a series of relatively flat boards that did not allow for large margins in IMPs. If you barely win all your matches, another team with a loss or two can pass you in the standings with big margins in their wins.

The plus side of VPs is that if you can keep a match close, even if you lose you get something. In win-loss scoring, you can lose by just 3 IMPs and get nothing for your efforts.

There are different VP scales depending on the sponsoring organization. In North America, most tournament organizers use the 30-point VP scale:

IMP margin	VPs	IMP margin	VPs
0	15–15	9–10	24–6
1	18–12	11–13	25–5
2	19–11	14–16	26–4
3	20–10	17–19	27–3
4	21–9	20–23	28–2
5–	22–8	24–27	29–1
7–	23–7	28+	30–0

You can see that winning by 7 or 8 IMPs gets the winning side 23 VPs. The losers get 7. Note that all scores add up to 30.

Bridge Lingo

When playing Swiss teams with victory point scoring, the ideal result for your side is to get the maximum number of IMPs. Beating a team by 28 IMPs or more will earn that 30–0 score, which is known in the bridge jargon as a blitz.

Knockout Teams

At one time, most tournaments featured an event known as board-a-match teams, in which all boards were treated equally. Only 1 point was available on each board, and any margin was sufficient for a win. The BAM, as it was called, was usually played on the last day of the tournament, typically a Sunday. The problem with the event was that it is a tough form of the game, so the best teams almost always won.

When Swiss teams came along, players realized that they could win some masterpoints just by winning a couple of matches. Further, because the matches were short, lesser teams often had a shot at winning or placing high in the overall with a bit of luck. Swiss teams swept the BAMs out of most tournaments almost overnight.

Then came a form of bridge competition known as bracketed knockout teams. This form of the game has supplanted Swiss teams as the overwhelming favorite of up-and-coming players.

The knockout is played just as the name implies—if you lose you are knocked out of the event.

Bridge Facts

It takes 500 masterpoints to achieve the rank of Life Master in the American Contract Bridge League, and the points must be earned in various levels of competition. The all-time leader in masterpoints earned is a Florida player by the name of Jeff Meckstroth. His masterpoint total is an awe-inspiring 75,000-plus, and he is still going strong.

Before bracketed KOs came along, knockouts were not so popular. At a large tournament, the organizers would run a Swiss teams' qualifier for two sessions, with the top sixteen teams advancing to play head-to-head matches. This was popular with the top players because the masterpoint awards were relatively high. Less-experienced players weren't interested because they basically had no chance.

The bracketed KO changed everything.

In this form of the game, at a large tournament there might be three hundred teams interested in playing KOs. The organizers accommodate everyone by breaking the field up into brackets of sixteen teams each. The event is played in four sessions as the field is cut in half with each twenty-four-board set. In the fourth session, the two remaining teams play for the championship.

Teams are assigned to brackets depending on their masterpoint holdings. At a well-attended tournament, the top couple of brackets are filled with top players. They get to enjoy the stimulation of competing against each other while the less-experienced players compete against their peers without fear of being completely outclassed by the experts.

At a 2011 tournament in one of the most popular venues, there were twenty-six brackets of knockout teams and more than four hundred teams.

Scoring in the KOs is the same as in Swiss teams—by IMPs—and the pairs line up the same as in Swiss: North-South at one table; East-West at the other. Teams compare at the halfway point of each match.

Strategies in Play

The two different forms of scoring are known to players as matchpoints (pairs games) and IMPs (team events).

At matchpoints, you might often risk your contract for an overtrick. At IMPs, no experienced player would ever do that.

Here's a classic example:

♠ 7 6 5
♥ J 4
♦ A K Q 8 7
♣ 5 4 3

♠ A K Q 9
♥ A Q 3
♦ 4 3
♣ J 10 9 8

West	North	East	South
			1NT
Pass	3NT	All Pass	

West leads the ♥9 to your jack, East's king, and your ace. In a pairs game, you might risk your contract to playing the top three diamonds, hoping for a 3-3 split. You would consider this line of play because if the suit does split favorably, you will take at least ten tricks, eleven if the spades also split to your liking—3-3 or three to the J10 with one of your opponents.

The contract at every table is certain to be 3NT, and you find on the opening lead that the heart finesse works. You could make a safety play in diamonds—ducking the first round—to guard against the more likely 4-2 split, but if the suit breaks 3-3 and the spades also provide four tricks, your score will not fare well when compared to the others.

If you duck a diamond and your opponents switch to clubs, cashing three tricks, your score of plus 600 (you are vulnerable) will likely be poor. Some players will go for the gusto and hope for a 3-3 diamond split, whereas others will not think of making the safety play because they don't know any better.

On the other hand, if you win the heart and go after diamonds by playing the top three, finding them to be 4-2, you will probably go down. It will not be a 0, however, because you will tie with the other players who take the risk going for a top or near-top. Minus 100 would not be a good score, but it would not be a 0.

In a team game, you would always make the safety play because of the consequences of going down in a contract you could have made. If you win the heart and play the top three diamonds, you may find that this is the full deal:

```
              ♠765
              ♥J4
              ♦AKQ87
              ♣543
♠J1083                      ♠42
♥9852                       ♥K1076
♦92                         ♦J1065
♣Q76                        ♣AK2
              ♠AKQ9
              ♥AQ3
              ♦43
              ♣J1098
```

Whatever you do will result in a minus score. For example, if you turn your attention to spades, hoping for some good luck there, you will have to cash your ♥Q and concede to avoid two down.

If the declarer at the other table takes more care and ducks a diamond at trick two, you will be recording a 12-IMP loss on this board. Your teammates will come back to compare with minus 600 on their score card to go with your minus 100. A couple more of those and you're out of the match.

At matchpoints, you will double the opponents for the penalty more aggressively because the payoff is handsome. If the opponents are vulnerable and you think they have overbid, even if it's a close decision, you might take a shot for a top by doubling a part-score contract.

Need to Know

It pays to be aggressive—not to say rash—in doubling your opponents when you are playing in a pairs game. For one thing, if it goes wrong, you and your partner are the only losers. In a team game, your teammates also pay the price. There's an old saying about aggressive tactics at pairs that has a lot of validity: "If you have never doubled the opponents in a maker, you aren't doubling enough."

If your opponents make it, you probably get a 0, but it's only 1/26th or 1/27th of your total score. You can recover from that relatively quickly. Further, when your double works, you get a top. So if you double three times and your opponents make it once, you have achieved 66 percent for your efforts. That's a winning percentage.

At IMPs, if you double a part score and your opponents make it, you have doubled them into game. For example, doubling a vulnerable 3♥ gives your opponents plus 730. If your teammates are allowed to play 3♥ unmolested and score plus 140, you have lost 11 IMPs.

There are times when you play safe at matchpoints or make a seemingly risky move at IMPs.

If you are in an unusually good contract at matchpoints—perhaps you bid to a slam you don't think the other pairs will reach—you would certainly play safe to make it, knowing that you don't need the overtrick and that going down will almost surely be a 0 for you.

At IMPs, you might feel you are trailing and need a big swing to get back in the match, prompting you to bid a risky slam or even chance a grand slam you don't think the opponents will bid at the other table.

You must be sure of your judgments, however. In most cases, it is wise to assume that your teammates are capable of doing the same brilliant thing your opponent just did that feels like a big loss. It is demoralizing for your partnership and team harmony for you to mastermind a situation and produce a disastrous result.

Game On

Another key strategy at IMPs is to be aggressive in bidding game when vulnerable.

Here's how the odds shake out:

When you are not vulnerable, if you bid and make a game that is not bid at the other table, you stand to gain 6 IMPs—your plus 420 compared to their plus 170. The difference of 250 is worth 6 IMPs. If you bid game and go down 1 for minus 50, when you compare it to the other table, where they stopped below game and scored plus 140, the net minus of 190 costs you 5 IMPs. It's about break even. Summed up, you don't stand to gain that much by bidding the game.

If you are vulnerable and you bid and make a game that is not bid at the other table, it's a 10-IMP gain—your plus 620 versus their plus 170, a difference of 450. If you bid game and go down 1 for minus 100, it costs 6 IMPs for the net minus of 240. The odds are now 10-6 in favor of bidding the vulnerable game.

The other factor is that if your opponents are experienced, they will probably bid the vulnerable game on the same rationale you used, so you stand a good chance of getting a tie board—or a push for your efforts.

At matchpoints, it is best not to push for iffy games because you can turn a good score into a near-zero by being too aggressive. If you turn a plus score into a minus by overbidding, you will turn an average result into a poor one. Rely on your superior card play to gain those extra matchpoints. Plus 170 on a board where most are plus 140 or worse will earn you just as many matchpoints as being plus 420 or 620.

CHAPTER 20

It's a Wrap

In This Chapter

➤ Key skills to acquire

➤ Rules, terms, and definitions

➤ How to improve

In this chapter, you will learn about how the top players of the game go about their business. You may not be able to play as well as they do, but you can emulate their behavior. You will learn more about the language of bridge and different types of games. If you want to improve, you will receive some advice on how to go about it.

Best Behavior

Bridge is a tough game. It's hard to play it well, at least on a consistent basis. The best players in the world make numerous mistakes, especially when they are playing against their peers. Most top players will tell you that they do not feel they will ever master the game. That is not to say, however, that no one should aspire to improve—and it certainly does not imply that you cannot enjoy bridge unless you are ready to contend for a world championship.

Bridge Facts

Bridge is a game that can be played for a lifetime. The American Contract Bridge League has many members still active in the game in their nineties and even past one hundred years of age. There is anecdotal evidence that playing bridge can help avert the onset of Alzheimer's disease, and it is a widely held belief that bridge helps senior citizens stay mentally alert because of the need to concentrate, focus, and recall what has happened at the table.

You can take immense satisfaction in doing the best you can, especially when your best efforts result in a winning line of play. The first time you execute a squeeze on purpose will be one of your biggest thrills, in bridge or in any other endeavor.

To get the most out of the game, you should strive to cultivate some of the characteristics of the top players.

Bridge Is a Partnership Game.

The best players strive to get the best out of their partners at all times. One of the top professional players in the world is Mike Passell, who splits time between his homes in Dallas and Las Vegas. Bobby Wolff, one of the all-time great players in the history of the game, reported on his experience in playing with Passell, noting, "He is a terrific partner—always supportive and positive." That is a high accolade indeed.

As an aspiring player, you may be lacking in confidence and unsure of yourself. Do not try to mask that with bravado and an aggressive attitude, especially where your partner is concerned. Consider that you are both on the same side, and put yourself in your partner's place when a mistake is made. When you goofed up, you probably already knew it, so do you think you your partner needs to remind you of your mistake? Of course not, and that applies to when your partner makes a mistake.

If you ever have a chance to watch the top players in action, you will note that they never discuss the boards during a session. When something goes wrong, they might scratch a brief note on their scorecard to remind them to discuss it later, but that's it. They do what every player should aspire to do after a disaster or, for that matter, a spectacularly good result. Concentrate on what's in front of you.

Keep It in the Past

Put what just happened—bad result or good—in the past, where it belongs. In his autobiography, Bob Hamman, the top-rated bridge player in the world for twenty years and still the all-time leader in lifetime results, described a situation where he started the second half of an important team match behind by a significant number of IMPs, only to have a lousy result on the first board out of the box. He and his partner misdefended a doubled game contract and let it make. His reaction? Go on to the next board.

If Bob Hamman feels that he cannot afford to use his mental energy rehashing an event that can't be changed, neither can you. If you are thinking about what a dunderhead you were on the last board, how will you be able to focus on the board you are playing now? If you are mentally congratulating yourself for your clever falsecard a couple of rounds ago that caused the declarer to misplay his contract and go down, you are asking for a bad result on the board you are playing.

Nothing is more frustrating and confidence-sapping than realizing you haven't seen any of the cards that have been played for the last three tricks because your mind was elsewhere.

Be Cheerful and Friendly

If you get to a table in a foul mood and convey that attitude to everyone there, the atmosphere will be tense. You concentrate best when you are relaxed, a bearing you can achieve by greeting your opponents with a friendly demeanor.

Duplicate bridge may be considered too serious by some who don't know much about the game, but there is a definite social aspect to the sport.

Bridge Facts

It may sound strange, but bridge has official recognition as a sport. The phrase *"bridge is a sport"* was spoken in 1999 by International Olympic Committee President Juan Antonio Samaranch at the Olympics Museum in Lausanne, Switzerland. The announcement was the culmination of years of lobbying by officials of the World Bridge Federation, an umbrella organization headquartered in Lausanne. Although bridge never made it into any Olympic Games, the recognition was viewed as important, and bridge is now one of the sports of the International Mind Sports Association, whose competitions have been held in Olympic years

Many bridge clubs look upon their members as family, and they are renowned for helping in times of trouble, fundraising for sick members, tending to older members, and generally just looking out for each other. It's not uncommon for players to meet their future spouses at bridge games. It is very healthy for a marriage when two people share a passion.

If you and your partner are having a bad game, focus on the good bids or plays your partner has made. At all costs, avoid giving lectures at the table. It is a futile, counterproductive activity that almost always annoys the other three people at the table and makes you look like an ass.

Rules not Meant for Breaking

There are certain actions at the bridge table that are frowned upon—some just covered in this chapter—and some that are forbidden by the laws of the game. The general principles cover matters such as not accepting a trick that your side didn't win or the concession of a trick the opposing side could not lose or waiving a penalty for an infraction. The most serious aspect of these proprieties involves communication between partners. The only legal way to communicate with your partner is through the calls and plays you make, not in the way you make them.

Nowadays, bidding boxes have replaced oral bidding in just about every setting. All tournaments and most clubs use the devices, which contain cards for every bid from 1♣ to 7NT plus green pass cards, red double cards, and blue redouble cards. These are much superior to spoken bidding.

In the old days, a loud double from one partner would make it clear that it was for penalty, or a firm four spades followed the slamming of the cards on the table could convey the message that the partner was to bid no more.

Bridge Basics

The late Ron Andersen, a top player and gifted raconteur, often told the story of his mother's bridge club, where the women had the communication down pat. According to Andersen, if one of the women in his mother's club opened the bidding with a meek "One club," it meant he had a poor three-card holding in the suit. If the opener instead said, "I guess I'll bid a club," that indicated a better club holding, and if the first shot was, "I'll start with a club," that showed a robust holding in clubs. The story was probably apocryphal, but it makes a good talking point for how not to communicate with your partner.

It is a serious breach of the proprieties to hesitate in such a way as to indicate possession of a card you do not have in order to deceive the declarer. Here is an example:

                        North

                        ♠ K 10 6 2

West   East

♠ 5 3   ♠ Q 8 7

                        South

                        ♠ A J 9 4

This is the trump suit, and South plays the ♠J, testing the waters, so to speak. If West hesitates and fumbles before playing the 3, South will probably play West for [S]Q and run the jack. He will be rightly aggrieved when East produces the queen and probably will seek—and receive—redress from the director. West has no problem at all and must play low smoothly.

There are other reprehensible actions that can result in serious sanctions against the perpetrators. For example, all players are permitted to ask the meanings of bids during the auction, but the timing of such questions can represent serious ethical violations.

West	North	East	South
	1NT	Pass	2♣
?			

If, before he calls, West asks the meaning of 2♣—a ridiculous question inasmuch as the entire world plays it as Stayman—and happens to have a hand with long, strong clubs, he probably should be thrown out of the event, as should East if he ends up on lead and starts with a club.

Dummy Stay Dumb

When you are the dummy, you have very limited rights. One of your rights occurs when your partner shows out of a suit. In order to prevent a revoke, you may ask if your partner has any of the suit just played: "No clubs, partner?' At the end of play, the dummy may call the director if he noticed an irregularity during the play, such as revoke by one of the opponents.

Other than those exceptions, the dummy must remain silent, and the dummy may not indicate any card to be played by the declarer or indicate disapproval of a card called by the declarer. The dummy may not ask for a review and may not ask the meaning of any bid by an opponent.

Not Supposed to Know

All players are entitled to information conveyed by the proper play of the cards and by the bidding. Partners are not entitled to information gained by variations in tempo—usually a protracted hesitation—or by gesture of indication of displeasure. It is not an infraction to convey information by a break in tempo, but it is a violation to make a bid or play based on such information.

All this—and there is more—may make bridge seem like a stuffy, unfriendly game, and sometimes the "lawyers" try to get something for nothing by invoking rules improperly.

Fortunately, these types are few and far between, and players in general are better educated about ethics and the proprieties. Most of the director calls, fortunately, are concerning leads out of turn or insufficient bids.

Bridge is meant to be fun, and the rules are aimed at enhancing that enjoyment by assuring a level playing field.

What Am I Playing In?

In times past, tournaments had little variety in the schedules. If you wanted to play, it was pairs games for most of the week, with a team game—probably board-a-match—on Saturday or Sunday.

Nowadays, there are a wide variety of events, especially at the three big American Contract Bridge League tournaments (in the spring, summer, and fall), where thousands of players can be found each year.

As already noted, the bracketed knockout teams are far and away the most popular for players who are trying to earn precious gold masterpoints. To become a Life Master, a player must earn a certain number of gold points, available only in events that have a regional rating. Bracketed KOs offer gold points, one reason that event is so popular.

Need to Know

The American Contract Bridge League organizes three eleven-day tournaments each year, in the spring, summer, and fall. They are known as North American Bridge Championships. The tournaments attract the best players from around the world, but they also place a major emphasis on providing games for all levels of players, including the newest beginners. These tournaments typically attract thousands of participants, many of them newcomers. Each of the tournaments features free lectures for newbies and lots of free food and postgame entertainment.

There are also games for new players and a form of pairs game that allows for less-experienced players to have a chance for masterpoints even while playing against higher-ranked competitors.

One such event is described as stratified, which means that players in three different strata play together but each is ranked with his peers when the final results are tabulated.

In this type of event, players enter in strats A, B, and C, A being the highest ranked. When all the scores are in, strat C players are ranked among themselves but also against the other two strats in case they did well enough to rank in a higher strat. Strat B players are rated by themselves but also against A. Strat A players are ranked only among themselves.

It is possible, therefore, for a strat C pair to come in first in A, B, and C, although the players receive masterpoints for only one of the strats (the highest). The higher the strat, the bigger the masterpoint payoff, so a strat C pair of players who happened to win overall, including A, would be very pleased with their masterpoint haul.

Getting Better All the Time

There are many ways to get better at the game of bridge. You can do it if you apply yourself and are not too proud to ask for help.

One great way to learn is to read, and there are many wonderful books available by fantastic authors who can help you sort out seemingly mysterious concepts and help make those lights come on as you finally "get it."

It's best to take any study of this kind in small doses. It's a mistake to try to become a world-class player in six months. For most people, especially someone who has not played a lot of cards previously, it's a slower learning process. Granted, there are some prodigies out there who seem to be able to see through the backs of the cards from day one, but that probably isn't you—or anyone you know, for that matter.

Need to Know

In two separate polls among expert players and readers of the American Contract Bridge League's monthly magazine, *The Bridge Bulletin*, the book selected as the favorite was *Why You Lose at Bridge*, by S. J. Simon.

Reading can prepare you for real-life situations. For example, it might not occur to you to eliminate side suits and throw someone in to "find" a queen for you or give a ruff and sluff, but if you read about it in a book, you would have a better chance of recognizing the situation when it came up at the table.

The squeeze might seem too esoteric for you to comprehend if you heard someone try to explain it, but if you see how it works on the printed page and you study the subject, you may understand enough to squeeze someone in an actual game.

Certain card combinations should be studied so that when you are faced with a key play you will know what to do. Here's a combination that comes up frequently:

♥ J 9 5

♥ A Q 10 3

You are in the dummy for the last time and need four tricks in the suit. How do you play this combination? If you read about it before it comes up, you will know the correct play—the play that guards against four hearts to the king on your right.

This may be the full layout:

♥ J 9 5

♥ 4 2   ♥ K 8 7 6

♥ A Q 10 3

If you play the jack and let it ride, it will win, but when you play another heart, you will have to overtake it with the 10 in your hand. With no further entry to the dummy, you will end up losing a heart trick.

It doesn't work to unblock the ♥ 10 from your hand because then East can cover when you play the ♥ 9, promoting him 8 to an eventual winner.

The correct play the first time you touch this suit is the 9. If East covers, you win, return the 3 to the jack, and then play back to your good AQ. If East plays low, you let the 9 run, then you can follow with the jack. If East plays low, you are still in the dummy to play a third round of the suit, and if he covers, your AQ10 are all good.

This is simple when you see it laid out this way, but you might not have known how to play that combination without reading about it first.

There are hundreds of items like this that when seen in print first become easy to spot when they come up in the heat of battle.

Classics

There are some masterful works that when studied carefully can take you a long way. A list of some of them is in the resources section, including *How to Read Your Opponents' Cards: The Bridge Experts' Way to Locate Missing High Cards* by Mike Lawrence, mentioned now only because of the story attached to it.

Lawrence was a young Californian recruited to be a member of the first full-time professional bridge team in history—the Dallas Aces, put together and paid for by businessman Ira Corn. The team members trained and studied and were coached by a bridge-playing former U.S. Air Force officer by the name of Joe Musumeci. The team was ultimately successful, winning a couple of world championships.

Corn could be a tough taskmaster, and he gave each of the team members jobs to do from time to time. One day he called Lawrence into his office and gave him his assignment: "Write a book." It was Lawrence's first attempt at such writing. The result was a classic that has as much relevance today as it had more than four decades ago.

Watch and Learn

You can also pick up a lot of tips by watching the good players in action. If you ever find yourself at a tournament of any size, plan to take a day off, and if you don't know the top players, ask a tournament director for a suggestion. The TDs know all the top players and they would be delighted to point you in the right direction.

As a kibitzer, you are not allowed to speak or make any gesture or comment about what has happened, but you could make a note or two and ask your subject when play is completed why he did this or that or made such and such a bid. Most top players are willing to help serious students of the game.

Get in There and Fight

Don't wrap yourself in the cocoon of the beginner games. Although the comfort of lesser competition may be soothing to your psyche, it won't do anything for your game. If you really want to improve, play up. In a way, it's like pushing yourself physically. If you never tax your muscles, they won't grow stronger. The same goes for your bridge muscle—your brain. If you never have to try hard to make a contract, you won't get better.

It may not be great for your self-esteem to get in there and mix it up with the big boys and girls, but if you keep trying, your efforts will pay off in a better standard of play. When the better players see you trying hard and actually improving, some of them may take you under their wings to help you get better even faster.

RESOURCES

Books

Bergen, Marty. *Points Schmoints!: Bergen's Winning Bridge Secrets*. Ridgewood, NJ: Bergen Books, 2002

Bergen, Marty. *More Points, Schmoints*. Ridgewood, NJ: Bergen Books, 1999.

Bird, David. *52 Great Bridge Tips on Declarer Play*. London: Batsford, 2005.

Bird, David. *Another 52 Great Bridge Tips*. London: Batsford, 2007.

Cohen, Larry. *To Bid or Not to Bid: The Law of Total Tricks*. Ontario Canada: Master Point Press, 2002.

Grant, Audrey. *Commonly Used Conventions of the 21st Century*. Louisville, KY: Baron Barclay Bridge, 2009.

Kantar, Eddie. *Eddie Kantar Teaches Modern Bridge Defense*. Ontario Canada: Master Point Press, 1999.

Kantar, Eddie. *Take Your Tricks*. Poughkeepsie, NY: Vivisphere Publishing, 2008.

Kantar, Eddie. *Test Your Bridge Play*. Chatsworth, CA: Wilshire Book Company, 1983.

Kelsey, Hugh. *Killing Defence at Bridge*. London: Cassell, 2001.

Lawrence, Mike. *The Complete Book on Balancing in Contract Bridge*. Louisville, KY: Baron Barclay Bridge, 2006.

Lawrence, Mike. *How to Read Your Opponents' Cards: The Bridge Experts' Way to Locate Missing High Cards*. Louisville, KY: Baron Barclay Bridge, 2006.

Lawrence, Mike. *Judgment at Bridge*. Louisville, KY: Baron Barclay Bridge, 2006.

Lawrence, Mike. *Play Bridge with Mike Lawrence*. Louisville, KY: Baron Barclay Bridge, 2006.

Love, Clyde. *Bridge Squeezes Complete: Winning Endgame Strategy*. Ontario Canada: Master Point Press, 2010.

Mollo, Victor and Nico Gardener. *Card Play Technique: The Art of Being Lucky*. London: Batsford, 2003.

Pottage, Julian. *A Great Deal of Bridge Problems*. Poughkeepsie, NY: Vivisphere Publishing, 2007.

Rodwell, Eric and Mark Horton. *The Rodwell Files: Secrets of a Bridge Champion*. Ontario Canada: Master Point Press, 2011.

Root, William. *Commonsense Bidding: The Most Complete Guide to Modern Methods of Standard Bidding.* New York: Three Rivers Press,, 1995.

Rubens, Jeff. *The Secrets of Winning Bridge.* Mineola, NY: Dover Publications, 1981.

Simon, S.J. *Why You Lose at Bridge,* Devyn Press, 1945.

Watson, Louis H. *Watson's Classic Book on the Play of the Hand at Bridge.* New York: William Morrow Paperbacks, 1971.

Woolsey, Kit. *Matchpoints.* Louisville, KY: Baron Barclay Bridge, 2006.

Websites

The American Contract Bridge League
www.acbl.org
Free downloadable software for learning to play and bid

Baron Barclay Bridge Supply
1-800-274-2221
www.baronbarclay.com

Bridge Base Online
www.bridgebase.com
Free bridge play, teaching software, extensive library of match play, vugraph presentation of major matches as they happen.

Bridge Guys
www.bridgeguys.com
A site with a wealth of information

Bridge Topics
www.bridgetopics.com
Daily news and hot topics co-hosted by World Champion Eric Rodwell

Bridge Winners
www.bridgewinners.com
Lively new site for online discussion, articles, and problems

OKbridge
www.okbridge.com
Online games

SWAN Games
www.swangames.com
Online games

GLOSSARY

Excerpted from the 7th Edition of the Official Encyclopedia of Bridge

Courtesy of the American Contract Bridge League and Baron Barclay Bridge Supply

Above the line – A phrase denoting all scores in rubber bridge entered above a horizontal line on the score sheet, including penalties, bonuses for game, slam and fulfilling a doubled or redoubled contract.

Arranging – Aligning the cards of the dummy as that hand is being spread on the table. Also a statement from a player indicating he is still sorting his cards, and the act of doing so.

Auction – The bidding sequence by the four players that determines the final contract. Dealer makes the first call and subsequent calls proceed in clockwise direction until there are three consecutive passes, which marks the end of the auction. See definition of Call.

Balanced – The description of a hand (13 cards) with no singletons or voids and usually no more than one doubleton. Balanced patterns are 4-4-3-2 (two suits of four cards each, one suit of three cards and one suit of two cards, 4-3-3-3 and 5-3-3-2. Hands with 5-4-2-2 and 6-3-2-2 are considered borderline cases.

Bid – A call by which a player proposes a contract that his side will win at least as many odd tricks (see definition) in excess of six (see definition of "book") as his bid specifies, provided the contract is played in the denomination named.

Blank – A void. Used as an adjective, it indicates lack of a protecting low card for an honor, such as a singleton or "blank" king. Used as a verb, it means to discard to the point that an honor has no more protecting cards, as in, "He blanked his king."

Blockbuster – A hand with tremendous trick-taking strength, either from a long, strong suit or high-card points in excess of 20.

Board – A duplicate board, also a synonym for the dummy, as in, "He took the trick on the board."

Body – The quality of a hand with more 10s and 9s than 4s or 3s to go with the face cards.

Book – The first six tricks taken by declarer. These tricks have no value in the score, but are used to calculate the number of tricks required for a contract. For example, a contract of 1♠ requires seven tricks: six for the book and one "odd trick." In the same way, a contract of 6♠ requires declarer to take 12 tricks.

Break – The distribution of outstanding cards held by the opponents in a particular suit. Declarer, playing in a trump contract with eight trumps between his hand and dummy, will be happy with a 3-2 "break" of the opposing trumps, indicating one opponent has three, the other two. A "bad break" would be 4-1 or 5-0. A synonym is "split."

Bust – A seemingly worthless hand.

Call – Any pass, bid, double or redouble. A bid is a call, but not every call is a bid.

Card sense – A special aptitude for playing card games, specifically (in this context) bridge.

Cards – Used in a colloquial sense, it usually means high-card strength, as in a "card-showing double."

Cheapist bid – The most economical bid that can be made in a particular point in the auction. Over an opening bid of 1♣, for example, the cheapest bid is 1♦.

Claim – Any statement by a player—declarer or defender—to the effect that he will win a specific number of tricks.

Clear a suit – At notrump play, to clear a suit is to force out, by continued leads of the suit, adversely held high cards so that the remainder of the cards in that suit are winners.

Closed hand – The hand of declarer. The "open" hand is the dummy.

Cold – Colloquial way of describing a contract that should always be made or always defeated, as in "It was cold for six" or "It was cold for down one." Similar terms are "frigid" and "icy."

Contract – The undertaking by declarer's side to win, at the denomination named, the number of odd tricks specified by the final bid.

Convention – A call or play with a defined meaning that may be artificial. The Stayman convention—2♣ bid in response to an opening of 1NT—is a convention because it does not indicate possession of clubs or the intent to play in that denomination.

Deal – To distribute all 52 cards; the privilege of thus distributing the cards; the act of dealing, and all 52 cards when they are distributed. A "hand" is 13 cards held by one player. A deal is all 52 cards held by the four players.

Defender – An opponent of declarer.

Discard – To play a card that is neither of the suit led or nor of the trump suit. As a noun, a card so played.

Double – A call that increases the scoring value of odd tricks or undertricks of an opponent's bid.

Down – Defeated, as in, "He went down in 4♥."

Drop-dead bid – A bid that tells partner that there should be no more bidding. Over a 1NT opening, a natural bid of 2♥ by opener's partner is a "drop dead" bid, meaning responder does not want opener to do anything but pass.

Dummy – The declarer's partner after he has placed his cards face up on the table. It is not a derogatory designation, but arose from an earlier card game in which the exposed hand was to remain silent (or dumb).

Duplicate – A term applied to the playing of the same board by more than one table of players.

Echo – A high-low signal by defenders.

Entry – The form used for taking part in a tournament or club game. Also, the means for securing the lead in a particular hand.

Face card – The cards that have a representation of a human figure (kings, queens and jacks), originally called coat cards, later court cards.

Falsecard – A card played with the intention of deceiving the opposition. A player with ♥J6 might play the jack when the opening leader starts with the ace and dummy hits with ♥Q82. Declarer's play of the jack is meant to discourage the opening leader from cashing his second trick (the king) for fear of a ruff by declarer and simultaneous establishment of the queen for a potentially useful discard.

Finesse – An attempt to gain power for lower ranking cards by taking advantage of the position of higher-ranking cards. An example is a holding A-Q in a suit in dummy and two low in declarer's hand. Declarer leads one of his low cards and "finesses" the queen, hoping the king is on his left. Leading up to a guarded king in dummy (hoping the ace is on the left) is also a finesse.

Flat – Another way of describing a balanced hand. Also, a deal in duplicate on which no variations in results are expected in the replays. For example, a deal on which every pair would be expected to bid 3NT and make exactly nine tricks.

Following suit – The legal obligation of every player to play a card of the suit led if possible.

Forcing – Description of a bid or call requiring further action by partner.

Game – The winning of 100 points below the line in rubber bridge.

Grand slam – A contract that requires declarer to take all the tricks—by definition a bid of seven of a suit or notrump. A bid of six is a small slam.

High-card points – The basis for determining the relative strength of a hand. The most widely used method is to assign values to the ace (4 points), king (3), queen (2) and jack (1). A hand is considered to be strong enough to open the bidding with 12 or more high-card points.

Leader – The person who makes the opening lead – always the player to declarer's left.

Level – The "odd trick" count in excess of book. A bid of 2♣ over 1♠ is considered to be at the two level.

Loser – A card that must be lost to the adversaries if led or if it must be played if the suit is led by an adversary.

Low card – Any card from 2 to 9. Sometimes inappropriately called "small card."

Make – To shuffle the deck in preparation for dealing; to succeed in a contract.

Matchpoint – A credit awarded to a contestant in a pairs game for a score superior to that of another contestant in direct competion.

Misfit – A situation in which two hands opposite each other are unbalanced, with each player holding two long suits with extreme shortages or voids in the third and fourth suits.

Natural call – A bid that indicate possession of the suit bid, as opposed to a conventional bid that may not indicate possession of the suit named.

Notrump – A ranking denomination in which a player may bid at bridge. Notrump is just above spades in precedence.

Odd trick – A trick won by declarer in excess of the first six tricks.

Open – To make the first bid in a given auction.

Overcall – In a broad sense, any bid by either partner after an opponent has opened the bidding.

Pair – A twosome or partnership of two players.

Pass – The call by any player indicating that, at that turn, he does not choose to contract for a number of odd tricks or to double an opponent's contract (or redouble when his side has been doubled).

Passed hand – A player who has passed as his first turn to bid.

Passout seat – The position of a player who can end the bidding by making the third consecutive pass.

Pianola – A contract that seems so solid that it requires no special care and could "play itself," as a player piano (or pianola) does.

Redouble – A call that increases the scoring value of odd tricks or undertricks of a partnership's bid following a double of your partnership's contract by an opponent. A redouble can be made only after an opponent doubles and only when the intervening calls were passes.

Revoke – To fail to follow suit when able to.

Ruff – To use a trump to win a trick when a "plain" (non-trump) suit is led.

Second hand – The player to the left of dealer. Dealer's partner is "third hand" or "third seat," to the player to declarer's right is "fourth hand."

Sequence – Two or more cards in consecutive order, such as AKQ, KQJ7 or QJ98.

Stiff – Colloquial for a singleton.

Stopper – A card or combination of cards that may reasonably be expected to stop the runner of a suit by an opponent. An ace will always take a trick in notrump, as will certain combinations of cards, such as KQ(x), QJ10(x), J1098, etc.

Tenace – Two cards in the same suit, of which one ranks two degrees lower than the other. A major tenace is A-Q, the minor tenace is K-J. More broadly, any holding of cards not quite in sequence in a suit. After most cards in a suit have been played, 10-8 can be a tenace.

Trick – Four cards played in rotation after a card has been led by the player whose turn it is to lead (play first).

Void – No cards in a suit, originally or after all cards in the suit have been played.

Vulnerable – A term indicating that the values of premiums and the severity of penalties are greatly increased. In rubber bridge, a pair become vulnerable after they have won a game. In duplicate, the vulnerability is arbitrarily assigned and is indicated on each of the duplicate boards (trays in which the cards are kept and moved from table to table during the game).

Zero – The lowest possible score on a duplicate board.

INDEX